S0-BDP-902

100 FACES OF MARIN

The Character of a County

Interviews by Peter Anderson
Portraits by Reggie Henkart

The development of this book was based on the experience and knowledge of the author and photographer with input from the numerous resources noted in the acknowledgements, introduction and from the subjects themselves. The information contained herein is true and complete to the best of the author's knowledge.

10 9 8 7 6 5 4 3 2 1

Printed in the United States of America

Library of Congress
Cataloging-in-Publication Data:

Anderson, Peter
100 Faces of Marin

Library of Congress Control Number: 2004114795

ISBN 0-9753645-053995 Hardbound

Project Management: Suzanne Dunwell
Design & Production: Gabe and Jennifer Anderson

Published by:
100 Faces Productions, LLC
314 Sandpiper Court
Novato, CA 94949
books@100faces.org
www.100faces.org

Acknowledgements

The book you are holding would not have been written and published without the brilliant endeavors of Suzanne Dunwell. As Project Manager for 100 Faces of Marin, she has labored fearlessly and relentlessly for almost three years to bring this book from conception to fruition.

I met her in 2001 when she was CEO of the Novato Chamber of Commerce. Partially on the strength of my first edition of 100 Faces of Marin (published in 1991), she hired me to write and edit the monthly newsletter for the Novato Chamber. Then, having taken a keen interest in the first book, she hatched the idea to write an updated version. Ten years had passed, she frequently reminded me, and Marin had gone through so many changes that the citizens needed a fresh new reflection of themselves.

I resisted for many months, but the more I got to know some of the newer people in Marin and their talents and businesses, the less I resisted. Also, there were many people who had been excluded from the first book only because the number 100 is so finite. Same is true of this edition—selecting 100 citizens is no easy task, and extremely limiting.

What Suzanne Dunwell has achieved is mind-boggling. What she went through passes and surpasses the rocket science test. Through sheer pluck, perseverance, extraordinary tenacity, an extremely well-honed organizational mind set, blind faith and rich humor, she has launched this rocket ship, and now we can enjoy its orbit around Marin. She is a great friend, and I thank her profusely.

The magnificent work of my collaborator, photographer Reggie Henkart, speaks eloquently for itself. Reggie is not only a consummate professional, but he is a total blast as a human being. Again, kudos to Suzanne Dunwell for discovering this rare gift of a guy (she had contracted with him to do freelance work for the Novato Chamber). Reggie has managed simply and with a great artist's touch to capture exactly the kind of spirit and substance we were hoping to find in each portrait. My thousand fallible words per profile could never be as profound as his single elegant shot.

I would like to extend deep and heartfelt gratitude to Novato writer Michael McCarthy, who appeared on the scene somewhat magically to help with research and interview skills at a time when deadline crunch was at its most severe. He is a multi-faceted, hard-working, fun-loving family man who helped save this project from deadline catastrophe.

My sons Gabe and Peter Anderson are the very beat of my heart. To have Gabe and his wife, Jennifer Deane Anderson, work on this book as the production team is one of the highlights of my life. Both Vassar College alums, they live now with their dogs Stella and Happy in Saratoga Springs, New York. They have provided calm, steadying, competent, top-notch professional advice to us concerning virtually every aspect of this project. They are both great writers and editors and they are fabulous human beings. I thank them both with all my heart.

My son Peter inspires me, as well. A recent graduate of the University of Arizona in Tucson, he is an aspiring writer living now in Los Angeles, where he romps on the beach with his girlfriend Becca Greenbaum and his dog Chase and feeds his imagination with new writing material. I envy both his warm heart and his writing style—brief, cogent, wry, witty, whimsical, compassionate, and very funny—and I am especially jealous of his golf game, which bears no resemblance to mine. My sons are God's greatest gifts to me.

My sons' grandmother, the late Ruth Pritchard of Sacramento (an accomplished publisher, editor, and good Democrat), idolized my children (and they adored her), and I thank Nana for the good influence she had on my boys.

Their mother, Kathleen Cory Campbell, is an accomplished writer and editor, as well. Not only has she been an absolutely wonderful mother to our sons, but she has also been a great friend and supporter of this book project. Her courage knows no bounds—badly hurt in a terrible car accident more than a decade ago, she has shown all of us how to handle life's challenges with grace, dignity, deep faith and class.

My parents, Joan and Elmer Anderson, lived in one of the first homes in Greenbrae. They both passed away in the 1990s and I miss them terribly. On their behalf, I thank their longtime next-door neighbor, Ray Poelstra, who generously helped support this project when my spirits were lagging. His late wife, Bonnie Poelstra, was a voracious reader who spent hours trading books with my mother and swapping literary opinions. I attribute my love of reading to my mother and Bonnie, two sweet and riotously humorous neighbors and friends. I only wish they could celebrate with me the publication of this book.

Warm acknowledgments, as well, to my late sister Patty (my family's little angel who died on March 24, 2003), to Michael Anderson and Suellen Miller Anderson, Tracy and Andy Armanino, Joseph Anderson, my Aunt Nora Tibbetts and my cousin John Tibbetts and their amazing family, Hart Doyle, Karen Iuppa, and to my incredibly bright and beautiful nieces and nephews.

Special thanks go to my landlord Michael Brionez and his partner Mark Partal who appeared out of nowhere to make a condo available to me at a critical juncture, thereby preserving the successful timing of the book's precarious deadline.

I also thank various friends and associates—Debora Abel (a miraculous muse), Rich Earle and his wife Ruthie, Kelly Weatherwax, Ron Benveniste, Julia Sarmiento of Colombia, Trudy Reynolds, Tim McGovern, Linda and Greg Maroni, Wencke Stromberg, Bruce/Sue/Mark/Mary Ann Chalmers, Tony Elshout, Clark Blasdell, fellow author Stuart Greenbaum, gracious '60s raconteur Charles Pintard, fellow 49er diehard Peter Farrell, Sister Patricia Lyons of Dominican Garden School, and all my friends at The Nossaman Law Firm in San Francisco, especially Bill Bagley.

Finally, many thanks to the 100 Faces of Marin for having me in their homes and minds in order to make this book a reality. It is an extraordinary experience and something of a free education to be an interviewer of so many fascinating people. I thank them for being forthcoming, informative, cooperative, and most importantly, themselves.

Suzanne Dunwell would like to thank the following people who bolstered her spirit, provided sage advice, mentorship, belly laughs, and the comfort of true friendship. Their kindness will never be forgotten: Tony Lazzarini, Heidi Kuhn, Jan Jensen, Norma Howard, Margaret Deedy, Jean Price Lewis, Joan Capurro, Rich Rubin, Michael Pritchard, Donnalei Sumner, Peggy Childs, Brian Sobel, Judi Joseph and an anonymous benefactor known only as "Deep Face."

The entire team of 100 Faces of Marin extends hearty thanks to the following individuals—dynamic winners all—whose companies are listed in the back of the book as sponsors: Roger Grossman, Marty Rubino, Richard Habib, Bob Griswold, Joan Capurro, Margot Fraser, Chuck Bennett, Bill and Aimi Dutra, Gary Giacomini, H.C. Jackson, Margaret Sabin, Romano Della Santina, Patty Garbarino, Randy Block, Mark Garwood, Bob Smoke, and Derek Knell.

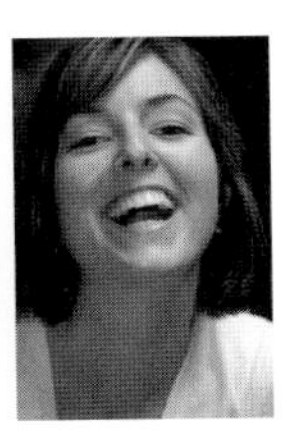

Contents

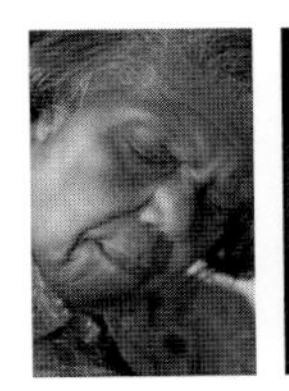

Contents

100 FACES OF MARIN

The Character of a County

Etta Allen

There was a time in the 1960s and 1970s when newspaper editors would occasionally assign a photographer and a reporter to cover what was, at the time, a social anomaly—the sight of a woman doing "a man's job."

Residue of the still-fledgling women's liberation movement, the phenomenon was still more of an eye-catching oddity than it was a seriously decisive step into a changing economy and culture.

So, every now and then, while flipping through the pages of the daily paper, the reader would come across a photo of a woman strapped against a telephone pole, in full blown uniform including a tool belt and hard hat. It would be up to the editor to create a catchy headline, something along the lines of "Climbing Toward the Glass Ceiling, This Woman Vaults Onward and Upward."

Or maybe the subject would be a female PG&E worker toiling diligently along a gas line in the aftermath of a storm or an accident. It was all still so new and somewhat awkward to see these pioneering women in traditionally male roles, so newspaper people could simply not resist the urge to publish stories and illustrations of these ground breaking women and events.

Marin County once even made national news when a young resident, Jenny Fulle, became the first girl to pierce the male bastion of Little League enrollment. We take all of this very much for granted these days, but you simply had to experience the newness and, sometimes, shock of these socio/cultural barriers crumbling in order to really understand their long-term significance.

In the case of Etta Allen, breaking into an all-male business environment in 1974 was not a frivolous novelty or an attempt to grab headlines. The motive was an absolutely resolute will to survive.

Etta and her husband, Jim Allen, had started a successful heating and air conditioning business, Allen Heating and Sheet Metal, in 1957. When Jim died in 1974 after a long battle with cancer, his widow Etta was staring at the bleak reality of how to raise and support her two young boys, Jim and Craig, in the style she felt they would have had if their father had lived.

"This was crunch time," recalls Etta Allen, who is now one of the most active and best respected women in Marin. "Jim had a small company, it was doing well, but I was suddenly faced with the option of taking some kind of office job or closing the company. So I decided to take on the formidable task of taking over the business.

"It was extremely difficult at first, as you might imagine," she says. "First of all, women just weren't in the construction business in those days. And secondly, in order for me to get my contractor's license, I would have needed to have 10 years in the field. At that time, apprenticeships were closed to women, making it impossible for me to attain that experience. I did some research and found that the Board could waiver the in-the-field experience requirement. I repeatedly wrote to the License Contract Board, sending them my resume and detailing my experience and qualifications. I was relentless in refusing to give up my drive to achieve.

"Finally, I received a letter inviting me to take the test. I became an instant pioneer, passing the exam and receiving my license. Since then, the laws have become more flexible."

Modest is the correct word for Etta Allen. She admits it wasn't frustration or overwhelming odds that made her feel conspicuous in a man's world. It was the debilitating feeling of shyness that would come over her when she would walk into a room filled with men. Back then, you never saw women on a job site. It was a novelty.

"I knew in my gut this shyness would be my downfall in this competitive new world I found myself in," she admits, "so I had to find a way to deal with it. Humor always works best for me, so I took this plain white hard hat, painted it hot, shocking pink, and began wearing it to all the construction sites. It was exactly what I needed to divert the attention to something else. Soon I became the 'lady in the pink hard hat.' Being a woman was no longer an issue for me."

It takes more than a pink hard hat to earn the respect of a business community, however, and Etta Allen was up to the task. Recognizing that she owed a debt for all the support she had received, she went on a mission to make her company as community-minded as possible.

"What I discovered," she says, "is how satisfying it is to return generosity back to the community, in all areas of Marin—serving on the boards of Marin General Hospital and Guide Dogs for the Blind, completing a term as president of the Marin Builders Exchange, working as board member for the Larkspur and San Rafael Chambers of Commerce, the Marin Community College District, and the Hispanic Chamber of Commerce. I was also the first woman to become President of the Marin Builders Exchange, and then went on to serve as the first woman on the Executive Committee of the California Builders Exchange

"What I discovered is how satisfying it is to return generosity back to the community, in all areas of Marin."

"It's just all extremely exhilarating and worthwhile. I can't tell you all the good things and great relationships that have flowed my way through active community involvement. I was born in Santa Fe, New Mexico, and was a member of a family that was very community minded, so a lot of this engagement comes naturally to me. But again, and most significantly, it goes back to running the company. I had been so well received at a time when men and women simply didn't know how to relate to a woman executive, so it was a no-brainer to express my gratitude in this fashion."

When she needs to get a break, Etta Allen retreats to her beloved property in Glen Ellen, where somehow she finds time to grow grapes—Cabernet and Merlot—which she then sells to the Benziger Winery for bottling. She has her own label—Sunny Slope. Her constant companion is nine-year-old Deanne, a lovely German Shepherd raised by Guide Dogs for the Blind and now in retirement.

"Being able to get away on weekends to Glen Ellen," says Allen, "is my saving grace. I can't tell you the benefits of getting away from it all to refresh both energy and spirit. When I come back on Mondays to tackle new challenges, it's like I have been completely restored and reinvigorated. I will always consider Marin my home base, but I am doubly blessed."

Marin, in turn, has been blessed by Etta Allen, shocking pink hard hat and all.

Isabel Allende

Author/activist/romanticist Isabel Allende is an angel living in the hills of Marin.

Perched delicately on a stuffed sofa inside her San Rafael home that is a testament to earth tones and to the rustic-elegant architecture of her homeland Chile, Allende speaks with quiet dignity and elegant strength.

"After being the daughter of diplomats, an exile and an immigrant, I have found a home in Marin for the past 16 years. I came here on a book tour and I met Willie, my husband, who was introduced to me as 'the last heterosexual bachelor in San Francisco!'

"I finished my book tour which took me to Spain and Venezuela, but I had in mind there was something I had to complete. So, I came back to San Francisco to spend a week with Willie, and I have never left. Then I forced him into marriage because I needed a visa! We've been very happy together.

"I've made a home here," says the accomplished novelist and lady of letters. "It's sort of an extended family/tribal/Latin American thing that's hard to describe. My son Nicolas lives across the lagoon, and my son-in-law Ernesto—whom I love like a son—and his new wife Giulia live down the hill in our old house. We cook for nine people. It's an open house on weekends. We celebrate family and life and we are all the time in each others' faces. This is a large house with a swimming pool, so all summer the house is full of people—I love that. The house sits atop a hill with a 360-degree view of the Bay and Mt. Tam."

Allende says she loves Marin because the community affords her the privacy to write—"People are really kind to me. Everywhere I go, at a restaurant, on the streets, people know me. The feeling that I can knock on any door and it would be open is just great. Yet, at the same time, there is space and privacy. In Chile, I would have absolutely no privacy.

"When my daughter Paula was married, she honeymooned in Spain with her husband Ernesto, and she got sick, falling into a coma and suffering severe brain damage because she was given the wrong medication. I brought her back here to Marin. Then began a terrible time, like a long winter. But there was so much help, so many people who showed up providing help and company. It was just incredible.

"Her doctors were caring, loving, and would visit daily even though they knew they couldn't cure her. When she died, I got a lot of help. People would stop me in the street to offer me prayers and help. Her husband was devastated when she died. I wrote a book called 'Paula' which is a memoir about the family and my sweet daughter. It became my most popular book. I did not want to receive any income from the book, so we put all the proceeds into a foundation. We have an old Victorian house in Sausalito which is where the foundation operates. We give awards and grants and scholarships. We have work in India, Guatemala, Chile, Bangladesh, and the United States. It is called the Isabel Allende Foundation and we work with people who are underprivileged in every way—education, health and protection for women.

"After Paula died, it was a very bad time. When I finished the book, 'Paula,' it was like a catharsis. After that, I couldn't write fiction. Then one day I met Anne Lamott in Book Passage. I told her I couldn't write, that I was just blocked. She laughed and said there was no such thing as writer's block—it's just that your reservoir is empty and needs to be filled up.

"That remark changed the whole thing for me. I realized I had been giving everything away. I remembered that I am a journalist by training, so I can write about anything if you give me a subject and enough time to research. So I gave myself a subject that was as far removed from death and mourning and grief as possible—I wrote a book about lust and gluttony called 'Aphrodite.' I did my research in all the porn shops in The Castro and I had so much fun writing the book that I came back to my body and got over the depression.

"The reservoir was filled and after that I have been writing a book a year. I start all my books on January 8 and I write until the book is finished. I write in Spanish. I cannot write in English. My book readings are usually attended by people who have read at least one of my books and know about my politics and the foundation, so it's a pretty liberal crowd.

"I write in a little house behind the main house. Being there alone for eight hours a day in silence makes things happen. I am very disciplined. The words start dancing, the characters emerge from the shadows, they tell you things you never expected, and the story unfolds. Inspiration comes to me from many places, often from some personal experience. I was raised to be somebody's wife in Chile in the 1940s, yet I went out into the world to do other things and somehow ended up in Marin County.

"The most important thing to me is gratitude. My life has been full of change, but this feeling of belonging here in Marin is a very new and wonderful feeling. Gratitude is like opening this chest full of stuff to give back to the community, and that is the whole point of our foundation."

"The first time I came here, Willie took me to Mt. Tam. It was October, a little cold, but a very clear day. I dismissed it, however, because I never thought I would ever live here, but this is where I have brought my children and grandchildren, after all.

"I fell in love with Willie because of his story, which I wrote about in a book called 'The Infinite Plan.' His story is also the story about California, and it always surprises me how young California is at 150 years old. It's truly amazing when you consider that it all started with the Gold Rush—all these greedy, disheveled people planted the seeds for this very sophisticated, cosmopolitan, elegant place called San Francisco.

"The most important thing to me is gratitude. My life has been full of change, but this feeling of belonging here in Marin is a very new and wonderful feeling. Gratitude is like opening this chest full of stuff to give back to the community, and that is the whole point of our foundation.

"I need to give because I have received so much."

Beth Ashley

Beth Ashley is one cool chick.

I have labored over that lead sentence for months. I like the irony and playfulness of those six words. Irony, because Beth, one of the most liberated women I have ever known, would "get" the blasphemy of being called a chick. She is, after all, a 10-year honoree of the Marin Women's Hall of Fame. And playfulness, because Beth is one of the few writers I know who absolutely delights in laughing at herself.

She is also one of those people in life you find yourself wanting to please. As a fellow columnist, I am acutely aware of the degree to which she goes to open her veins to let the feelings, thoughts and words bleed to shed enlightenment, hope and joy to her readers. Led by her insatiable curiosity, her strong heart and a resourceful journalistic m.o. that elicits pearls of stories from the most tightened clams, she abhors stuffiness of style. She has a charming, irresistible, girl-like quality about her that keeps her innocence intact, her curiosity buoyant. I admire her, I respect her, and in my thrashing about for words trying to find something that might please her, I came up with "chick." She has a great big intoxicating laugh. That's what I was going for.

When I first came to the Marin IJ *in 1985, I was going through a divorce. I had this beautiful new job as a daily columnist in the county of my birth, yet I was hurting badly on the inside from separation from my spouse and loneliness for my two sons. I guess Beth grew tired of seeing my scowling face in the newsroom, because one day she came over to my desk and said, "Come on, we're going for a ride." She whisked me away mysteriously and explained in her car that I needed a pet to take my mind off my sorrows. I couldn't have a dog where I lived and I am allergic to cats, so at the pet store she introduced me to two matching, chattering, miniature Greycheek parrots from South America whose names were Peru and Chile.*

Miraculously enough, each bird's behavior and moods, in a way, matched my sons' distinct personalities. It wasn't complete healing, obviously, but the fact that she cared enough to do something for her unhappy colleague has stuck with me for the past 20 years. That's another reason why Beth Ashley is one cool chick.

In the crazy, extremely difficult, mind-torturing, hair-pulling world of trying to make it as a professional writer, Beth Ashley pulls it off effortlessly. In her inspired way, she keeps things simple, expressing only what she knows, never betraying her own voice, writing with passion and sometimes outrage, and always with an eye toward helping someone out there in Reader Land. She is evidence that easy reading is damned hard writing.

Though most of her columns demonstrate a homespun quality to her work that has gained for Beth a reputation as a leading voice of Marin, it has been her extensive travel escapades that have strengthened the spine of her somewhat considerable resume. After she earned a journalism degree at Stanford where she was editor of the *Stanford Daily* and a *Phi Beta Kappa* graduate, Beth spent a year traipsing around Paris and stringing for the *Los Angeles Times.* When she moved on to Germany, she was hired as reporter/editor for a U.S. State Department journal.

It was during her German sojourn that she married her first husband, an American newspaperman who later worked for the *San Francisco Chronicle*. Much later, in 1990, she worked as a guest editor for the Moscow newspaper, *Komsomolskaya Pravda*, firing off two articles a week to the *IJ* describing the dire conditions of Russian citizens struggling with the early days of *Glasnost.* It was this experience, weaving accounts of economic depravity amid political upheaval, that really solidified Beth's credentials as a writer with *gravitas*. Marinites, long used to enjoying her highly entertaining columns about shopping at the supermarket or raising her sons, were witnessing the growth of a first rate-journalist coming into her own.

Shortly after the Soviet excursion, Beth seized an opportunity to travel to Beijing in 1992 as visiting editor of the *China Daily*. This trip tested her mettle even more than the Russian stint, given the obscurity of the Chinese world and the turbulence of the time in the wake of the violence at Tiananmen Square. Her Marin readers may have missed her lighthearted takes on county lifestyle, but they gained immense understanding of a strange world far away yet interpreted vividly by their favor local columnist.

In the latter part of the 90's, Beth was assigned as a loaner to *USA Today* in Washington, D.C. where she worked on the Life section of that paper at a time when D.C. was embroiled in all things Monica and Bill. Beth Ashley has always demonstrated an uncanny knack for being in the right place at the hot time.

"When you write a column, you sometimes think the whole world is your canvas, and often it's hard to separate idle chat with friends from potentially new column material."

Significant trips in the past two years have included travels to Antarctica, Afghanistan and most recently, Iran.

"I dearly love what I do," she says, "and I am constantly seeking fresh voices, new stories. When you write a column, you sometimes think the whole world is your canvas, and often it's hard to separate idle chat with friends from potentially new column material. In other words, if you see me coming, watch out—you might end up in the pages of the newspaper!"

After her first marriage, Beth met and married Ross Ashley, a journalist and widower who had two sons. Beth had one son from her previous marriage, and soon she would give birth to two more, so just like that she and Ross had five young boys to raise. Once again, perfect column fodder.

Sadly, Ross died of cancer in 1971, so the challenges facing Beth, now a widow with five mouths to feed, were substantial. This was the time in her life when she reached down deep, summoned all the strength she could muster, and put together a very successful public relations firm. But shortly after this is when the *Marin IJ* wooed her away from public relations and asked that she work as a features writer, editor and occasional columnist, which is who she has been for the past 30 years.

Journalism is nowhere near as lucrative as public relations, but if Beth Ashley hadn't chosen to accept the more modest journalism offer, can you imagine how many lives would not have been touched by this cool chick with the magical pen?

Bill Bagley

If Mt. Tamalpais had a voice, one suspects it might sound like Bill Bagley.

The man commands attention with his pipes. That is a severe understatement. His mellifluous vocal artistry is sort of like Barry White meeting James Earl Jones. When he announces his presence, women have been known to swoon, children scramble, deer scatter in terror.

Enough levity—Bill Bagley is nothing if not the very embodiment of *gravitas.* Raised in a two-room (post-1929 bankruptcy) Woodacre cabin, he worked as a summer Marin County fireman to pay his way at U.C. Berkeley, commuting from West Marin by ferry, and became *Phi Beta Kappa* valedictorian and permanent president of his 5,000-member graduating class of 1949.

A graduate of Boalt School of Law, he ran successfully for the State Assembly in 1960, and served Marin and Sonoma Counties in that capacity for the next 14 years. President Jerry Ford appointed him as the First Chairman of the Commodity Futures Trading Commission. California Governor George Deukmejian "drafted" Bill as a California Public Utilities Commission (CPUC) member, appointed him Chairman of the California Transportation Commission, and then to a total of 13 years as a Regent of the University of California. Presently, Bill is a Trustee of the Marin Community Foundation (the Buck Trust) appointed by the U.C. President.

Colleagues and critics alike—he's too lovably bear-like to have enemies—swear to his swarming, engaging charisma.

The man epitomizes the practicing attorney who dedicates himself to *pro bono* public service. His knowledge of Marin history, political infrastructure, family ties, and his grasp of how to navigate one's way through the often baffling labyrinth of government and bureaucracy is breathtaking.

The same can be said for his love and understanding for the State of California. That love is being severely tested these days for the moderate

Republican, because it sickens him to witness how the Legislature and most of government have become dysfunctional and paralyzingly ideological.

He comes from a legislative tradition of true collegiality in the State Legislature when members of both parties could argue vigorously during the day over vital state issues, then respectfully party and jostle together after hours. They worked together to make this a great State—this was the era of giants who built university systems, waterways and dams, superhighways and mass transit complexes. They fought like hell when the taxpayer's clock was ticking during the day, they accomplished great things, then they clinked glasses at dusk in celebration of their creative differences.

Bagley is a moderate Republican who loathes ideologues. He knows that state governance is about people, not agendas. It literally breaks his heart to see how California has descended into the gridlock and paralysis of dysfunction.

Today, at 76, he is still pro-actively engaged in a myriad of issues and causes around the State. Based in San Francisco, he is a partner in Nossaman, Guthner, Knox & Elliott, a statewide and Washington, D.C. law firm widely respected in national transportation, water, infrastructure, real estate and environmental legal matters.

He gazes out at Alcatraz from his 34th floor corner office which affords diagonal transbay views of both his beloved Marin home and his *alma mater* in Berkeley. He points to the island prison and with squinty eyes states flatly: "That is my moral compass. I never stole while I was in public office, so I have to keep working now." His eyes twinkle at the sober jest.

Later, in the Le Regency Deli on California Street (where Bagley has been a customer for 25 years), the Armenian owner, Paul Ayanian, comments in an aside that Bagley's eyes, squinting and kind, are "the eyes of a very wise man—Herb Caen had the identical look."

After his family and the State of California (the man's face could easily pass for the State Bear), Bagley's primary passion is the University of California. He was named UC Alumnus of the Year in 2003, an honor which still makes him teary-eyed. As a Regent, he was best known for being the champion of diversity, keeping "my University as open as possible." His foe on the Board of Regents was a black man named Ward Connerly. It is one of the most compelling debates in the State that a moderate white Republican from Marin would be champion of racial equality at odds with a conservative black businessman who has befuddled political observers for years with his odd stance on race issues.

Bagley received a higher vote record scorecard from the NAACP than either his colleagues Willie Brown or John L. Burton. When you're more liberal than those two and you're a registered Republican, that makes you, at the very least, fascinating. Bill states that of all legislative accomplishments, his proudest moment came when he "killed" a bill to repeal fair housing (the Rumford Act) in California. This he did by simply refusing to convene the two-house conference slated to approve the repeal.

Colleagues and critics alike swear to his swarming, engaging charisma.

Equally fascinating is that his pace as a public servant and now as an attorney with juice has actually increased over the years. His law partners marvel at his stamina, his ever-growing sense of the world, and his absolutely ironclad determination to leave a legacy vividly branded Bagley. His current project is leading a statewide bipartisan organization called the Voters' Choice Open Primary, which is an effort to break partisan gridlock in the legislature and return non-ideologues to the Capitol to truly represent the voters. He is president of the group which also includes former Clinton Chief of Staff Leon Panetta, former L.A. Mayor and fellow moderate Republican Dick Riordan, former South Bay State Senator Becky Morgan, and current Democratic State Controller Steve Westly. The organization has collected more than 900,000 valid signatures to put their work, Proposition 62, on the November 2004 ballot.

Living in San Rafael, Bill Bagley is married to the former Diane Oldham, and is the father of five children—Lynn, Bill Jr., Walter, Shana, and Tracy Bagley-White.

His trademark legacy is open government, having authored all Freedom of Information Acts since the 1953 Ralph M. Brown Act. These statutes include the Bagley-Keene State Open Meeting Act, the Public Records Act, anti-discrimination amendments to all meeting acts, and a constitutional amendment opening the meetings of the U.C. Board of Regents.

Margie Belrose

Around 1962, when my little sister Patty was nine, I vividly recall attending a performance of "Oliver" at the Belrose Theatre in San Rafael. Patty was my family's starlet. She would dance on the coffee table at our home in Greenbrae. Tutu afloat, legs pretzeled, toes on tippy, she pretended she was Tina the Ballerina. When Margie Belrose assigned her to the cast of "Oliver," Patty felt like she had been called to Broadway. I will never forget her singing one of the signature songs from the musical, "Where Is Love?" A single oval light circled my sister as she chirped her little heart out to a totally rapt audience at the Belrose Theatre. It was a stunning moment. Patty Anderson Weber died in 2003. I dedicate this page to her, and I thank Margie Belrose for providing me with such a sweet, poignant memory.

"Of course I remember Patty," Margie Belrose tells me, "and I remember the courage it took for her to get up there and perform a solo. I am so proud of her and of the thousands of Marin girls and boys who have come to me in their formative years to learn about dance and song."

Margie and her husband David Belrose opened their prized theatre nearly 42 years ago inside the vacated Trinity Lutheran Church across the street from the San Rafael Library. It was a longtime dream the two of them had shared for years as they tried to figure out their niche in life.

As an orphaned young girl in New Jersey, Margie has vague recollections about dancing on a hillside and knowing in her heart she wanted to be a dancer when she grew up. The years and circumstances are a blur, but Margie somehow moved from the East Coast to Lodi, where she worked for a family as a housekeeper doing odd jobs. She also worked for another family whose children were dance students, so she joined them in their regular classes.

After high school, during which she continued to dance, Margie had saved enough money to come to San Francisco, where she schooled at the Mason-Kahn Studio and the San Francisco Ballet, and learned ballroom dancing at the Greg Moore Studio. It was during these lessons that she met David, her private instructor who was also a student of psychology at San Francisco State.

After falling in love and getting married, David and Margie moved to Marin to pursue their dream of opening a community-wide studio to teach and celebrate their cherished dance passions. Margie says the availability of the old church on Fifth Avenue was very much like a divine omen.

"I knew this was the place," she says, "especially after viewing the pews and the stage-like altar. I didn't know how we were going to afford it. Our children were three (Dea) and five (David), the mortgage was substantial because we had to bring the building up to code, but I was absolutely determined to make this happen.

"I had an attorney friend in Ross, Sol Abrams. David and I had taught his children, so he knew about our talents. I called him late one night and implored him to help us with the down payment. After very little convincing but great emotion, he agreed to help us. I will never forget this wonderful man's generosity."

The '60s were really great days for the Belrose Theatre. It was truly a one-of-a-kind Marin experience. The theatre was a beehive of activity, offering lessons in jazz, ballet, tap dance and drama to Marinites of all ages. It wasn't uncommon to see an earnest little ballerina protégé showing up for lessons at the same time an octogenarian gentleman would arrive for acting class. Margie and David were at the top of their game, and the Belrose Theatre became the embodiment of all things theatrical in Marin. Under Margie's dutiful approach as an instructor and David's skills as a wordsmith who penned original scripts and scores, this was a dream that had come alive.

At the crest of their hard work and newfound success, David Belrose dropped dead in the middle of the night on October 15, 1971.

"I was paralyzed," recalls Margie. "He was only 45 years old, which today sounds so young. Fortunately, however, we had been such close partners, both business and personal, that I didn't go into the kind of financial shock that a lot of widows experience. The emptiness our family felt was emotional, but we knew we had to go forward.

"The first thing the children and I resolved was that the school and theatre would go on. It would be very difficult, because we had always relied on David's original plays and scripts. Now we had to pay for professional scripts like 'The Miracle Worker,' 'The Lion in Winter,' 'The Wizard of Oz,' 'Peter Pan,' and all the rest. But we were up to the task. The empty hole without David was enormous, but we just viewed it as the opening of new opportunities for us."

The theatre was a beehive of activity, offering lessons in jazz, ballet, tap dance and drama to Marinites of all ages.

New opportunities, indeed—over the ensuing years, the Belrose Theatre became The Performing Arts Center, an umbrella for all the acting, improv, and dance classes; in 1977, the company opened a highly regarded costume shop, which today boasts the most complete inventory in Northern California and which provides over 3,000 costume rentals for participants of the Arizona, Georgia, Colorado, Atlanta, Texas and Northern California Renaissance Faires.

Today, a thriving Belrose Dinner Theatre offers a full evening of entertainment ($37.50 per person tops) with waiters and waitresses turning into lively performers, dancers and singers. Margie has been made countless offers to expand her venue into larger presentations like auditoriums and civic centers, but she is determined to maintain the intimacy of her little theatrical gem.

In 1981, she converted the business into a non-profit organization, thereby enabling even more students to qualify for scholarships.

"I'd be remiss if I didn't mention Rodney Sheriff," Margie concludes. "He filled a great void left by David's death, and when he came to us in 1975 as a comedian and actor—he'd performed at the Punch Line, the Holy City Zoo, and had worked with Robin Williams—he brought light and brilliance. He has also expanded his skills to include set designing, lighting engineer, technical director, writer and teacher."

Margie Belrose is a jewel of Marin. Inducted into the Marin Women's Hall of Fame in 1996, she has brought joy and entertainment, magic and hope into the lives of thousands of Marinites.

Chuck Bennett

If Chuck Bennett's ego were the same size as his frame, he'd be the King of Marin. Fortunately, like many people with girth and gravity, he's a teddy bear/puppy dog deep inside.

"I don't have a big enough ego," says the bearish man with a heart of a lion, "that I have to get out in front, but I am concerned about my community and I do whatever I can to make it better.

"As a businessman," continues the longtime head of Cal Land Title (Marin's leading title business), "I recognize the importance of schools, and from a business standpoint, the importance of educating our children. We see the difficulties of finding capable, intelligent new talent. It's appalling, and I put it back on the schools. Unfortunately, the schools have become a babysitter rather than an educator.

"As a high-profile businessman, there are so many opportunities to get involved. Frankly, it's hard to decide where to focus, but all the issues are important—the environment, the stability of business in general, certainly the schools and the education of our youth, and the aging of our population. They're all vitally important."

Bennett's Marin roots are deep, especially in Novato. As a child, he lived in Lanham Village or what later became Lanham Village at Hamilton Air Force Base. His father was the Provost Marshall at the military base, and the family really liked living at what was at the time considered to be a garden spot of military bases.

After living at Hamilton for three years, the family bought a house on the outskirts of Novato on Bradley Avenue across the street from where the old Novato Hospital used to be.

"I was going to St. Raphael's grammar school in San Rafael," recalls Bennett, "and was scheduled after high school to go to Japan with my Dad. He was slated to be transferred there in mid-1956. But the day before school began, my Dad died, so I stayed in Marin, went to Novato High, and graduated from there in 1960.

"After high school, I went to the University of San Francisco for a year and a half, but soon quit and went looking for a job. The first people to hire me were the folks in San Rafael Title Insurance and Trust, where I made $250 a month. I thought that was big bucks—I was a clerk, but the opportunity to move up happened quickly.

"In 1970, Cal Land recruited me. I worked here until 1981 when I bought the company—actually, a group of us bought it. It was basically in bankruptcy at the time, so we changed it around and have done very well ever since.

"What's fun about the title business is that you get to witness firsthand all the changes that occur in your community. I worked on the Marincello project down in the Sausalito Headlands (the ill-fated development that would have built a virtual city atop and to the west of the Waldo Tunnel), the San Marin project when Sunset International was the developer of that, the construction of Peacock Gap, and all sorts of pockets of development around Marin."

Bennett is as blunt-spoken as he is formidable. He minces no words when it comes to the quality of political leadership in his beloved Marin County: "I think political leadership here is terrible," he says. "Clearly, there are very, very few leaders in this community, except for Cynthia Murray, among others, who is a standout. We have many problems, and very few of the so-called leaders have risen above or have a command or understanding of what has to be done, of where the soft spots are.

"I think there is a terrible lack of balance. Most of the *quasi* leaders have a specific agenda. So they focus on that and fail to see the consequences of their actions."

Does he feel comfortable confronting these leaders?

"In a heartbeat," he responds. "I've given up being a nice guy. For so long, a lot of people have said you don't want to piss anybody off, you don't want to make enemies out there. There's a great slogan that came out of the California Association of Realtors—'Get into politics or get out of business.' I realized then that if you don't stand up for yourself, nobody else is going to do it.

"So, yes, I've taken that on. I don't shy away from the conflicts and I certainly don't always win, but at least people know where I stand. A large part of the problem is term limits. Then there's the very structure of politics, whereby politicians are not only in the limelight but are also under the microscope. Therefore, everyone's afraid to make a move. They take the public pulse, then they make a decision.

"I don't shy away from the conflicts and I certainly don't always win, but at least people know where I stand."

"Meanwhile, we have critical issues—transportation is a regional issue. Fiscal viability is a huge issue. So is water. And the lack of sensitivity with the people in this community in regards to the homeless and affordable housing is downright scary."

Bennett, who is overextended himself with community service, sits on the boards of community organizations like the Novato Chamber of Commerce and North Bay Family Homes. He finds the biggest challenge facing him is learning how to balance family, business and community activities. Bennett, who was named Novato Citizen of the Year in 2001, is married to Patty Bennett. Their daughter Cathryn goes to San Marin High and is involved with basketball, volleyball and soccer.

His business is doing "very, very well. I have a core group of absolutely dedicated people who are under a lot of pressure because of the re-finance mania, but we take care of them and support them as much as we can. We have three branches—Novato, Greenbrae and Mill Valley. We have 90 employees, some of whom have worked with us for 20 or 30 years. Basically, we handle the paperwork on real estate transactions—the documents and the money. We act as a disinterested third party."

Ending the interview on a positive note, the affably quiet-spoken Bennett says: "If people stay connected and don't give up, Marin's got a chance. I see a lot of longtime Marin County residents growing increasingly frustrated with all the problems we have. Yet, as for me, despite the over-regulation of everything—which drives me crazy—I still get up in the morning loving what I do."

Al Boro

San Rafael Mayor Al Boro is far too modest a human being to ever take seriously the suggestion that he is the "Man Who Saved San Rafael," but there are many, many citizens of this central Marin hub who would happily grant him this distinction.

Life has a miraculous way of making sure that certain vectors in history intersect artfully, melding trying times with skilled individuals.

It wasn't too long ago that San Rafael looked bleak, lifeless, drab, like a once-promising starlet who had lost her way. For a city that is basically the centerpiece for a county that is nationally envied and internationally renowned, San Rafael was on the verge of losing its soul in the early '90s.

Fourth Street, long heralded as the main vein of a sense of community that thrived here in the '50s and '60s, suddenly looked boring, depressed, out of focus, disjointed, wholly without a theme or look of consistency.

The country was in the throes of a recession, and the dispirited look and feel of downtown San Rafael did not give buoyancy to people's outlook or merchants' ledgers.

Then-San Rafael City Councilman Al Boro, a Marin resident since 1960 when he and his wife Pat moved from San Francisco to Corte Madera, decided to step up, seize the reins of leadership, and actually do something about his city's sinking plight.

"It's all about citizen participation, really," admits the quiet-spoken Boro, whose strength as a civic leader rests largely in his ability to bring out the best in others, building a consensus for change, and driving the right elements together to effectuate badly needed transformations.

"Getting the community involved was the easy part," he says, "because the problems were right in front of us. Vagrancy was on the rise, physical deterioration of buildings was more than evident, and shoppers were deserting Fourth Street in droves for malls both new and old.

"So it was simply a matter of fathering a vision for the city and rallying the troops behind it. Once people sensed we were serious about change, there was a tremendous buy-in."

An entire litany of physical change ensued, including the razing and reconstruction of the Macy's block into a bright, cheerful work-live space; the restoration and revitalization of the Rafael Theater (behind the leadership of the Mill Valley Film Festival's Mark Fishkin and Ann Brebner); the creation of a street fair-like Farmer's Market that brought life and vitality to a once dreary boulevard at least one night a week; the renaissance of the Italian Street Painting Festival, which gives a small town artsy look to San Rafael with its amazing creativity (including reenactments of the Sistine Chapel and other classic works of art); and the birth of the San Rafael City Plaza, which grew from the public's hunger for an upbeat gathering place.

San Rafael, named for an archangel and apparently looked over with extremely caring arms from above, was becoming a new city before our very eyes.

The diverse population of this core of Marin's multiple-city makeup became something to celebrate, not to fear. If 22 percent of the populace were Hispanic, this presented a challenge, not an obstacle, to give new thinking to mixed-use, affordable housing.

"Our goal was to keep downtown alive," says Boro, "and this is done by inclusion and smart growth, accepting reality for what it is and making the most of it. Of course, we are blessed with an absolutely great, astute, and savvy public, a very solid, forward-thinking City Council, and a very talented City staff. We've managed to make things happen, maybe not as swiftly as some people would like, but we've accomplished things in a way that sets San Rafael apart as a city that knows how to get things done. It's been extremely gratifying for me."

Leadership is not always born; sometimes it is shaped on the anvil of experience. Boro is of solid stock, having been raised and educated in San Francisco, where he went to St. Igantius High School, and was student body president of the University of San Francisco in 1957 at the crest of that school's meteoric rise to national acclaim when they were NCAA basketball champions featuring the likes of Bill Russell and K.C. Jones.

Boro started work at an early age, earning the kingly ransom of $49 per week with Pacific Bell in The City. He and his wife Pat, who was born and raised in San Francisco, have four children (all products of St Raphael's grammar school in San Rafael)—Al Jr. is an attorney in San Francisco; Maureen is a pharmacist in The City; Mike is a lawyer in New York; and Gena is a mother in Pleasanton.

Civic engagement has always been a significant part of Boro's makeup. He was a homeowners' association president and served on the Planning Commission when he was a Corte Madera resident. He and his wife, Pat, moved to the Dominican area of San Rafael in 1966. In 1968, he was appointed to the County Parks Commission by Supervisor John McInnis. Later, in 1971, he was appointed to the San Rafael Planning Commission, and was elected to the San Rafael City Council in 1987. In 1991, he was elected to his first term as Mayor, and has been reelected to three subsequent terms.

Life has a miraculous way of making sure that certain vectors in history intersect artfully, melding trying times with skilled individuals.

"Personally, even through the most difficult stages of revitalization," says Boro, "this has been a very rewarding job and an overall great experience. How else would I have been able to meet three Presidents? These types of experiences make up for all the long hours you work on striving to make housing and traffic issues flow more smoothly. Sure, issues like these will always be with us, but the important thing is to make progress and try to have fun in the process."

Making things happen could very well be Al Boro's theme song. Like many people with vision and organizational skills, he's not afraid of the tedious grinding that comes with big plans; in fact, his best talent may be in recognizing the talent in others, then delegating effectively—and that has always been the universal definition of successful leadership.

One need only take a short walk down history's most recent path to recall the kind of limbo stagnation that was stunting San Rafael's growth and driving people away from the city. San Rafael just didn't seem like a very fun place to visit in the same way it did in the '50s when everyone knew each others' name.

Today, there is tone, identity, flavor, distinction, character, maybe even a bit of creative edge to San Rafael's personality. This renaissance will forever be linked with the name of Al Boro.

Larry Brilliant

When asked to summarize his somewhat serendipitous philosophy of life, Dr. Larry Brilliant of Mill Valley calls upon the words of his equally enchanting friend and fellow hipster, Wavy Gravy of Woodstock/Haight-Ashbury fame: "Put your little bit of good where it will do the most real good."

Talk about keeping things simple. And Dr. Larry is nothing if not simple. And Brilliant.

Many baby boomers who submerged themselves in the hippie era eventually took deep sighs, measured their mortality, and settled for lives far less exciting yet more monetarily rewarding by taking on jobs and careers they once fiercely denounced as "selling out."

Brilliant, now 60, had all the trappings of a career hippie—Hog Farm commune veteran. Friend of counterculture writer Ken Kesey. A pilgrim to India to consult with Baba Ram Dass' guru, Neem Karoli Baba. Medical advisor to rock stars like David Crosby, Mama Cass Elliott, and Jerry Garcia. And a fellow inhabitant of Alcatraz when it was taken over by an Indian uprising—Brilliant, a doctor, was one of a handful of white guys living on the seized former federal island; he had been invited to deliver an Indian baby on the island and lived there with the Indians for weeks thereafter

Limited space cannot possibly or accurately chart the zig-zagging meteoric path of this Brilliant man's race with the galaxies, so simply strap on your reading belt and try to catch fleeting glimpses.

Most recently, Brilliant, who founded the Well, one of the first online communities, has been CEO of SoftNet Systems Inc., a San Francisco broadband firm that offers high-speed Internet access to small cities, airports and rural towns. He oversaw 1,000 employees and a company with almost a billion dollars—pretty much the type of guy he once may have scoffed at in his hippie years, except it is fair to say that Dr. Larry Brilliant is still part hippie.

Despite his business success and his life's work, his heart

is still entwined with the Seva Foundation, which he founded in 1978 to restore vision to poor people in Africa and Asia, for which he has received numerous awards, including an honorary doctor of science and being named by University of California as its 2004 "International Public Health Hero."

The way Brilliant tells the story of how he got into international health, he was sitting under a tree at his guru's ashram in the Himalayas, meditating and contemplating the vagaries of life following recent surgery to remove a cancerous para-thyroid gland. The guru, Neem Karoli Baba, would disturb Brilliant's search for peace by throwing apples at his testicles.

"What the guru was attempting," laughs Brilliant, "was to disturb my peace, and push me into what my life's work ought to be. My guru was quite specific—after waking me up, he said my mission was to vaccinate people against smallpox in India."

Brilliant never questioned his guru. He boarded a bus and was soon hired by the United Nations World Health Organization to begin administering smallpox vaccinations to India's besieged citizens. This was a plague of monumental proportions—India was devastated, corpses were causing rivers to flood, the disease was epidemic.

Talk about daunting—Brilliant was a member of a tiny team of physicians battling an epidemic that threatened to explode from the hundreds of millions of people in India and re-infect all of Asia. Village leaders throughout the land were taken by this strange foreigner and his focused mission. Brilliant—who has been described as two-thirds Dalai Lama, one-third Chauncy Gardiner—tried to explain to village chieftains that it was his *dharma*—his destiny—to fight the disease. He said it was simply his guru's wish that Brilliant fight to eradicate smallpox in India.

And so it went, from village to village, Brilliant battling seemingly insurmountable odds. Working in conjunction with a formidable team from the United Nations, Brilliant toiled in this battle for more than three years.

Starting off as the "mascot" of the United Nations team, Brilliant somehow found himself supervising a medical program employing 100,00 workers offering vaccination house calls throughout the entire country.

Of this mind-blowing experience blending blind trust with major accomplishment, Brilliant explains: "Greater things have happened to me by accident than by planning—getting to India, meeting my wife, finding myself at the head of the India smallpox program. I could not have planned any of those things."

When Brilliant and his wife, Girija, returned to the United States following the successful effort against smallpox, he became a professor at the University of Michigan, she got a PhD. in public health, and they raised three children (Joe, Jon and Iris). They then set up the aforementioned Seva Foundation, which for the past quarter of a century has allowed 2 million cataract victims to see again.

As Brilliant explains it, Seva "started primarily as a spiritual organization—the work we did to alleviate blindness was a consequence of our spirituality. It was motivated by a desire to serve God by doing good."

"The point of life is to transcend the smallness of the finite self by identifying with things that last."

The work of Seva attracted U.N. diplomats, major foundations, professors, and also the Grateful Dead's Bob Weir and Danny Rifkin, who became Board members of the organization. Brilliant also convinced Apple's Steve Jobs to lend financial and technological support to the organization.

All of this is quite a bit to absorb, but Brilliant, a Michigan native who studied philosophy as a youth and decided to use his life to change the world, has done precisely that. In a musing moment, he says he has devoted his life to trying to grasp this one mysterious mantra—"Live your life without ambition. But live as those who are ambitious."

Confused? Let this unique Marinite explain more fully: "Say you decide that you like Chevrolets and not Fords. Or you decide that you like *Yahoo!* and not Google. It's all the same. In my case, I felt that it was more important to stay in the monastery and deepen my spirituality rather than work in the world. But in the long run, your small preferences don't matter to your happiness. They distract you from seeing what is most important to you.

"The point of life is to transcend the smallness of the finite self by identifying with things that last. From my preference for a certain path comes confusion, and from that confusion comes inability to reason, and from that inability to reason comes *pranshiti*—total destruction of the cognitive process."

Is that Brilliant. . . or what?

John Briscoe

John Briscoe of Ignacio is a master storyteller, a poet, a *bon vivant,* a diversified writer, an impassioned Californiaphile, a devoted father (he has two children from a previous marriage—John Paul has served in the Army for three years and is beginning college, and daughter Katherine is a Junior at Tulane College), and an affable hobnobber who also just happens to be an. . . attorney.

"I am a poet," he says over dinner in one of the hallowed wooden booths inside the Tadich Grill in San Francisco. (Did we mention he is also the official biographer for that famous restaurant? The book is on sale at the bar. It is truly not only a masterful profile of one of The City's most historic eateries, but it is also a brilliantly spun tale of San Francisco's most famous events and personalities.)

It is compelling that such a successful, respected lawyer (whose expertise is land, water and natural resources work with the Stoel Rives firm in The City) would first describe himself as a poet, but he says his love of poetry has deep Marin roots.

"In 1974, I vacationed at Stinson Beach, and stopped at the book shop to look for new poetry publications, and found an intriguing volume by a fellow named Robert Hass. The book had won the coveted Yale Younger Poets Award of that year, which is the most prestigious designation any young poet can receive." (Hass is a Marin native who served as America's Poet Laureate under Bill Clinton; his profile is also in the pages of this book.)

"As I got halfway through his poetry, I realized this man loved Marin as much as I do. Who was he? He was writing the kinds of things I wished I could write."

Briscoe soon befriended Hass, and the

two have been very close friends for years—Hass once recited a poem in honor of Briscoe and his wife, Carol Sayers, a controller for a San Francisco law firm, an artist and a former professional ice skater who was born and raised in The City's Mission District.

"A few years ago," Briscoe continues, "I was teaching law at Boalt Hall in Berkeley, and Hass asked me to be a guest lecturer at his U.C. undergrad class. He and his wife Brenda Hillman and I are members of the Advisory Board of St. Mary's College MFA Program of Creative Writing. We consult frequently on fun writing issues—now if I can only quit my day job! I was extremely honored that America's foremost poet, Bob Hass, had planned on reciting poetry at my wedding; a conflict occurred and he couldn't attend, so we used Hass-inspired verse instead."

The Stockton native started out as a newspaper writer. At 16 years old, he brashly walked into the sports editor's office of the local paper and talked himself into a job covering virtually everything—high school and college football games, big fires, Bobby Kennedy's assassination, book reviews, obituaries.

"I've done a lot of academic writing," says Briscoe, "all the stodgy footnote stuff, and I love doggerel, historical pieces and, of course, poetry. If you allow me to name drop, again, former San Francisco Mayor Joe Alioto and I used to meet regularly at Tadich and compare poetry notes. Not many people realize this, but the man was a true romantic who penned some breathtaking poetry about his wife.

"I am also a *bona fide* lover of California history, something like State Librarian Kevin Starr who is a walking treasure of state lore. I am a mere dilettante next to him. But I am truly fascinated by the history of our state, and I am on the Board of the Bancroft Library at Berkeley where I can continue this pursuit of California."

Alas, everyone has to make a living, which is why Briscoe is also an attorney, but one should not be fooled by his self-deprecating jabs at "day job." His colleagues and peers say Briscoe is possessed with a razor-sharp legal edge, and he also practices law with the most vital legal requisite firmly in place—integrity. He has done extensive legal work for the State of Alaska, he has spoken before the United Nations tribunal that is hearing the environmental claims against Iraq, and he has written articles for the *Law Review* on relevant First Amendment issues of the day.

Try as we might, however, the conversation keeps getting pulled out of law and into literary. "Being a lawyer is hardly writing," Briscoe explains. "Writing a brief is not so much the silver-tongued oratory you might think it is. It's a lot of grunt work, very tedious. If you heard *Gore v. Bush* in the U.S. Supreme Court, for example, or if you've heard Solicitor General Ted Olsen argue a case for Bush, it's not exactly William Jennings Bryan."

Luckily for Briscoe, the Tadich Grill loomed like a plum ready to be plucked into his literary grasp. This was the place where, as a kid who had moved from Stockton to North Beach, he watched in awe as The City's movers 'n shakers made deals, exploded in fraternal laughter, banged shoulders, slapped backs and clinked glasses.

Poet, raconteur, husband, father, historian, biographer, attorney—John Briscoe is truly a multi-dimensional figure living the good life in Marin.

"The food story about Tadich is essentially this," Briscoe says. "In 1849 at the beginning of the Gold Rush, there were fewer than 500 people living in San Francisco. By the end of the year, there were about 100,000 living here. Imagine that! It was chaos and vigilantism, yet, get this—less than 20 years later, in 1869, the most popular French writer of the era, Dumas, wrote on his deathbed that the city with the most and best restaurants in the world after Paris was San Francisco. Isn't that remarkable?

"This comes directly from his deathbed manuscript, *Le Grande Dictionaire de Cuisine,* and he makes this assertion about a 20-year-old brash young city still drunk with Gold Rush Fever. How could this have happened? That was one of my motivating factors weaving San Francisco history in with the story of the Tadich Grill.

"There's a back story to all of this, and it's about California wines, which really didn't make it on the world scene until nearly 200 years later when, in 1976, California beat French wines at a tasting in Paris and suddenly the whole world was taking notice. But that's another story and, in fact, another book that I am shopping around."

Poet, raconteur, husband, father, historian, biographer, attorney—John Briscoe is truly a multi-dimensional figure living the good life in Marin.

Mary Jane Burke

Mary Jane Burke, nearing her first decade as Marin County Superintendent of Schools, conjures memories of another California educator, the late Superintendent of California Public Instruction Wilson Riles, whose eloquently simple guiding principle in life was his first campaign slogan: "For the Children."

Mary Jane Burke exudes the same sense of simplicity and devotion.

"My values are instilling pride and a good work ethic in kids," she states. "And accountability, an understanding that the educational process is getting kids ready for life. It doesn't matter what your background is—I would say that in this profession, you are reminded that the role of a teacher is to empower and motivate others, especially when it comes to Special Ed. My daughter Jane is teaching Special Ed at Long Beach, and that makes me so proud. My son Bob is in his third year at Hastings Law School. My husband Larry died four years ago, and he, too, was an educator—he was superintendent of the Dixie School District."

Burke was born in Stockton and moved to Marin in 1970. The oldest of eight kids in her family, she attended St. Luke's Elementary and St. Mary's High School. Math was always her favorite subject. She attended Dominican, where she had some great teachers—like James Boitano, in political science, and Sister Conlan, a woman, says Burke, of deep faith, integrity and a passion for learning.

"I knew I wanted to be a teacher when I

was in high school," says the Superintendent, who is now ultimately in charge of the education of 40,000 Marin students. "I started working as a volunteer, helping special needs kids, and became a Special Education teacher for four years. Then I became principal at Forest Meadows School in San Rafael, so this is my 30th year working in Marin schools."

And how is the forecast?

"We need to have a continued and clear and articulated vision of what we want Marin to be," she replies without hesitation. "What kind of community do we want to be? Everyone I know is working towards that. I wake up in the morning every day feeling good about what I do, and I continue to be inspired by my job. I feel full of life because there is so much to do and so many challenges. Thinking of the days when each kid is a success is my motivation. I'm always clear about what I think is the right thing for the kids. In that sense, this is the perfect job for me."

What are the hot button issues today?

"One of the challenges we have in Marin is a lack of diversity," she answers. "Our role as teachers is to make sure that the kids are ready to live, work and play in a very diverse world—and to offer a vision of what everyone can do. It's critical when we look at the educational system to make it better for all the students, then to remind the community that it's important to support public education.

"Diversity is the gift of the human race—that we're all different. That's what 'celebrating diversity' means.

"Our commitment must be working," she adds, "because in statewide test results, most reports show Marin County as ranking number one in California. We have a very low dropout rate, we consistently maintain high scores, and kids are going on to college with a great foundation and even greater enthusiasm. The reason those scores are good is because we have good teachers, good stable families, and a great community."

So you like living in Marin, as well?

"I like the visual and performing arts in Marin. I go to plays, read good books, and enjoy museums. I work long hours, but I enjoy community activities. I belong to the Alumni Association at Dominican. I am on the board of the YMCA and several state organizations.

"As for a down side, well," she smiles, "the traffic has really grown. But," she adds, back on the education beat, "there are higher expectations for the schools, which is really not a negative. We can't rest on our laurels; we have to make the schools better all the time. I feel that there is a stronger sense of community here now. Most people I interact with are concerned, really genuinely concerned, with each other. The number of non-profits in Marin is always growing. People are really giving back to the community, and people in The County give of themselves in so many different and very significant ways."

Teachers urgently need their vacations and, someday, retirement. What about you?

"Retirement seems so far off, it's not even in my plans," she responds "I'd probably continue doing the same kind of work, but in a volunteer capacity. We need to get more volunteers into the schools, by the way. If I am to be remembered, I hope it is as someone who worked tirelessly to ensure that all children had the opportunity they deserved."

"I would say that in this profession, you are reminded that the role of a teacher is to empower and motivate others..."

(Readers will note she ignored the vacation query!)

Burke, whose tenure in the Marin County Office of Education included several years as an instructional assistant under former Superintendents Virgil Hollis and Byron Mauzy, feels that she's far less visible, politically and PR-wise, than her predecessors, but that it isn't necessarily a bad thing.

"I realize very clearly that my role calls for a balance of politics and education," Burke continues, "and my definition of politics is, basically, to offer a vision. As for education, I have always viewed my primary responsibility as simply to do the right thing. It is wonderful work and I cherish it. I absolutely adore my job. My job gets me back to the core, and I am very clear about expectations. Again, if I can inspire and motivate the kids, then I am doing my job, no matter how small the small things may seem.

"I am always restless, and, when I say I am 'never happy,' it simply means I am always looking for improvement, maintaining the edge. I am forever thinking ahead. I want so badly to instill a sense of vision and passion in every kid. Then, at the end of the day, I ask one simple question—Is this good for the kids?"

The answer is obviously yes—For the Children.

Jim Canepa

Jim Canepa is a Mill Valley gem.

It feels good—hell, it *smells* good—being around him. Cloistered for this interview in the cozy upstairs office of his beloved Mill Valley Market, one cannot help but be surrounded and soothed by the incredibly fresh aromas of wholesome groceries that waft upstairs, conjuring daydream memories of what it must have been like when all markets were small, neighborly, healthy, community-oriented and centrally located.

Yes, that's it—Jim Canepa, in looks, accent, family connections, attitude, values and career choice is like a Sinclair Lewis character oddly transferred out of time from the pages of "Main Street" into the bustle of 21st century Marin.

The man exudes Jimmy Stewart, Henry Fonda, perhaps a pinch of Jack Lemmon—a native Mill Valley son born in 1932 who has flourished doing what he knows and what he enjoys best in life, serving his customers excellence and affability.

"My father had a store in San Francisco," says Canepa, "but he and my Mom sold it and moved in with a butcher on Throckmorton. There were seven other grocery stores spread around Mill Valley at the time, so he decided he wanted to put a produce department in the old butcher store. He had his grand opening in 1929, the day of the historic Mill Valley fire.

"So there he was, all dressed up to celebrate the opening, fresh off the boat from San Francisco with his load of produce, and the fire chief told him the party would have to wait until after he joined so many others in helping to fight the fire. So, in his suit and tie, he grabbed a shovel and headed for the front lines. Luckily, the wind reversed itself, and the fire was diverted from downtown.

"My Dad had that original store until 1955, when we moved to our current location, the year I got out of the Army. So I got involved in the business and he retired. He still liked to work, however, so he worked produce from 5 a.m. until 8 or 9 in the morning—some retirement!"

The Mill Valley Market has expanded in increments over the years. Patrons who are familiar with the deli area may know that was once the location of Quinn's Bar, a colorful joint that attracted many Mill Valley raconteurs and hooligans. Customers have also been used to shopping with celebrities like Danny Kaye, Grace Slick, Sammy Hagar, Francis Ford Coppola, Dan Hicks, Dana Carvey, Tommy Smothers, Andre Agassi and former Senator Bill Bradley.

"Over time, all these folksy stores with their neighborly policies disappeared," laments Canepa. "As a high school kid, I used to do delivery, so that's one thing we have saved from the old days—although today it is by taxi. This service is mainly for our customers who are sick or shut-in.

"The biggest change currently discussed among the merchants downtown—and I consider myself a resident-serving merchant—is the loss of other resident-serving merchants in the area. That includes the druggist, the hardware store, the men's clothing store, the shoe shop—they're all gone. They've been replaced by art galleries and gift stores—not resident-serving businesses, and that's my major grievance about how downtown Mill Valley has changed. I object even having to go to the freeway to Goodman's to buy nails or other items."

Canepa says he is sort of semi-retired himself nowadays—his son Doug runs the wine department and son David handles the produce—but he still works for the corporation. Four of his five grandchildren also work at the store during their summer breaks.

"They all enjoy it," he says fondly of his offspring's attachment to the market. "I would never force them to become involved unless they wanted to.

"My wife and I have property up in Glen Ellen where we grow organic produce. We had a vineyard in 1980 and produced Chardonnay until 1991, but then a fungus ran through the valley which wiped out a lot of vineyards, ours included. So now we stick to olives, tomatoes, peppers, spring onions and basil. It's just enough so that I can work as much as I want or as little as I want. It's a good life."

Canepa doesn't flinch when asked if he's the "ultimate people person." You'd think after a half century of service he might want to flee customers' queries. On the contrary—"The success of this business," he explains without hesitation, "is that when we are open, at least one of us is always here to field a complaint or provide extra customer service. We are always getting suggestions for products to sell, or people will tell us what to stop—they feel very comfortable giving us their opinions."

His philosophy is profoundly simple—you live in the town, you make your living off the town, you participate in the town.

As a fundraising tool for the Mill Valley Chamber, Canepa and the Mill Valley Market have sponsored for the past 23 years the Wine and Gourmet Food Tasting event which is held in the Mill Valley Plaza.

"It began as the kickoff party for the newly redesigned Mill Valley Plaza, which had been the depot parking lot for Greyhound buses. That first year's event was in November, and we braved the iffy weather, pouring wine and offering cheese and crackers. It cost only five dollars to get in. Ninety minutes into the event, it began to pour like crazy. People went across the street to Lockwood Drugs and bought all the umbrellas, standing in the rain sipping wine. We decided if people would stand in the rain to drink wine, then we should make this an annual event. It now costs $35 per person, and we feature 70 top-notch wineries and gourmet foods. It is considered the number one wine tasting event in the Bay Area."

Even though his life sounds idyllic and storybook, Canepa does harbor some regrets about how absurdly expensive it has become for people to live in Marin. But he continues to give back to the community, nonetheless, donating to the Little League, the Redwoods senior facility and the Kiddo! school foundation. His philosophy is profoundly simple—you live in the town, you make your living off the town, you participate in the town.

Sinclair Lewis could not have said it any better.

Joan Capurro

Iowa-born Joan Capurro, Vice President and Director of Community Relations for Bank of Marin in San Rafael, is the embodiment of an independent-minded, strong woman whose dedication to hard work and community service has reaped rewards both personal and professional.

She came with her family to Southern California (Monrovia/Arcadia area) in 1948 when she was a seven-year-old toddler. After graduating from Burlingame High School, she took classes at both Golden Gate College in San Francisco and the College of Marin in Kentfield. She moved to San Francisco in 1959 and started working as a page girl at Wells Fargo Bank in 1961.

"It was still a very traditional time in the banking industry," she recalls today. "The males would make the loans, and the pages would deliver the paperwork for them. But I kept my eyes and ears open, my mouth shut, and learned all that I could about the banking business."

Like many San Francisco working girls at the time, Capurro lived modestly, occupying a flat at 44th & Balboa. One night, she went on a blind date to Marin County to meet a fellow named Bob Capurro, who was an auto parts salesman—"We went to the Motor Movies in San Rafael and Juanita's Galley in Sausalito," she laughs.

To the newly arrived or to the uninitiated of all things historical in Marin, "Motor Movies" was the appellation given by Marinites to drive-in "theaters" that were popular in those days; and Juanita's Galley was a raucous den of dancing and drinking anchored in the mud at the northern end of Sausalito near Gate 5.

Joan and Bob Capurro apparently hit it off, because they have been married now for 41 years and live in San Anselmo.

"I had this dream, like many of us did," muses Capurro, "to have 10 children—I was raised in a family of 10—and be one busy Mom. But I was captivated instead by work and career. I have always had a great work ethic, and I have never been afraid of working hard to attain what I want and need in life. To my great joy, the banking business opened me up to an entirely new extended family, and I have mentored scores of 'children' in the business who very much feel like my own.

"Gratitude is everything to me," she says, "and I am so extremely grateful to be healthy, to have a wonderful husband, a great job, and lots of friends. The best bank I have ever worked for, Bank of Marin, has afforded me all the opportunities I could possibly have, to brainstorm with people, to network and mentor, and just simply be with so many wonderful people in Marin."

After her page girl stint at Wells Fargo in San Francisco, Capurro transferred to Crocker-Anglo Bank in 1962, working there for 23 years in Corte Madera, Novato, San Anselmo, San Rafael, and the Marina District in The City. It was this nearly quarter-of-a-century stretch of hard-time banking years that truly solidified her status as a service-oriented, people-first business woman who had already made the mental connection between banking and benefit to the community.

This awareness was allowed full bloom when she was named Branch Manager at the Bank of Marin's San Rafael office when the "new" Bank of Marin was launched on January 23, 1990, and it's hard to imagine a person anywhere in Marin who is happier in their work. The bank is located at the crux of San Rafael socializing on Fourth Street, and Capurro delights in the fact that she can literally stick her head out the front door and meet 'n greet a handful of folks she has known for most of her adult life.

What is most impressive about Joan Capurro is that her "giving back to the community" philosophy is gilded in platinum. Her list of favorite worthwhile causes, agencies, boards and civic involvements is mind-boggling—American Red Cross (past Chair), Marin Grantmakers, Marin Senior Coordinating Council Advisory Board, Mediation Services Advisory Committee, Ross Valley Rotary, Salvation Army, United Way of Marin, and Whistlestop Advisory Board.

"It's one thing to have been able to amass all this experience in my career choice, the world of banking," explains Capurro, "but it's quite something else to then be in a position of giving, to take all the good stuff that banking has taught me and be able to share my achievements and insights and resources with people who are doing so many wonderful things for the Marin community. It's a cliche, forgive me, but I sometimes do pinch myself."

"Being rich in spirit is the truest measure of wealth. I am a huge proponent of life's simple things."

And, in case you thought the above list of attachments kept her busy outside of the office, there's more—Capurro has been a principal of the Art Works Downtown project in San Rafael, a member of the advisory board of Nexus (now called Center for Volunteer and Non-Profit Leadership of Marin, where she has served as a corporate volunteer), past president of Marin Forum, an advisor to the Marin History Museum, a member of the development committee for Petaluma Ecumenical Properties and graduate of Petaluma and San Rafael Chamber Leadership programs, San Rafael Board member and chair of the Workforce Investment Board.

"Being raised in a family of 10 and being the third eldest," she says, "gave me a spirit of joy. Being with my siblings meant the world to me. We were so busy and caring, we simply didn't know we were poor. Being rich in spirit is the truest measure of wealth.

"I am a huge proponent of life's simple things," she adds. "I am extremely happy living in Marin, but not for the obvious material reasons. Yes, Marin is a very special place, but mainly because there are so many giving people here. There is an abundance of money, of course, but it is the generosity of spirit that impresses me.

"And, just to keep myself humble," she concludes, laughing, "I still drive my 1965 Ford Mustang with the rebuilt engine. And, if I wished for anything that might come to pass in Marin, it's for less traffic, especially in Fairfax, Mill Valley, San Francisco, and the beach—so that I can really let my Mustang fly!"

Kit Cole

Fiery, tiny, passionate about life, family and business, Kit Cole is as blunt and direct and no-nonsense as her name is short. Twenty-seven years ago, she founded Kit Cole Investment Advisory Services. Her purpose was then—is now—to specifically help women and their families by giving them financial counseling and sound investment management.

"What I am all about," she says from her strikingly handsome and casual office in downtown San Rafael, "is being a force for changing and increasing the economic opportunities for women in Marin County. That has been my passion in life—to help women lead bigger lives by understanding how to use their own personal and financial resources even more effectively."

Her initial investment management business, Kit Cole Investment Advisory Services, was followed by several other successful enterprises, beginning with the formation of New Horizon Savings, which was one of the first successful financial institutions in the country ever founded by women and governed by a board primarily comprised of local women leaders.

"That event was a watershed moment for Marin County," she states, "for how the community perceived women and their ability to create and finance a viable and successful economic venture. In fact, I think it surprised the women themselves!"

Starting from scratch and taking one step at a time, these pioneering women raised $2 million to start the bank. They hired management, provided board oversight through the formative years, and then sold the bank to Luther Burbank for 10 times their original investment—in the meanwhile laying to rest the world's notion that women were not likely to be successful in a financial arena.

New Horizons was followed by Tamalpais Bank and Circle Bank, both of which were also substantially founded, financed and governed by women—thereby removing all doubt about the growing economic involvement of women.

Was there a defining moment in Cole's upbringing that would unleash this pioneering spirit?

"Yes, there was," she says. "When I was growing up, my model was Ma and Pa Kettle—live on a farm and raise 15 kids. I almost made it! I got married, stayed home, had children and baked cookies. I married early, and by the age of 27, I already had five children under the age of seven. Then my marriage ended. There I was, a single woman with a covey of children, totally unprepared to fend for myself economically. Naturally, I sought out financial advisors for help, but they were all men, with no idea what it was like to be a single woman with five children, no job and few immediate prospects.

"At my first successful interview at a major stock brokerage firm in Los Angeles, I was asked by one of the firm's partners—'How do we know that you don't want this job as a broker just to find a husband?' 'Easy', I answered—'What man in his right mind is going to marry a woman with five children under seven years of age?' I got the job! Then I promptly married another man with his own five children under 12. Now, at 31, I had 10 children under 12 years under one roof. Go figure! We had eight children at Ross Grammar School at one time—a record, I suspect."

With all of those children, Cole continued working as a stockbroker.

"I still expected my husband to take care of me, however," Cole admits. "I got a reality check one night when I arrived to find my home had been gutted by fire. There we were, 10 children with no place to stay. Hopelessly overwhelmed with the entire situation, my husband proposed divorce. He later recanted, but the damage was done. It became crystal-clear that I could no longer avoid taking responsibility for my own financial outcome. I could no longer delegate my life's choices and be limited by another's view or prospects.

"I finally understood that it is impossible to have personal peace of mind unless you can take care of yourself financially. Throughout my journey of 35 years in the financial community, I have experienced formidable obstacles, challenges, glass ceilings, naysayers and setbacks. I have also had help, encouragement and support from so many places.

"My goal in life has been to be a model for positive change for the role of women within the financial community. I have been a mentor, a cheerleader and an enabler, to make it easier for all women to achieve their own economic successes and lead the lives they themselves want to lead.

"My goal in life has been to be a model for positive change for the role of women within the financial community."

"The firms that I have helped to create are based on the premise that 'everyone gets a chance to rise according to their own capability and performance—no hidden or real glass ceilings.' I embrace the philosophy that the individual is responsible for her/his own personal and financial outcome. It's that simple!

"Today, one can see women as CEOs of financial institutions and not think twice. In fact, we have two women in Marin County who are bank CEOs. One of them is my daughter, Kimberly Petrini, who is Chairman/CEO of Circle Bank in Novato. There is a third bank in the community with a woman Chairman of the Board, and there are several women serving as Directors of these local banks. That is extremely gratifying.

"I hope that I have inspired women to secure their financial prosperity and security. I believe that it is important for women to take charge of their financial lives: educate themselves, understand their alternatives, learn to obtain financing for their ventures, and invest their resources effectively.

"There simply aren't enough women who really understand finance and economics, or who have fundamental financial skills to represent themselves adequately. When financially literate, a woman becomes an even better partner, in life and in business. The current educational system has failed to prepare women adequately. This has been the basis of my work. When a woman is economically empowered, the less likely her actions will come from fear and the more prepared she will be to create the life she wants.

"I want to be part of women's progress. I might be making just a dent, but it's what drives me."

Nora Lee Condra

As a kid growing up in Greenbrae, I always felt culturally deprived. That's not sour grapes. It's just that we baby boomers were spoiled. We were the first generation of post-war all-Americans to reap the largess of a victorious country. Our parents, God love 'em, felt that since they had won the war, they could choose to live any way they wanted. That's how I found myself as a kid wandering around the crime-free, lily-white suburbs of Marin. The first black woman I ever saw was a noble, elegant, tall and thin young woman named Celeste. She took a Greyhound bus from Marin City five days a week to and from Greenbrae, where she worked as my best friend's housekeeper/nanny. I was fascinated by this person with dark skin who was stern, no-nonsense and commanded so much respect. I was intrigued by the fact that my friend would sass his wealthy parents but would cower in fear if Celeste caught him doing something inappropriate. Her story interested me much more than the frivolous chatter I would overhear at Greenbrae cocktail parties and swimming pool soirees. In retrospect, I thank Celeste for triggering in me a lifelong curiosity about other races and cultures and for opening my mind to peer beyond the highly acquisitive nature of many of my friends and neighbors. We had plenty of characters in Greenbrae, but what really inspired me was the essence of character I saw firsthand in this lovely young woman named Celeste.

Try as I might, I could never find out what happened to Celeste, but I resolved someday to give honor and tribute to her long misunderstood, much feared and sadly ignored neighborhood of Marin City, which for so many years was upscale Marin

County's hushed-up and ostracized ugly little sister that nobody wanted to talk about. It was my great privilege during the organization of this book to meet Nora Lee Condra, who from all reports is something of a much-revered, admired, respected and beloved legend in Marin City. Through her voice, through the lens of her fascinating life in this precious yet underrated corner of Marin, my best hope is that we come to appreciate her and people like my old friend Celeste even more.

On a sunny Sunday afternoon, Nora Lee Condra sits propped up on some pillows inside her modest Marin City residence. There is a steady stream of visitors coming and going through the stretch of the interview. This is the Lord's Day and Nora Lee greets each guest with open arms.

"I first came here in the summer of 1949," she recalls. "I came from Mississippi, I was in my 30s, and it was a big adventure for me. My baby brother was in the service, stationed at Hamilton, so that was the cause of my coming here. I am the oldest of three and I was worried about my baby brother. I took a train all the way here, and soon after arriving, I did some domestic work for a family in Sausalito. My first marriage had ended back home, but I met a man out here who worked for Custom Builders, and pretty soon we got married.

"His name was George Condra. He laid all the pipes for the plumbing projects for the construction company that was building homes in Mill Valley, Terra Linda, Corte Madera, the then-growing suburbs. George passed in 1984.

"When I first moved to Marin City, believe it or not, it almost seemed like 'out in the country' to me—little brown houses with what I called 'turtles.' The tops of the houses were green. It was nice. The people were closer in those days. You could leave your door open and go to San Francisco and come back and everything would be the same when you came home. We all watched out for each other when a neighbor was gone for the day. If someone wanted a beer or a Coke while you were out, they'd come in and help themselves, then tell you about it when you came home.

"I loved riding the ferries to San Francisco and Oakland—it felt like the high seas to me, a kid from the South. I'd stare into the water and just refresh my spirit. You could even eat on the deck of the ferry, too."

A deeply devout and religious person, Nora first joined the Powerhouse Church of God and Christ in San Francisco when she came to the Bay Area. There was no church yet in Marin City in the early 50s, but after a while a room inside the schoolhouse was set aside for worship.

"I helped organize a group of worshipers," says Condra, "who started selling chicken dinners and chicken and fish sandwiches, and pretty soon we raised enough money to build our own church, which is now the cornerstone house of worship here in the community, the Church of God and Christ.

"I loved riding the ferries to San Francisco and Oakland—it felt like the high seas to me, a kid from the South. I'd stare into the water and just refresh my spirit."

"I am a Deaconess at my church and I serve communion, so I get to know a lot of people in the community through that service."

When asked about her family, Nora lets out a joyous "Whoooooeee! I have 28 grandchildren and 17 great grandchildren, and still counting. I have 12 children of my own. Every Thanksgiving Day we have a family reunion, so I invite them plus all my other friends, and we all celebrate in a grand way."

(One of her special Marin friends is *Marin IJ* photographer Frankie Frost, an Alabama transplant who loves Nora Lee's cornbread and who allows himself to get conned into documenting on film the Thanksgiving Day festivities at the Condra residence.)

As for how Marin City suits her today, she chooses her words carefully and with toughness:

"With the new housing, shopping mall and influx of white families in the new apartment/housing subdivision where all the houses are too close together, Marin City has lost that Southern sense of family. We no longer leave our doors unlocked. Although the community had a say in the new development, a process which took many years, it is not the way most African Americans wanted it. We just couldn't make up our minds, so the decision process was taken out of our hands. If you look around, you do not see many African Americans owning or renting the shops and *that* was what was supposed to happen. It was supposed to reflect our culture and that isn't the way it is."

Charles Daniels, Jr.

Someday a rollicking, raucous book will be written about Prohibition days in both San Francisco and Marin County. It will be a fascinating study, laced with wonderfully rich anecdotes and vignettes about bootleggers, rum runners, speakeasies, trap doors in dark houses of questionable repute, and the somewhat vacillating relationship between cops and moonshine peddlers.

Ironically, because he is the epitome of honor and dignity and integrity, one of the purveyors of this oral history should be Charles Daniels, Jr., whose father no doubt shared with his son many of these rich tales. Charles Daniels, Sr., the family patriarch, had been a prosperous San Francisco businessman who came perilously close to losing everything in the dark days of the 1929 stock market debacle.

Determined not to let the Great Depression get the better of his spirits (so to speak), the elder Daniels waited patiently until Prohibition ended, then started selling Rainier Beer to Marinites in 1933. If you think the paranoid days of marijuana growth and use gave birth to a counterculture of whispered secrets and mind-bending suburban legends in the '60s, then you would be amazed at the cornucopia of subculture lore that sprang from the days of Prohibition.

If bottles could speak, Charles Daniels, Jr. holds the key to one liquid library. After the sad passing of Frank Galli several years ago, Daniels inherited from the merry Ignacio Mayor and restaurateur his entire supply of "Galli's—A Place to Eat" liquors. These are historic bottles that graced the back bar of Galli's restaurant in Ignacio, the family steak house owned by Frank's father, Sal Galli, another Prohibition character who unfortunately brought many colorful secrets to his grave.

Countless Marinites have wondered about these bottles—most of them are decades old, they were never dusted, and rarely opened. Because the collection has reached almost legendary status, Charles Daniels, Jr. says he plans on making them available for viewing someday in a gazebo-style glass-and-redwood showcase at a location yet to be announced.

After making a reputable name for himself distributing Rainier Ale and Coors beer in Marin, Daniels, Sr. soon thereafter established the House of Daniels, one of the pioneers in a liquor distributing business that has now become commonplace and highly competitive in a region so heavily saturated in restaurants, hotels and motels, an ever-burgeoning wine culture, and in a lifestyle easily conducive to entertainment and celebration.

Charles Daniels, Jr. took the reins of the family business in the 1960s after a stint as Vice President and Treasurer of Robert Mondavi Vineyards. Daniels has great admiration for Mondavi—he witnessed him overcome huge obstacles, like the time in his life when he was asked to leave the Charles Krug Winery and start his own small winery.

Today, Daniels proudly boasts that House of Daniels was exclusive distributor of Opus I wine, a joint effort of Baron Philippe Rothschild of Bordeaux and Robert Mondavi Wineries that is widely heralded as a magnificent, unique vintage.

Daniels is equally proud of the fact that his son, Peter Daniels, is COO and Executive Vice President of House of Daniels today, which is located at Black Point and is home to a highly sophisticated operation with huge warehouse space, proximity to a railroad, and a drive-through-sized refrigeration walk-in that can hold nearly a half million cases of beer.

"The wine and spirits industry," he says in sober, measured tones, "is a responsible corporate citizen, and we have worked very hard to promote moderate drinking among a responsible public. We wholeheartedly support schools that foster educational programs about alcohol abuse and holiday overindulgence. We are very proud to sponsor the schools' 'Taxi Time' safe driving program during the holidays."

Ever mindful that alcohol sales have declined dramatically in recent decades due to stiffer drunk driving legislation, less tolerant service on the part of lawsuit-fearful restaurants and bars, and an increasingly aggressive campaign by organizations like Mothers Against Drunk Drivers (MADD), Daniels doesn't view the trend as a seriously damaging confrontation that threatens his business, but rather he takes the high road.

"I feel very good about how drinking patterns are changing," he says. "The health-conscious consuming public is merely switching its preference from hard liquor to more benign spirits like wine and beer. We distribute both ends of the spectrum with responsibility and caution.

"And, contrary to what severe proponents of total abstinence like to tell the public, we have full confidence in the drinking public's maturity and how it seeks its own level."

Under his guidance, House of Daniels has expanded into three separate sales companies—Golden Gate Distributing, Blackpoint Marketing, and Trellis Vineyards—which span almost the entire length of California and which provide sales to 20 states. Some of Daniels' favorite prized labels include Trellis Vineyards, Sonoma appellation wines, Dry Creek Sauvignon Blanc, Alexander Valley Merlot, Cabernet Sauvignon and Russian River Chardonnay, a stable of varietal wines from Chile, Villa Magi Chianti and, in the distilled spirits category, Peter Jake's Private Keep, a 10-year-old Kentucky bourbon, and Los Arango Reposado Tequila.

If bottles could speak, Charles Daniels, Jr. holds the key to one liquid library.

Charles Daniels has been married to his wife, the former Carol Lund, for 48 years, and they have three sons—Peter, who has two children, Anya and Peter Jake; Jonathan, who works in beer sales for the family firm and who has one daughter, Katie; and Chal, who had been with the family business but who now owns Harvest Financial and who has five children—Christina, Chase, Taylor, Tovae, and Cael.

Daniels, a longtime Marinite who frequently points out that the celebratory nature of his business fits so perfectly with The County's enhanced lifestyle, is a strong believer in giving back to the community. Not only is House of Daniels actively engaged in countless youth sponsorships and charitable giving, but Daniels himself is personally involved in St. Vincent's School for Boys in Marinwood, where he serves as Vice President for Youth Activities, and at Dominican University, where he serves on the President's Council. He is also on the Advisory Board of Marin Council Boy Scouts of America, and serves as Chairman of the San Rafael Fire Commission.

Shirley Davalos

San Jose-born and raised Shirley Davalos came to San Francisco when she was 16 years old to see a performance of "The Sound of Music" at The Orpheum. She was smitten with the North Bay immediately.

"I fell in love with The County instantly," she recalls. "How could I ever go back to San Jose?"

Not that she didn't know the way to San Jose, but how could she resist the allure of all that the North Bay had to offer?

Davalos was determined to sink roots here, somehow, some way. She took all sorts of jobs at first, opening her life to opportunities in the media-rich days of late '70s San Francisco. Media, if you recall, was the buzz word of the moment—still undefined and vastly untapped, sort of like the dot-com revolution that came into fruition in the '90s.

Davalos is a doer, so she talked and walked her way into many high-exposure situations. She was a friend of Steve Silver before he became famous for "Beach Blanket Babylon." She worked with Silver at the hungry i and put on shows with him on street corners—the precursor of "Beach Blanket Babylon." She worked for both KGO and KRON TV, producing "AM San Francisco" and live—*very* live—New Year's Eve shows set in The City.

Today, she is a media consultant, a widely respected one who has seen the business from virtually every angle available. She has coached a variety of executives, authors and professional speakers who benefit from her creativity and grasp of TV production and programming.

A Marin resident ever since discovering Sausalito while house sitting, Davalos has two daughters, Simone Pilar and Arianna.

Something of a local media pioneer—her vast, varied experience dates back to 1982 when she began producing live talk/magazine programs for both ABC and Chronicle Broadcasting (Channels 7 and 4)—she is still at the top of her game today. Most recently, she has produced health and financial news reports for CNX Media, which produces Dr. Dean Edel's "Health Reports" and "Health Central Web Site."

"I like to brag playfully," she says playfully, "that I am the one who brought Gilbert and Dilbert together."

Translation: Both Gilbert Amelio (former CEO of Apple Computer) and Scott Adams (creator of the insanely popular "Dilbert" cartoon strip) were students of Davalos' Broadcast Media Training, experiences that made them "interview ready" for dealing with big-time media.

Shirley Davalos' specialty is identifying the core message of each of her clients who come to her for coaching, and working with them on an agenda that comfortably positions the clients—celebrities, authors, and CEOs alike—into the interviewee's seat in any interview situation.

How important is this kind of training?

Hear it from San Francisco author Curt Gentry, who felt he had a weak public persona prior to working with Davalos—"You stopped my mumbling and made this book—*J. Edgar Hoover: The Man and the Secrets*—a best seller."

Clients are served intense media training sessions, including on-camera training, disciplines of the mind—forget your purpose, establish your focus, identify your audience, outline your agenda—and all the various elements of the interview itself, including the art of styling yourself visually (wardrobe and make-up review), practicing camera techniques, crafting sure-fire introductions, creating exciting verbal pictures, and learning how to summarize so that your audience is spurred to action—that is, buying your book, joining your membership, purchasing your products.

Davalos keeps her fundamentals simple and sound—Reach Your Audience, Create Clear Messages, Control An Interview. That's how 25 years in the business looks in print when it is boiled down to its most effective essence.

A significant piece of her training revolves around Guided Imagery as a way to completely revolutionize your outlook and preconceptions in life. The focus is on the formulation of new habits and the execution of new life changes that will help you control and shape the issues in your life.

"Habits can make our lives simpler," says Davalos, "by helping us perform acts without thinking. It's like being on automatic pilot, which can be extremely beneficial in the daily routines of life. However, we can change unwanted activities by becoming aware of the unconscious automatic response we perform when we fall into a non-thinking activity."

With her direction, you will discover new ways to use self-talk and affirmations to create new routines and attitudes; you will find out how to focus your energy to cultivate enthusiasm and courage in order to use them to promote your new lifestyle; and you will discover how your intuition can enhance your awareness.

"I like to brag playfully," she says playfully, "that I am the one who brought Gilbert and Dilbert together."

Davalos is completely sold on the concept of Guided Imagery not only as a tool for effective professional enhancement of one's skills, but also as a generator of good things flowing into one's personal life, as well.

"The process is about relaxation," she says, "and letting go of so much garbage we accumulate in our heads—those talking tapes that keep us distracted from easy performance. We are all victims of inner city stress, probably the greatest malady of the day. Guided Imagery can help bring about a different perception within ourselves. I like to describe it as the process of creating good habits so that you can see the good that happens. It works, it really does work."

Her formidable client list—Apple, Chevron, Fisher Investments, authors Daniel Ellsberg, Peter Burrows, Kathy Kamen Goldmark, Carole Adrienne, Ron Hansen, to name a few—and various testimonials from happy students attest firmly to her ability to make constructive changes in one's personal make-up.

Davalos even became something of a fictional heroine through her successful work with author Bonnie Hill Hearn (who wrote *Intern*). Swears Hearn: "I was so impressed by you that I actually wrote a media trainer into my next book!"

Romano Della Santina

Marin Joe's isn't really a restaurant—it is a definitive Marin experience.

From the steaks sizzling on the open-air grill to the drinks clinking inside the cavernous, convivial bar, this is a ritual every bit Marin-ish as hiking Mt. Tam, strolling Bridgeway, sunning at Stinson, or sailing to Sam's.

It's also the very life of Romano Della Santina, a papal-like presence, and his close-knit family with deep Italian roots.

Marin Joe's is the basilica of Marin restaurants. Since 1954, when The County was a sleepy suburb with a handful of coffee shops and few top-flight dining houses, the Della Santina family has carved a niche as the preeminent place to eat.

Fad foods have come and gone. Stylized temples of dining have made a flash impact on the terrain and vanished. But one thing is constant on the Corte Madera/Mill Valley border that is home to Marin Joe's—the telltale sizzle of the grill sparking forth scallops and prawns, Piccata and Scallopini, sirloins and filets, burgers and pot roasts, Joe's Specials and Zuppa Maritata, Chicken Caccciatore and Liver Venetian.

Marin Joe's is the cathedral of garlic, fine wines, celebratory dining, and enduring dependability. In an age when the worship of fine food has reached an almost absurd level of reverence, the Della Santinas have never forgotten that families eating together, friends gathering to celebrate comprise the first order of restaurant business. Fine food and drink are essential, but the never-ending buzz of folks clinking glasses and sharing hearty laughter give definition to Marin Joe's soul.

Romano Della Santina—a wise, kind, jovial man who presides over his tables not unlike a merry Pope—measures his success not by numbers of dinners sold or cases of wine consumed, but rather by the progressive march of generations who file through his doors displaying decades of loyalty. Romano never forgets a face.

"We've watched generations of Marin people come and go," boasts Romano, a happy, serene man who is a master table-hopper. "Parents love to come in with their young kids and brag to them how they were raised in Marin, and how part of that experience was eating here. They even point out the booths where they used to sit. It's very satisfying to see people I knew and served in the 50's maintain their loyalty and continue to come in today."

Original owner of Marin Joe's in 1954 when it opened was Adolph Della Santina. It has stayed in the family's hands since then, and current co-proprietors are Romano and his two sons, Paul and Ralph. Like many Italian restaurants we have all come to patronize in the Bay Area, family allegiance, tradition and loyalty are more like a religion than a business. In fact, if you think about it, they teach us very clear and simple lessons about life—work hard, play together as a family unit, welcome guests into your home graciously, serve excellent food at fair prices, treat people with warmth and respect, remember your guests' names, and show a genuine interest in their welfare.

No think tank analyzing human relations can present a better social formula for healthy interaction than does Marin Joe's—day after day, lunch after lunch, dinner after dinner. The secret ingredient in Marin Joe's fare has very little to do with food but everything to do with how people relate to one another. Simply sit at the counter and observe the drama unfolding around you—old friends happily bumping into each other, total strangers sharing bites of pasta, wisecracking chefs bantering in their native tongue about love and life, waiters and waitresses squeezing past each other good-naturedly and whispering terms of endearment out of diners' earshot. It's a fiesta.

A native of Lucca, Italy who came to the United States in 1948, Romano Della Santina very proudly sports the designation "Cav." on his restaurant business card—that is an abbreviation for "Cavaliere," which is the most esteemed honor Italy can bestow on a countryman for generosity of spirit and work toward Italian people and organizations. The proprietor extends his generosity to a wide ranging index of Marin County schools, non-profit organizations, youth sports teams and other worthy causes.

Romano has been married to his wife, Maria, since 1950, and when the two of them work the door at the fabled Marin eatery, they would resemble royalty if the reference were not such an insult to their working class spirit. Romano is especially proud of the sense of continuity so evident in his restaurant.

"My son Paul learned the business since his days in high school," he says, "and my other son Ralph started six years ago. They have been working here steadily for almost 40 years. Same thing for many of my waiters and waitresses. The turnover rate is very low, and my customers really like the fact that they've been served by the same person for almost a quarter of a century."

The Della Santinas have never forgotten that families eating together, friends gathering to celebrate comprise the first order of restaurant business.

In addition to the always bustling dining room and the extremely cozy confines of the home-like bar, there is the counter where curious diners can observe expert cooking firsthand and there is a private room for any number of Marin businesses, political groups and community organizations to hold secluded meetings and banquets.

In an era when people's tastes have wandered far from the standard steak and hamburger diet, it is truly remarkable that Marin Joe's continues to pride itself on what may be the best hamburger on the planet. Premium beef sizzled to perfection and served on a hollowed out section of sourdough and presented simply with a bed of French fries and a handful of pepperoncini, it is sheer heresy to add anything as garish as garnish to this supreme delicacy.

That's right—add a pepperoncini or two with each bite, no mustard or ketchup, no salt or pepper, no onion or lettuce—it will change your world view of hamburgers instantly.

The piano bar at Marin Joe's, a testament to a sadly vanishing craft, is alive and pluckin' five nights a week, and an entertaining jazz group performs on Sunday evenings as a mellow way to prepare for the work week ahead. In a nod of the head to the strong Irish-Italian bonds that exist in Marin County and in celebration of all the wonderful Irish-Italian marriages that still thrive (and which may have begun in the romantic bar), Marin Joe's continues to serve on Thursdays one of the finest corned beef 'n cabbage dishes this side of County Cork.

Words fail. Eat at Joe's.

Carola Detrick

There is an angel living in our midst.

Carola Detrick—a modest, deeply serene woman from Germany who moved to Marin in 1979—was so profoundly moved by her mother's death from breast cancer in 1987 that she became fiercely committed to finding meaning from one of life's most jarring lessons.

Embarking on a mission that can only be described as inspired and fever-pitched, Detrick, in an embrace of life that would put to shame self-pitying doubters and hardened cynics everywhere, founded an organization called Meals of Marin.

Starting in her own kitchen on March 3, 1993, Carola began to prepare and deliver home-cooked meals to Marinites afflicted with AIDS. She had been a volunteer at a similar organization in San Francisco, Project Open Hand, so shifting her focus to Marin County struck her as a natural way to honor her mother's life.

"I was tending to my mother during the final months of her life," says Detrick, "and I was alone with her when she passed on. This profound experience which changed my life forever and for the good made me feel so grateful about life and all of its mysteries. The choice I made at that time to help others was the easiest decision I had ever made."

Detrick had been working as designer/president of her family's handcrafted leather good business (HCL-Kaspar Roth America), a century-old firm that creates purses, trunks, attache cases and other quality merchandise. She left the business in capable hands once she discovered her newfound passion of feeding the sick, and, she says: "Meals of Marin is now my only professional focus."

Five years after non-stop devotion to Marin AIDS patients—delivering two high-caliber meals a day to sick people from Marin City to the Sonoma border—she was approached by Marin doctors and asked if she could possibly expand her services to include cancer victims, as well.

"How could I say no?" she asks rhetorically. "Once you let the goodness in and the power begins to flow, it clearly becomes the grace of God. I may be helping others live, but this journey has saved my life, as well."

Meals of Marin—or MOM, as it is called, in possible veneration of Detirck's deceased mother—has served nearly 400,000 meals to Marinites suffering from debilitating illness since 1993. That's two meals a day (lunch and dinner), seven days a week, 365 days a year, focusing primarily on homebound people under the age of 60 living with illnesses such as AIDS/HIV, breast cancer, MS, or Hepatitis-C. Meals have never been missed, thanks largely to the 80 volunteers it takes to get the food prepared and delivered.

The genesis of Detrick's awe-inspiring charitable work came at a time when she was a divorced, single mother of two children—Christopher and Michelle—who got up early to help their Mom do the kitchen prep work before their school day began. Her children, she says, gained a great deal from the experience—"Not only was it a wonderful way for us to bond every day, working in the kitchen together, but it also helped them see how blessed we were and how they should never take anything for granted in this life that is so sacred to us all."

MOM receives no government funding, but relies primarily on private donations and community support to serve its approximately 70-80 clients on a daily basis. Working out of a kitchen at 1495 East Francisco Boulevard in San Rafael, volunteers are asked to peel and chop fruits and vegetables, prepare sandwiches, assist the lead chefs with the hot meals, then package, deliver and serve the meals to the recipients around Marin. (The sandwiches are left for the next day's lunch, and they are bagged with care, displaying a little heart and the MOM logo.)

Joe Parenti is a volunteer for MOM, and he describes how some of the donations are generated: "Twice a week the Marin Farmers Market is held at the Civic Center in San Rafael. There you can find organic vegetables, fresh fruit, and delicious baked goods. In the afternoon, MOM volunteers go through the market collecting donations from the farmers. It is truly mind-blowing to see the incredible food donated to us each week.

"There is no shortage of ideas to keep the cooks busy—fresh pasta, homemade pies, and meals that cater to the special dietary requirements of each client, like no salt, no dairy, no wheat."

Volunteer opportunities at MOM are never-ending since meals need to be cooked, delivered and served on a daily basis—drivers are always needed, and it is an easy way to get involved, since routes can be completed to and from one's place of work; high school students required to perform community service are urged to contact MOM to fulfill their hours; and people are needed to sit in the MOM booth at the Farmers Market to get the word out about the organization.

"Once you let the goodness in and the power begins to flow, it clearly becomes the grace of God."

With the nationally noted high incidence of breast cancer among Marin women which has vexed and troubled both medical experts and residents alike, there has occurred a natural bonding between MOM and the Marin Breast Cancer Council. "Stepping Out" has been a highly successful, if not healing, annual gala in Marin since 1996 that features breast cancer survivors modeling designer clothing.

As Council president Kathleen Clark explained in a *Marin IJ* story: "It's just glorious. The idea is to have an evening that makes you feel like there's life after breast cancer and which makes you feel special when you're feeling not sure about your appearance, and you're feeling self-conscious, like you've been given a real jolt."

Since its inception, the wildly successful "Stepping Out" has raised hundreds of thousands of dollars that go directly to cancer-fighting organizations in San Francisco, Marin and Alameda Counties. In 2003, MOM received $12,500 from the Marin Breast Cancer Council.

"We are so grateful for this help," says Detrick, "and we are always grateful to other fund raising sources, as well. The Human Race, which has become such a fun and worthwhile Marin tradition, has been very good to us, as has The Feinstein Challenge, a nationwide food bank that has a very effective matching donation program. The people of Marin and the surrounding Bay Area are the most generous people in the world. They have hearts of gold, and they are keeping us—and, more importantly, our clients—alive and thriving."

Linda Dunn

One of my favorite spots on earth is the top of Mt. Tamalpais. I have so many vivid memories of hiking up there as a kid, partying at the old Mountain Home Inn, and enjoying the splendor of the amphitheater performances of the Mountain Play, which has, quite simply, the most beautiful backdrop of any theater on the planet.

Many newcomers to the Marin scene won't know this, but in 1967 or thereabouts was a swiftly produced rock 'n roll weekend fest called the Magic Mountain Festival held in the amphitheater and headlining Jim Morrison and The Doors. The image of Morrison stumbling and prancing on stage, seemingly in a slow-mo trance, has stayed with me for years.

But that show was an anomaly. What makes the top of Tam so special year after year is the Mountain Play. This is a genuinely Only-in-Marin experience hiking up the mountain to enjoy theater, spreading picnics on the smooth-topped seating boulders, sipping wines out of bota bags while drama unfolds a stone's throw away. It is a distinct honor to include in this book a woman who spent a portion of her career making this heavenly theater such an endearing local success.

"I was teaching at the College of Marin," says Linda Dunn, "and one of the instructors there, Jim Dunn—no relation—was the director of the Mountain Play. I've been involved ever since. I don't think I have what you would call a favorite play. There have been so many and they are all interesting in one way or another, but I remember 'South Pacific' as being the most exciting. We had these vintage World War II fighter planes fly over the performance, and my job was to get them coordinated, and set their timing, using radio. Another of my favorites was 'Fiddler on the Roof.' Each show has its own little flavor."

Dunn has worked with the Mountain Play for 17 years as stage manager, assistant director and sound engineer. Countless numbers of local acting talent have graced the boards of the Mountain Play stage, and Dunn has been an up-close witness to how terribly daunting it is to master the profession.

"There's a phenomenal level of acting talent in Marin," she explains. "but for every Robins Williams there are a lot of people who don't get famous for one reason or another.

"It's a very difficult career and you need some luck to make it. I've seen so many good actors here. Sean Penn and Robin Wright Penn live here, and Peter Coyote, but there are also many people acting regularly who aren't necessarily household names.

"I'm a Texas gal," she continues. "I moved to Marin in 1975. My husband at the time graduated from Heart Institute and we both got jobs in San Francisco. We moved to Marin because it was so beautiful, but we didn't like the commute, so we moved into The City. We moved back after my first son was born. I wanted a yard for them to play in. I love Marin. I separated from my husband and moved to Larkspur. We've lived in San Rafael for the last 23 years. My son Damien is now 28 and a teacher; and my son Jeremy, 23, is co-editor of his college newspaper.

"I taught theater arts at the College of Marin for 10 years. Then I became principal at Marin Primary in Larkspur where I also taught drama for 11 years.

"Then I went to Marin Catholic and ran the theater department there—'Amadeus' was our biggest accomplishment. I have also directed performances for the Ross Valley Players, and am a member of its board.

"I'm not teaching right now," says Dunn. "I'm working as a public speaking coach and 'presentation developer' for the Kerry for President campaign. I'm putting together workshops for their local speakers in the Bay Area. I went to a meeting and there seemed to be a need for some help and guidance. I teach the speakers how to use their voice and body, and how to take advantage of their material.

"My educational experience plays a huge role in all this. Many people don't know how to reach out to the whole group.

"People joke to me: 'Maybe you ought to go teach Kerry that.' Some people have that gift. He's an intelligent man and kind. Public speaking is something of a gift, and sometimes it comes from a genuine love of people. Others just seem to have a gift of gab.

"It is really important," she continues, "to know your audience. A lot can be accomplished by using a good director. A lot of research has gone into that. I'm from the directorial side myself. Fear of public speaking gets down to the personal level. 'Am I going to be accepted or rejected? Will there be a positive or negative response?' You make yourself very vulnerable by speaking in front of a large group of people.

"One of my favorite arts is storytelling. What I love most about it is the creativity. My grandfather was a great storyteller. Whenever we would go camping as kids, we would sit around the campfire and he would keep us all on edge with his terrific stories. The use of imagination is so important, especially for kids in today's world of television and computers."

"There's a phenomenal level of acting talent in Marin, but for every Robins Williams there are a lot of people who don't get famous for one reason or another."

Dunn's voice rises in enthusiasm as she underscores the following point, clearly her most impassioned sentence of the interview:

"*We have to do everything we can to encourage the use of imagination.* We have to teach our children how to create it, build it and share it. I always told my kids bedtime stories when they were growing up, not just reading books. They loved it.

"Robin Williams used to be a student at the College of Marin. I met him as a student. He got his acting start there. That manic energy that you see from Robin in films and on stage is the same manic behavior that he shows in real life. He doesn't turn it on and off; he's always like that.

"I am going to stay with what I am doing now. When my last son is finished with college, I'd like to do some travel. In particular, I'd like to live in London for a while. I'm also interested in helping others. I enjoy being with people. I am a volunteer with various organizations.

"It's so beautiful here, everywhere you go," concludes Dunn. "I like the fact that we are so close to San Francisco, the mountains, the oceans, Tahoe, and Yosemite. It's so easy to get to those beautiful places from here."

Aimi and Bill Dutra

One of the most impressive business teams operating in Marin County is a father-daughter partnership made up of Bill and Aimi Dutra.

In conversation and in business thinking, they complement each others' words and thoughts.

The firm they manage—The Dutra Group—has a heritage of over four generations providing services to an ever-expanding client base in the San Joaquin Delta and the San Francisco Bay Area. Dutra Dredging and Dutra Materials provide a solid organization of experienced professionals—as well as the latest technology and equipment—to ensure that client demands are met in dredging, marine construction and aggregate manufacturing and transportation.

"The San Rafael Quarry," says Aimi Dutra, "has been in operation for over a century, since the late 1800s. Our family business started as a dredging and marine construction company in the Sacramento Delta. We purchased the San Rafael Quarry in 1986. Prior to that, our family was actually a customer of the quarry, purchasing rip rap materials that were then placed by our equipment and crew in various locations of the Sacramento Delta and San Francisco Bay."

The Dutra Group's resume is a formidable one, indeed. Projects include:

Pier 39, Sea Underwater World—Dutra Dredging placed 54-inch concrete cylinder piles, 140-feet long, driven to support a 36-inch thick concrete deck upon which the Waterworld Aquarium was built.

Bay Bridge Earthquake—On site within four hours of the collapse of a portion of the bridge following the 1989 Loma Priete temblor, Dutra's 500-ton derrick barge removed and rebuilt collapsed sections, then reopened the bridge to traffic in 30 days. Reconstruction was designed and built by The Dutra Group.

Pac Bell Park (Now SBC Park)—On December 30,1999, The Dutra Group's Heavy Lift Division conducted the unique lift of the Coca-Cola bottle for San

Francisco's new Pacific Bell Park. Due to its unique size and shape, the 120,000 pound, 80-foot long structure required special rigging and expertise.

"The quarry," explains Aimi, "is full of what is known as 'blue rock.' Our quarry is unique not only for its quality of rock, but most importantly because it is the only quarry in northern California that has waterside shipping capabilities. The San Rafael Quarry provides rock product to various locations in the San Francisco Bay Area; we also ship product up to the Sacramento Delta. Currently, we ship about 40 percent of our material by barge and 60 percent by truck."

"Neighborhood opposition to the quarry's operations," explains Aimi, "only started back in the late 1990s. The operational noise of blasting and dust, however, had already been there for nearly a century.

"But it's important to remember that, given the information we have today, there are only about 15 years left in the operational life of the quarry. At that time, the quarry is expected to shut down, and we envision a mixture of residential and commercial development in the quarry property at that point. I think it would be mostly residential with a touch of commercial, with perhaps a yacht harbor. We have 250 acres of land available for development."

"Throughout this most recent controversy involving our neighbors," says Bill Dutra, "we've honestly tried to reestablish that common thread of trust which used to be so prevalent in Marin County. We're genuinely concerned about what's fair for both sides. We are not a Wal-Mart or K-Mart-type squabble *versus* the community-at-large. We are a long-term family sharing the same neighborhood with other families, and we simply want to get along."

Interjects Aimi: "I perceive my job as educating the community, and being educated by them at the same time. My outreach to the community is like a full-court press—100 percent of my time is given to reaching out for discourse, keeping dialogue open between what we are about and what the community needs and wants.

"Ours is not a positive business, PR-wise, which is why I am constantly vigilant. But the experience has empowered me to give trust and confidence even to our detractors."

Says Bill: "What we are always seeking is that pendulum of balance that should rock smoothly and reasonably between one side and the other."

Laughs Aimi: "Now I know why I am so much my father's daughter—I am all about balance! Seriously, I could not be doing this without my father's guidance. I've learned my values from him, and my passion for the business. I just want to continue working hard to resolve these community issues so that both we and the citizenry can contribute to each others' well-being.

"Our plan for possible future development," she continues, "has been in the works since 1982. Yes, it

"I just want to continue working hard to resolve these community issues so that both we and the citizenry can contribute to each others' well-being."

needs to be updated, but basically what we plan to do is the same as what happened at Larkspur Landing. We want to build a community, a destination community.

"The time to start planning this development is now," Aimi Dutra emphasizes. "It took 10-13 years at Larkspur Landing (which The Dutra Group had built). There was the whole planning process, the politics, getting the approval process, and everything else. The time to start planning for the future of the San Rafael Quarry is now."

Dutra Materials' primary source of long-term aggregate reserves is strategically located in one of the fastest growing areas in the Western United States, the San Francisco Bay. The San Rafael Rock Quarry has in excess of 50 million tons of aggregate reserves with the only waterside distribution center in the Bay Area.

The San Rafael Rock Quarry is on a unique piece of property with both deep water and land accessibility. It encompasses 750 acres and accommodates the manufacturing of high quality products for the road industry, the ever-expanding regional infrastructure, as well as the protection of our vital Delta waterways and shorelines.

Dutra Materials also supplies stone protection to ensure the integrity of the Sacramento River deep water channel, the San Joaquin ship channel, and over 1,500 miles of waterways.

But, in the end, it's the continuously strong bond between father and daughter that keeps this company a solid force in the commerce of The County.

Jill Eikenberry and Michael Tucker

They weren't born here, of course, and they haven't resided here for a very long time, either, but there is something especially comfy and soothing about the feel and fit of Jill Eikenbery and Michael Tucker living in Mill Valley.

They are low-key, respectful, reflective, caring people whose very faces emit the kind of rural civility (or is it civil urbanity?) that is such a good match with the casually sophisticated fellow citizenry of the village beneath Mt. Tam.

It's only been a decade of living here, but Jill and Michael have woven themselves into the community tapestry of Marin seamlessly. They are, in a word, much more Mill Valley Film Festival than they are Grauman's Chinese Theater. L.A.'s loss has been a decidedly rich gain on the part of Marin.

They might be best known for their roles on "L.A. Law"—he played the lovably huggy but internally simmering Stuart Markowitz, and she played activist attorney Ann Kelsey, whose brooding impatience and self-searching *persona* collided in an inevitably marred relationship with Markowitz.

Theirs was, perhaps, the most credible pairing on the show—two seemingly ordinary individuals plowing their way through the mini-dramas of their lives, always played in low pitch and tentatively calm, but somehow masterfully keeping their believably raw and vulnerable feelings just barely beneath the skin of their characters. Kind, sweet, solid but not totally predictable, they acted their way through the series more by keeping within what we were dying to see from the outside. Weird dynamic, but it worked.

Being married to each other in real life, to say the least, was perfect dress rehearsal for playing their roles. Any memory of their episodes is devoid of the legal cases with which they were so intricately involved. When you think about Markowitz and Kelsey, you don't think about how they prevailed or lost in court—you think about the interaction between the two of them.

They hadn't started out on a similar path prior to their marriage. Eikenberry had been an anthropology student at Barnard College in New York before switching to acting at the Yale Drama School. Tucker, a Baltimore native, burned the stage boards at Carnegie Tech Drama School, where he appeared in more than 40 dramatic productions. He has also claimed to be the youngest stand-up comedian on the Catskills circuit.

While Eikenberry embarked after college on a winning streak of theater and feature film credits, Tucker was chasing fame at theaters all across the nation. Their stars were somehow crossed in a positive way when they met at the Arena Stage in Washington, D.C. and discovered compatibility both professional and personal.

Jill Eikenberry won four Emmy nominations, two Golden Globe nominations, a Golden Globe award for her work on "L.A. Law," and one special award that makes her most proud—an Obie for her work in two off-Broadway plays, "Lemon Sky," by Lanford Wilson, and "Life Under Water," by Richard Greenberg. But one of her most significantly compelling works was hosting and co-producing "Destined to Live," a one-hour documentary for NBC-TV. This gripping piece delved into the heartbreaking aspects of breast cancer, covering the range of emotions subjects feel from diagnosis through surgery and recovery.

A breast cancer survivor herself, Jill's courageously valiant work on this documentary helped untold numbers of women realize that they could break apart the fear, then learn how to guide their recovery through the various stages of the illness, thereby restoring both their emotional and physical integrity enough to lead active, full and normal lives once again.

It was a breakthrough act of personal courage on the part of the actress at a time when there were still many hush-hush stigmas attached to the malady.

Part of Michael Tucker's appeal to women fans is his finely tuned-in sensitive side, revealing him to be more of a compassionate listener than a brash talker or fumbling doer. In 1986, when his role on "L.A. Law" was just beginning to take off, he was honored with the Good Guys Award from the National Women's Political Caucus, spotlighting his quiet behind-the-scenes work on behalf of a number of causes involving women.

In his career, Tucker has had three Emmy nominations and two Golden Globe nominations.

Although he will probably wear the role of Stuart Markowitz for the rest of his life, he has shown his distinct versatility with roles in Barry Levinson's "Diner," in a Universal movie called "For Love or Money" with Michael J. Fox, and in an HBO special titled "Tracey Takes on New York," with Tracy Ullman (speaking of versatile). He has acted in two Woody Allen movies, "The Purple Rose of Cairo" (1985) and "Radio Days" (1986), and, for rabid trivia buffs, a couple of '70s classics, "The Eyes of Laura Mars" and the widely acclaimed "An Unmarried Woman."

When you think about Markowitz and Kelsey, you don't think about how they prevailed or lost in court—you think about the interaction between the two of them.

Even more grist for trivia buffs—Tucker was a classmate at Carnegie with Stephen Bochco, who produced "L.A. Law." And—the husband-wife acting duet of Tucker/Eikenberry also teamed in two made-for-TV movies, "Assault and Matrimony" and "The Secret Life of Archie's Wife." Tucker has also authored a book, "I Never Forget A Meal: An Indulgent Reminiscence."

Speaking of food, Jill and Michael light up when they boast about their daughter, Alison, who is, they say, "a brilliant cook who's in the catering business." Their son Max, fresh out of college, is now a full time professional musician in New York. He plays mostly jazz, but he also has an Afro-beat band, a rock band, and is a member of a church in Harlem where he plays snare drum and tambourine in a gospel trombone choir.

As for their life in Marin, both chime in together to say how wonderfully they have been treated in The County—"We feel so welcome here," beams Jill, echoed by Michael's eager assent. "We get lots of smiles and plenty of approval. The people just couldn't be any better. We are enjoying doing theater in the Bay Area—at Marin Theater Company, at ACT, the Theater on the Square, and the Napa Valley Opera House, to name a few.

"We have a home in Umbria, Italy, where we spend six weeks in the autumn and six weeks in the spring, and we've found a smaller place to live in Mill Valley recently—we're learning how to scale down, in all aspects of life. And we plan on being here for a long time. Marin is home."

Mervin Field

One of the really fun things about living in Marin is the occasional discovery of someone famous who has lived here for years seemingly without notice.

It would surprise many local observers, for example, to know that one of the household names of political polling, Mervin Field, is a resident of the Tiburon-Belvedere Peninsula, and has been for many years.

"My wife Marilyn and I were living in The City in the late 50s," says the 83-year-old Field, "and she saw some ads about Marin County. We were quite taken by what we could see from Tiburon, first-rate views of San Francisco, Angel Island, Raccoon Straits—it was all so beautiful, we couldn't resist."

His name has been recognizable long before Lyndon Johnson would be seen stuffing Field Polls into his back pocket, but it makes him feel very secure that he can come and go in his hometown with a minimum of fanfare. People in stores, for instance, never hesitate to ask a TV weatherman about the impending forecasts. Can you imagine how burdensome it would be to be one of the nation's top pollsters and being accosted in the produce section of Mollie Stone's for a thumbnail prediction of the presidential race?

So—how did the polling bug, a wholly modern American science, first bite Mr. Field?

In 1937, while he was a high school student in Princeton, New Jersey, he had a chance meeting with polling's pioneer, Dr. George Gallup. Fascinated by this new concept of survey research, he conducted his first-ever poll measuring student preferences during the presidential campaign of his senior class.

His name has been synonymous with American polling ever since.

After attending Rutgers University and the University of Missouri, he worked for Opinion Research Corporation and the Gallup Poll in 1942. During World War II, he served in the Merchant Marine in both the European and South Pacific theaters of operation. It was during this three-year service stint that he immersed himself in a course of self study examining various technical aspects of survey methods.

In 1946, he founded Field Research Corporation (FRC); then he started The Field Poll in 1947. The Field Poll is a unique continuing public opinion news service, widely recognized as an authoritative source of public opinion utilizing sophisticated survey methodology. Since its inception in 1947, The Field Poll has published more than 2,200 reports on a wide variety of political, social and public policy issues.

FRC now has a permanent staff of 50 professional and operations people, and employs a large contingent of part-time interviewers.

The company, which regularly conducts surveys embracing regional, national and international scope, maintains a close working relationship with the University of California and California State University campuses where all Field Poll survey data is regularly deposited.

"The importance of this," explains Field, "is that the extensive and continually growing body of survey data has become an invaluable resource for scholars and public policy makers. The body of research has become a unique and rich archive that is used in political science, journalism, sociology and survey research courses."

While Field is best known for his work in the political and public policy arena, much of his professional life has been devoted to the direction and development of hundreds of marketing and consumer research projects conducted by FRC.

The 2003 recall of the Governor election, which resulted in the unprecedented ouster of one Governor, Gray Davis, and the landslide coronation of a new leader, Arnold Schwarzenegger, captured the imagination of Field the same way it fascinated constituents and political wags alike.

The public's distaste for Davis, soon after reelecting him in 2002, coupled with the sudden enchantment for the inexperienced, charismatic, former body builder-turned-movie actor resulted in an unprecedented political upheaval.

It represented another sign of the public's unhappiness with politics as usual, Field explains further, warning that if voters were seizing a quick-fix remedy in embracing Schwarzenegger, they better take a long reality check.

The verdict is still out on Schwarzenegger being an effective Governor, of course, but Mervin Field has been around too long and polled too many people to settle for such instantly simplistic answers to incredibly complex policy matters when governing such a highly dysfunctional California.

Since its inception in 1947, The Field Poll has published more than 2,200 reports on a wide variety of political, social and public policy issues.

In addition to authoring his polling methodology, Field has written, lectured and spoken extensively on many business and public policy issues. He has directed numerous studies which have been introduced in U.S. District and other Courts where he has offered expert testimony on a variety of business and governmental practices. He has also appeared frequently as an expert witness before House, Senate and California State legislative committees, as well as federal and state regulatory agencies.

California Journal, the most respected political periodical in the state, marked its 30th anniversary issue in 1999 by selecting 30 men and women who have had the greatest influence on California government and politics in the 20th century. In its selection of Field as one of the 30, the magazine stated: "Over the past half century, Field and his poll have defined California politics. He has been the man who explained Californians to one another and the nation. His nearly 2,000 reports have been carried by newspapers and television stations across the state.

"In the national media, the myth grew that if you want to see America tomorrow, look at California today. And Field became the lens through which most of the nation viewed California."

In 2002, Field was appointed a Regents' Professor at UC Berkeley. He is also a member of the Advisory Council of the prestigious Institute of Governmental Studies on the UC Berkeley campus.

Mark Fishkin

You will forgive my indulgence—right?—if I cut into Mark Fishkin's valuable space and wax nostalgic about the Mill Valley Film Festival, which has always brought out the ham in me. From 1985 until 1990, when I was an extremely popular columnist for the *Marin IJ*—right?—one of my favorite assignments was to cover the festival. When that time of year approached, I'd say to no one in particular in the newsroom—"Yes! That's what I'm talking about!" even though that wasn't even the streetwise parlance of the day.

One year, I brought my then-girlfriend along to interview glamorous actress Sally Kirkland, who said, "Interviews suck—let's go get a drink!" So there I was between two dazzling blondes marching down the street from the Sequoia Theater into a local watering hole. Another time, I interviewed Peter Fonda, on hand to screen his film, "My Own Private Idaho." He grew bored of the interview, too, and said, "Let's take a spin on my chopper." How cool was that, being asked by Easy Rider himself to grab a seat on his hog?

On a more serious note, the fest introduced me to then-Festival President Ann Brebner, whom I included in my first edition of *100 Faces of Marin*. I was honored to attend one of the productions of her Tam High School's Ensemble Theater, and was able to witness up close and personal how deeply she impacted her students aspiring for careers in drama.

The Film Festival for me always signified a brief respite from the more mundane aspects of writing newspaper columns, and with this slight indulgence, I now raise the curtain upon the man who was largely responsible for its inception and continuation—Mark Fishkin.

What a cool dream Mark Fishkin had nearly 30 years ago before Mill Valley was synonymous with "Film

Festival." How awesome it must have been to survey the surroundings, take stock of the environment, process the inventory of potential success, then wake up one morning and announce to the world—"I think Mill Valley would be the ideal spot for its own film fest."

He could not possibly have imagined that 25 years-plus later, the vision is not only still intact, but also joins Cannes, Sundance and San Francisco as four of the hippest, most sophisticated, savvy and sought-after festivals of film in the world.

"All I knew," says Fishkin somewhat humbly today, "is that I was absolutely passionate about what I was doing. It really did seem like a very good idea at the time. I take my position very seriously, not only because I cherish the perfect backdrop of Mill Valley as the ideal venue, but also because, as a non-profit cultural organization, we are able to contribute something of lasting value year after year.

"I am a firm believer in the extraordinary power of film, and the Mill Valley Film Festival has managed to attract some of the more compelling films of the past quarter of a century. Great films have a message, and for us to be the carrier of that message is a noble task."

The festival has long held the reputation of championing independent films, and it is this sense of risk that has carved its unique character over the years. "Strictly Ballroom," for instance, was premiered at Mill Valley at a time when there was much head-scratching over the film's somewhat novel subject matter. Same with the appearances over the years of "The Crying Game," "Like Water for Chocolate," and "My Left Foot." "Stand and Deliver" (originally titled "Walking on Water") was another bright birth child of the festival, premiering in 1987 with the appearance of actor Edward James Olmos.

The Mill Valley Film Festival is now one of three parts of an umbrella organization, the California Film Institute—the others being the Christopher B. Smith Rafael Film Center and California Film Institute Outreach. The latter is a great asset to both the Bay Area and global film communities in that it offers plentiful opportunities for aspiring filmmakers and community screenings alike; the former, named after benefactor/philanthropist Smith, has taken up residence inside the fabulously restored Rafael Theater, whose classic movie house looks of its birthday in 1918 had crumbled, deteriorated, been damaged by fire in 1937 and by the Loma Priete earthquake in 1989 before its happy restoration.

"The Rafael Theater conversion to the Smith Rafael Film Center," says Fishkin, "is an enormous labor of love. In addition to Ann Brebner and myself, we worked side by side with dozens of board members, donors, volunteers and, of course, Chris Smith. The success of the Film Center also speaks to the kind of community we have in Marin. People here are doers. They are well-educated and crave the nourishment that comes from the arts. The Smith Rafael Film Center is a huge asset to the community of Marin and a fitting evolution of the Mill Valley Film Festival."

Fishkin told writer Greg Cahill a few years ago:

"I am a firm believer in the extraordinary power of film..."

"We have a hidden agenda where we illustrate what an amazing medium film is and how it can influence people. We've all heard about how it can influence people negatively in terms of children viewing violence; one would also hope that you can influence people positively. I believe film gives us the ability to see who we are, where we are, and how we relate to each other, to the planet, to political, environmental, and social issues."

Fishkin, whose personal love of the arts extends to his family—his wife Lorrie is a singer; his daughter Lindsay is an artist, singer, actor at Marin Academy; and married daughter Tia Whiteaker of Fairfax is head of the Art Department at San Rafael High—shakes his head in disbelief when he thinks that his beloved film festival now has a nostalgia factor of its own.

"Many local festival followers," he says, "will vividly recall Robin Williams' amazing trailer in 1988 which caused such a hilarious stir that it actually upstaged some of our principal offerings that year. Then there was the time Robin ran down the aisle and jumped into the arms of Jonathan Winters on stage. One of my favorite poignant moments came when we were giving homage to Jack Arnold at the Sequoia Theater for his 'The Creature From the Black Lagoon,' and, when he stood up in a frail fashion because of his ailing health, the audience—all wearing 3-D glasses—gave him an ovation that made Arnold cry and almost brought the roof down."

(Note: Fishkin is not a prophet, but part of the Sequoia's roof did come down in a mysterious accident in the summer of 2004.)

Phil Frank

If life were fair, Phil Frank would be declared a local treasure.

The Sausalito-residing cartoonist for the *San Francisco Chronicle* is nearing 30 years in print as the creator of "Farley," which began as a nationally syndicated cartoon but which for the past 19 years has been an exclusive *Chronicle* feature, the only local daily comic strip in the country.

Phil and his wife Susan, an accomplished author in her own right, are Sausalito fixtures. Both are intimately involved in the ongoing nurturing of that town's development and they are closely linked to the preservation of their city's history.

"We love the town," raves Frank. "We've both been involved with local history—Sue as a member of the Local Landmarks Commission and myself with the Sausalito Historical Society. Our own history here is pretty rich itself. In 1972, we rebuilt one of the old arks, the 1890s houseboats, at Waldo Point. It was sinking. We refloated it and restored it into a comfy houseboat and moved in. My studio is a pilot house on an 1880s ferryboat, plus I have an office at the *Chronicle*, too.

"As much as I love working from home, I really like going into the paper once or twice a week. I gather material, put out fires, and just love the energy in the newsroom. Talk about being blessed. I'm a little over 60 years old and just signed a 20-year contract to produce a seven-days-a-week syndicated comic strip about aging in America. It'll be called 'Elderberries.'"

The Franks now live on land in Sausalito after many years afloat, but their love of the South Marin waterfront community remains very much intact.

"It's amazing how much history there is in this relatively small area," says Frank of the Sausalito/Marin City acreage he calls home. "It's a history shaped by people—more specifically, the wonderful *machinations* of people. From ship building during the wars to the growth and development of little theater groups, artistic and literary cultures, and of course the Beatnik era—this is one fertile landscape."

It's also a landscape upon which Phil Frank has embossed his still-growing legacy. Beyond the reaches of his cartoon strip and book illustrations, works around the Bay Area bearing his indelible stamp include the de Young Museum, BART, the San Francisco Giants, the San Francisco Water Conservation Department, the Small Business Bureau, the San Francisco City Treasurer's Office, numerous regional utility companies and extensive educational materials for a wide array of state parks and historical landmarks.

Trying to define Phil Frank's work would be a disservice, sort of like attempting to categorize the late Herb Caen's inimitable style. Both have been part of the local diet for so many years that, in typical Marin/San Francisco tradition, we don't gloat over, trumpet or glorify our favorite sons. But, as with Caen's loss, take 'Farley' out of the *Chronicle*, and it's simply not our beloved local rag anymore.

What gives Frank's work special distinction are the poignant tugs of the heart—Farley, the strip's hero, pining after Irene the Meter Maid in an Only in San Francisco romance that somehow seems perfect for us readers. Or Orwell T. Cat's adventures in the White House. Or the four bears who operate the Fog City Dumpster for their furry gourmet friends in The City. Again—description fails Frank's brilliance.

"Farley" offers welcome, heartwarming mirth as we follow the unpredictable adventures, calamities, pratfalls and hijinks of our beloved line-up of local troops and luminaries.

Phil is particularly proud of his wife Susan's writing. She has written—with Phil as collaborator—four guide books to national parks, covering the Grand Canyon, Yosemite, Yellowstone and Muir Woods.

Phil's own book, "Fur and Loafing in Yosemite: A Collection of Farley Cartoons Set in Yosemite National Park," is a scream, the fifth of six published collections of "Farley" cartoons. Frank paints a wonderfully rich confrontation between park bears and summertime campers, especially one Mrs. Melmac, equipped in a monstrous RV and armed with battle-ready anti-mosquito canisters. Urban bears from San Francisco, who have hijacked an SF Muni bus to join Melmac for summer fun, add to the Yosemite culture clash.

Because of his strongly held environmental convictions that boil fiercely just beneath the surface of his humorous jibes, Phil has been invited to be a member of the board of the Yosemite Association, and he is also an honorary California State Park Ranger.

Another of Phil Frank's books is "The Dog Lover's Companion to California: The Inside Scoop on Where to Take Your Dog." In collaboration with author Maria Goodavage, Frank has illustrated this very detailed manual—in actuality a series of 12 that have been localized for different areas of the country—on California lakes best suited for canine swimming and dipping, dog-appropriate beaches, and scores of dog-friendly cafes, hotels, restaurants and leash-free parks throughout the state.

Humor, especially as it is delivered through the barrel of Frank's quill, is always the best medicine.

As evidence of his ever-shrewd ability to hook his talent into cutting-edge contemporary issues whose relevance begs for Frank's wit and humor, the cartoonist has also collaborated with author Beverly A. Potter in her book, "Overcoming Job Burnout: How to Renew Enthusiasm for Work."

This book's topic is an especially troubling concern in an era beset with financial stress, global uncertainty, and the individual's ever-daunting struggle to maintain stability and job continuity in an increasingly competitive workplace. Typically and refreshingly, Frank's illustrations lend the seriousness of the topic a much-needed element of levity and hope. Job burnout is a malady—much like depression and anxiety—that needs to be treated. Its symptoms just don't vanish without care.

While author Potter demonstrates eight proven strategies that work to turn job burnout around—increasing self-empowerment and cultivating a renewed enthusiasm for work—it is Frank's wholesome, inspirational and self-poking humor that renders badly needed comic relief in this compassionate guidebook that puts things in proper perspective and offers burnt out workers a fair shot at surviving. Humor, especially as it is delivered through the barrel of Frank's quill, is always the best medicine.

And that's another reason why Phil Frank is a gem, an authentic local treasure.

Margot Fraser

German-born Marinite Margot Fraser has told the story so many times, she laughs at the thought that it may have the ring of an urban folk legend.

The woman whose name has become synonymous with Birkenstock Footprint Sandals, Inc.—headquartered in Novato at the jagged-roof former home of McGraw-Hill Publishing—says: "In 1966, I was vacationing at a health spa in Bavaria. I had a chronic foot problem, and I complained about it to the fitness person at the spa who suggested that I try on a pair of Birkenstock sandals. So I put on a pair of the strange looking footwear, and my life changed instantly."

It was like Cinderella donning the glass slipper—"The pain I had endured for years," she says, "disappeared after a few months. To say I was impressed would be a huge understatement.

"I moved to Marin in 1971. My best customer at that time was June Embury, who with her husband Howard owned San Rafael Health Foods on Fourth Street. We formed a partnership and started to operate the wholesale business out of the health food store. Pretty soon that space proved to be too small and we had to move out as business expanded."

It wasn't as if this particular brand of shoe had been invented at the same time as lava lamps or macrame plant hangers. In fact, Johann Adam Birkenstock is the family patriarch listed as shoemaker in the German archives as early as 1774. In 1897, Johan's direct descendant, Konrad, really made a breakthrough in shoe styling that would serve as the foundation for the Birkenstock formula.

Konrad developed a concept that was revolutionary. Although the soles of our feet are curved, shoes were always manufactured flat on the inside. Konrad came up with the theory that if the shape of the shoe better reflected the shape of our feet, the result would be infinitely more comfortable. He thereby designed the first known shoe with a contoured insole; several years later, he added the first flexible arch support.

By 1925, the popular new arch supports maximizing personal comfort were being exported from Germany to Austria, Switzerland, France, Italy, Belgium, Czechoslovakia, Holland, Luxembourg, Denmark, Sweden and Norway. In 1932, the company became sophisticated enough to start offering seminars and lectures throughout Europe. Leading medical specialists of the day endorsed the seminars, and the Birkenstock system's popularity soared oversees.

It wasn't until 1964, however, that the company took the contoured arch support concept one step further—as a shoe, thereby creating the first Birkenstock sandal.

Fast-forward two years, and enter Margot with her foot problem. "That little health food store which sold my first boxes of sandals started the whole thing rolling," she says. "Business grew so rapidly that pretty soon I had to open a small warehouse in San Rafael in 1971, where I stored all the sandals I was importing from Germany."

The '70s were the defining years for the rustic-looking footwear. People, especially in Marin, were focusing more on comfort and laid-back casual than they were on high fashion or dress wear vamping, so the Birkenstock was a perfect complement to hot tubs and futons, tofu and granny gowns.

"It was amazing," says Margot. "What began as emergency care for my feet turned into this multi-million dollar business. And I had no formal business training or even any money to get going. All I had was a 100 percent belief in the product, a very strong work ethic I inherited from my German ancestry, plus a natural market that fell absolutely in love with this extremely simple product. Pretty soon, even the warehouse wasn't big enough. When the building in Novato became available, we jumped at the opportunity.

"So, from my tiny business inside a health food store, we are now a major firm with 160,000 square feet of warehouse and office space, 250 employees (who since 2002 are also the owners), more than 3,000 retail accounts, and over 200 licensed specialty stores."

As founder and CEO/Chairman of the Board, Margot's imprint is permanently fixed on the company's culture (er, counterculture). While she no longer needs to show up for work every day, she is fast to credit her employees' energy and loyalty as the key to the company's sustaining success.

"We began as a people-oriented business," she says, "and that's the way we are today. It is vital to any company that the employees are not only engaged in what they do, but are *happily* engaged, so that they see the positive results of their hard work on a day-by-day basis. That's Birkenstock's."

It wasn't as if this particular brand of shoe had been invented at the same time as lava lamps or macrame plant hangers.

While the signature two-strap sandal, known as the comfort icon, is now over 30 years old, other styles include the Aberdeen slip-on, the Wellington loafer, and the Kensington for more formal wear. Birkenstock has also invaded the hiking boot craze with its Footprint line, which is well suited (or booted) for either light hiking or long treks. The Arizona is one of the most popular Birkenstock offerings, providing a hip, on-trend style for the fashionable set.

Birkenstock is a firm proponent of the power of giving back—their so-named Giving Back program focuses a good deal of time and resources to human needs, health and wellness learning, and the environment. Each of these areas has a company committee assigned to it, and members are empowered to make decisions on donations, organization of volunteer events, and the education of employees about such socially conscious concerns.

Grants and product donations are also a part of the Giving Back function of the firm, and there is a Corporate Giving program, an Employee Matching Gift program, and a Birkenstock Volunteer program, all designed to strengthen the bonds between the company and non-profits, humanitarian agencies and medical support groups that look to the corporation for support.

Margot Fraser sometimes can't quite believe her good fortune. She has managed to create a highly regarded firm with solid business sense and a good deal of "sole," one that began from a modest back room of a health food store no bigger than, well, a shoe box.

Candice Fuhrman

Candice Fuhrman has made a solid name for herself throughout both the Bay Area and national literary circles, and her roots were planted deeply in Marin soil at the outset of her career.

An arrival from New York City in 1972, she and her then-husband, Boyd Jacobson, a San Francisco advertising man, first settled in Kentfield,

"Where we had an apartment with a pool and a view of Mt. Tam, and I was bored silly." (Hard to please those manic New York urbanites when they first settle in a Far West outpost, isn't it?)

Candice had already begun a publishing career in the Big Apple as an editor for Dell Publishing Company. So, when she was divorced from Jacobson and moved to Mill Valley with her daughter Karie, she found it relatively easy to find freelance jobs in the Bay Area.

"I worked for small publishers," says Fuhrman in her cozy and compact downtown Mill Valley literary agency, "who had all sorts of publicity and marketing needs. It was very much on-the-job-training, and I started to build a stable of clients in the publicity arena. Then, gradually, I did more and more books and special events, like the Sausalito Art Festival, the Marin County Fair, and the Harvest Festival. But, as my business grew, I realized I was drifting further and further away from publishing, which has always been my first love."

As fate would have it, Candice met and married Charles Fuhrman, a graphic designer whose career naturally guided her back into publishing.

"We started a book packaging company called Wink

Books, Inc.," she says. "I would get an idea, we'd hire a writer, then Charles would design sample pages. It was a great collaboration. We had an agent in New York who sold the proposals to publishers.

"But book packaging is very labor-intensive, and it was very difficult to make a living. Besides that, our agent in New York was very disagreeable and would often make me cry. So we fired her and I declared myself my own literary agent, flew to New York, and agented our own projects and eventually those of other writers.

"That was 16 years ago. The first book that I sold, titled *Smart Love*, was in 1987. It is still in print. Since then I've sold literally hundreds of books, many by first time writers. I've had a number of *New York Times* bestsellers and scores of *San Francisco Chronicle* bestsellers. But I still get excited when a new manuscript comes in over the transom. You just never know what wonderful book is out there."

Fuhrman traces her love of books and reading to her childhood. Both her parents were avid readers, and she says she did nothing but read until she was 15. She laughs when she recalls sitting in a tree all weekend, reading up to 10 books which she hoisted above to her perch by way of a clever little book pulley. She also laughs when she says she discovered boys at 15 and her reading sagged a bit.

Candice and Charles Fuhrman lived in Forest Knolls until his untimely death in 1995. That's when Candice moved back to Mill Valley for three miserable years—until she met Gary Fiedel, whom she married in 2000.

"Being a literary agent is a lot of fun," she says. "and I certainly can empathize with writers. I wrote a book myself called *Publicity Stunt! Great Staged Events That Made the News,* published by Chronicle Books in 1989. It is a history of publicity, going back to the 19th century when penny newspapers were creating stunts themselves to create news and sell newspapers. I appeared on Larry King's show and 'Entertainment Tonight,' and the *New York Times* even reviewed it."

The biggest book Fuhrman has ever represented is *The Rapture of Canaan*, by Sheri Reynolds. It became an Oprah Book Club selection and number one *New York Times'* bestseller. Fuhrman vividly recalls reading Reynolds' first manuscript, *Bitterroot Landing*.

"The sun was shining through the skylight on my white bedspread and I was reading this beautiful prose and I was just knocked out. I was crying. At the time Reynolds was only 24, and I called her and said I must represent her. I sold it to Putnam, then Putnam made her an additional two-book deal. The first two books received rave reviews but didn't sell well, so Putnam canceled the third book.

"Fortunately and out of the blue, we received a call from Oprah Winfrey's people that same day saying they had chosen the second book for Oprah's Book Club. Putnam got wind of this and begged us to get her back on their list. But of course we said no. Revenge is sometimes sweet. We turned down a huge amount of cash from Putnam and went with an editor who truly believed in the author."

"Those of us who live in Marin and who enjoy its breathtaking beauty are often guilty of taking it for granted. We forget that there are young people who have never been on a hike."

Another exciting deal was made for the author of a self-published book. Marlo Morgan had printed more than 300,000 copies of *Mutant Message Down Under*, and Fuhrman heard about it from a number of friends in Marin. She found a copy for sale at Book Passage and contacted Morgan at her home in Missouri. Subsequently, she made a multi-million-dollar deal for the author with HarperCollins, and the book went on the *New York Times* Bestseller List for 19 weeks. In 2004, it was reissued in a special 10th anniversary edition, and it continues to be a bestseller around the world.

Where she finds time from the hustle of being a literary agent is a mystery novel of its own, but Candice is especially proud of her volunteer position in Marin as a docent for the Audubon Canyon Ranch. This is an extremely worthwhile organization that hosts kids from the inner city and takes them on all sorts of nature trips.

"Those of us who live in Marin and who enjoy its breathtaking beauty," she explains, "are often guilty of taking it for granted. We forget that there are young people who have never been on a hike. When I see kids' faces after that experience, I resolve never to take Marin for granted again."

Fuhrman says that although she has clients all over the country, she gets a thrill still out of walking from her home to her office in Mill Valley.

Leon Galleto

Leon Galleto has a way of making his presence known and felt. Call him Mr. Irrepressible. Charming, engaging, filled to the brim with anecdotes and vignettes based on an astonishingly full life, it's only fitting that he be such a success in the newspaper business in Marin County.

As vice president of Public Affairs for *Marin Scope Community Newspapers*, Galleto brings energy, insight, creativity, humor and resourcefulness to a business that sorely needs all of the above.

The 73-year-old European-born Galleto first came to America to interview with a company in Los Angeles.

"I had visions of Los Angeles being the same as the South of France," he recalls, "but L.A. was a bitter disappointment. I had itchy eyes from the smog and all that pollution. Someone told me that if I came to the Bay Area, I would love it, and that's been true."

It's been true, in fact, for more than 40 years, the span of time he's been serving the community of southern Marin, which has a charm all its own and which is quite distinct from the South of France. His reputation throughout southern Marin is that of a man thoroughly involved in his community's interests and a shrewd businessman who brings savvy customer service and marketing acumen to a newspaper group that must always remain cutting-edge competitive.

"I moved to Marin in 1958," says Galleto. "Marin was very laid back in the old days. After the war, a lot of artists were attracted to Sausalito, because there were many cheap places to rent. Basically, some of them were just squatting because the military left behind a lot of empty buildings. Sausalito was a light industrial zone at the time. Most of the roads were unpaved. The artists loved the waterfront, the empty boat lofts and the cheap rents.

"That's how Sausalito, and Marin, all changed. It attracted Bohemians. Jean Varda was a well-known artist at the time, and he lived with Alan Watts on a houseboat in Sausalito. Varda was always surrounded by beautiful women, and there were parties all the time on the houseboat. I met a lot of artists through Jean Varda. Sausalito was not commercial at all in those days. Now, like everything in Marin, it has become terribly gentrified."

How he got into the news business is a story worthy of Galleto's own colorful first-hand account:

"I was working at the Valhalla restaurant in Sausalito as a maitre d'," he says. "It was owned at the time by Sally Stanford, the famous madam. She had run for office in Sausalito seven times, always using her real name, which was Marcia Owen. When she ran the eighth time, she used her madam-ish alias, Sally Stanford, and won. I was the one who had told her that she should run under her own name, and she did, and she won by a landslide. She would say to me: 'If you wait long enough at the door, eventually you will see your enemy go by in a hearse.'

"A bit later, I was general manager at Heath Ceramics in Sausalito and was approached by a gentleman by the name of Paul Anderson, who wanted to start a local newspaper. In order to support him, I bought a full-page ad. That became the first issue of the *Marin Scope* newspapers. When I left Heath Ceramics in the early '80s, I was a fan of Paul Anderson, so I hired him to do public relations for my ventures. We've been together ever since.

"In fact," he continues, "I'm still involved with *Marin Scope* papers in community affairs. I belong to all the chambers of commerce, and I go to the monthly mixers and everybody knows me. In the old days, people would come to the *Marin Scope* office and ask for free publicity for their non-profit groups. It was my idea to give a free, full-page ad to many community functions, and then ask certain businesses to put their names down as sponsors for maybe $100 each. I still do that, for events like the Fourth of July, the Chili Cookoff, Easter and Halloween. I am retired these days, but I still love to help in community affairs. I am involved with the Art Festival in San Anselmo, the Magnolia Festival in Larkspur, and the Jazz Festival in Fairfax. I think the *Marin Scope* papers are doing very well these days—they have a new owner and he is well connected and affiliated with other newspapers."

Though his worldly manners and first-rate people skills would make him a success in a variety of professions, some observers might be surprised to learn that his formal education consisted of study at the Royal Academy of Fine Arts in Copenhagen. A noted ceramicist in the 1950s, Galleto was quite a famous artist around the European circuit as he exhibited his creativity in ceramic sculpture.

It was this artisan's talent that attracted him to Heath Ceramics in Sausalito in 1958, a company led by noted ceramicist Edith Heath, whose trademark work in stoneware, dinnerware and custom-glazed tiles was a perfect fit for the impending trend of simplicity and back-to-nature earth tones that would mark the decade of the '60s and beyond.

"I feel lucky to have had such a long career, and I am grateful to all the people I have met. Luckily, there is no chance of my retiring from the community."

Meanwhile, back in Sausalito, Galleto was experiencing relationship problems with the firebrand former madam-turned-mayor Sally Stanford. Again, in Leon's words:

"I had a falling out with Sally Stanford. She had a famous parrot named Loretta. One day, in the middle of a heat wave—I still remember the date, September 11th, 1981—I went to the restaurant and the poor parrot was lying on its back on the floor, near death. She had knocked over her water dish and she was dying from dehydration. Loretta died that night.

"Sally had a furious temper, and she lost it with me—as if it was my fault—and I couldn't tell you the names she called me. It was only a year later that I ran into her at a local restaurant, and she apologized. But later on, when I was on my honeymoon in Italy, I was buying gas coupons with my wife for our rental car, and she said there were two guys pointing at me. They said: 'Look, there's the guy that killed Sally's parrot.' The incident had taken on international proportions! That story was told at Sally's funeral and brought great laughter.

"I am very happy in my retirement," concludes Galleto. "I feel lucky to have had such a long career, and I am grateful to all the people I have met. Luckily, there is no chance of my retiring from the community!"

Patty Garbarino

With its highly touted, well-documented geographic charm and lifestyle splendor, Marin is sometimes forgotten as an innovator of a far more mundane life-enhancing phenomenon—recycling.

In 1981, Joe Garbarino took a pioneering step into the then-untested waters of massive community recycling. Marin Recycling and Marin Resource Recovery Center at 535 and 565 Jacoby Street resemble a movie set for some kind of monumental Schwarzenegger vs. Garbage blockbuster—bulldozers moving at high rates of speed saving waste from landfill, a monstrous wood grinder known as "The Hog" converting wood and yard excess into mulch, fertilizer and fuel.

Patty Garbarino is one of four daughters of Joe and Sally Garbarino, and she is the President of Marin Sanitary Service, a company that has consistently managed to recycle a whopping 68 percent of its clients' waste, placing it well in the vanguard of comparable sanitation agencies in both the state and the nation.

Born in San Francisco's North Beach to a very large and tightly knit family, Patty moved to Marin nearly 45 years ago. Her 1973 senior class at San Rafael High School was, with 555 students, the largest graduating class in the school's history.

"That experience at San Rafael High," says Patty, "is the nicest experience of my life. We have all stayed so close to each other. When we were kids, we were shaped forever by John F. Kennedy's inaugural message to ask what we can do for our country, and we were all branded with that.

"Just as importantly, we were influenced by a lot of very strong female role models during the Women's Movement while we were growing up, and their efforts need to be applauded.

"We were lucky to have grown up in Marin—that's what makes it so easy and fun for me and my company to give back to the community now. I went to Cal, then Dominican, and earned my degree in education. I taught the handicapped at the Forest Meadows Development

Center at Dominican, spending 11 years working in Special Education, exploring new techniques and joining forces with Superintendent Mary Jane Burke, who shares a passion for giving back."

Garbarino is married to prominent Marin attorney Dave Freitas, who brought to the marriage three daughters—Diane, Megan and Nancy—and four grandchildren.

After years as an educator, Patty accepted an offer from her father Joe to work a part-time job at Marin Recycling in 1987—"There were not many women in the waste industry," she laughs, "The first time I negotiated with the Teamsters, the union rep blurted out, 'I don't negotiate in a room with a woman.'" In 2000, she served a two-year term as the first woman president of the California Refuse Removal Council.

While the company had been around since 1949, Marin's growth and the changes in solid waste management made it essential to divide the firm into three divisions—Marin Sanitary, Marin Recycling, and Marin Resource Recovery.

This transformation increased efficiency in trash removal and made for an environmentally sound, economically feasible plant.

Marin Sanitary Service initiated the countywide curbside collection program that was the first of its kind in the United States.

Marin Recycling Center operates a permanent household hazardous waste facility as a joint program with the City of San Rafael and the Marin County Waste Management Joint Powers Authority.

Marin residents (except Novatoans) are encouraged to bring to the facility, free of charge, such items as paint, adhesives, motor oil, pesticides, household batteries, latex paint, computer monitors, and televisions. Businesses may make arrangements to dispose of small quantities of hazardous waste by appointment, and for a fee.

Marin Resource Recovery Center is an indoor facility the size of three football fields. All types of non-hazardous solid waste from commercial sources are accepted, including yard waste, dirt, rock, concrete, demolition debris, and large appliances.

Every month, the Resource Recovery Center processes almost 4,000 tons of recyclables, using state-of-the-art equipment. A customized system of screens, conveyors, blowers, magnets and hand-sorting separates dirt, sand, metal, wood, concrete, paper, and other materials for recovery. The sheer volume of visitors from around the world attests to the fact that this somewhat amazing facility is really one of the most sophisticated systems of its kind anywhere.

Over the past 10 years, collections and educational outreach efforts have resulted in a 68 percent increase in recycling, which surpasses the state mandate and saves the equivalent of 2 million trees and 900 million gallons of water through recycling.

"I consider it such an honor to work with my Dad," says Patty, "because he is such a kind, gentle, and strong leader. Because of his perseverance and reputation, we are widely respected in Sacramento. That is hugely important, because that is where we advocate legislation protecting the smaller trash collecting businesses. We also fight to make certain that landfill operations protect the environment and avoid ground water pollution."

The sheer volume of visitors from around the world attests to the fact that this somewhat amazing facility is really one of the most sophisticated systems of its kind anywhere.

In Patty Garbarino's tenure as President of Marin Sanitary Service, she has artfully capitalized on her position by helping to generate over $500,000 from the Marin business community, and others, to support her favorite cause—public education.

She credits her time as Chair of the Education Committee of the San Rafael Chamber of Commerce as the catalyst for aiding public schools—she organized three parcel tax campaigns and two bond measure efforts to raise badly needed funds for San Rafael city schools.

Garbarino has also served as chair of the Marin County Planning Commission, and she has served on the boards of the Marin Association for Retarded Citizens and the Rafael Theater Renovation Project. She was also a 1999 inductee to the Marin Women's Hall of Fame.

A thoroughly modern Marinite who has kept true to the values she learned at San Rafael High School, Garbarino brings an inspired leadership savvy to her role in the family business, whose employee-friendly atmosphere keeps its nearly 300 workers happily vested with full benefits and long tenures, some for as many as 30 years.

Donna Garske

The initial reaction upon speaking with Donna Garske, Executive Director of Marin Abused Women's Services (MAWS), is shock. She sounds so happy and free, it jolts the preconception of what the first meeting might be like.

Domestic violence is such a dark, secretive passageway to slavery, the listener braces oneself for what he expects will be a voyage to doom, debilitation and depression.

Donna Garske defies these myths. She radiates light, joy, inspiration, power and freedom.

The much-traveled community activist (North Dakota, Minnesota and Oregon) first came to Marin in 1976 following a career stint as a prison reform architect. The similarity between domestic violence and prison reform was not lost on Garske; within a year, she founded MAWS, a two-year-old fledgling organization which for the past quarter of a century has served as a model for similar organizations around the country, around the world.

"Marin," she says, "was rife with domestic violence cases in the late '70s, and women and children had no shelter from the disease. It's still very much present—in fact, people would be shocked at what goes on in this tranquil, serene county—but we have created a safe harbor, a vehicle for hope and safety and renewal. Our work is far from over, but I shudder to think what may have happened to so many displaced women and children had we not created a safe haven for them."

The motto for MAWS is "Creating Safety and Justice for Women and Children." The idea, so simple and profound yet so daunting to achieve, has spread to over 2,000 communities nationwide.

"Since the inception," says Garske, "thousands of lives have been saved; numerous state and federal laws have been passed to protect battered women and their children, and to uphold their unequivocal right to live in safety."

The Mission Statement of the organization reflects both the urgency created by the crisis of domestic violence and the effectiveness of MAWS:

Provide for the immediate safety of women through our programs; alert the community to the epidemic of violence, abuse and intimidation of women; educate the community about the social and political roots of violence as a tool of oppression and control of women; mobilize the community to create innovative and dynamic solutions to end violence, abuse and intimidation of women.

Garske is a bright-eyed, motivated angel of hope, but she is far from being naive about this deep-rooted social malady that has been America's secret curse.

"Violence against women continues," she explains, "and girls are now experiencing more abuse, at a younger age, than ever before. Our movement is continually confronted with new challenges. There has been an upsurge of sexism and violence in the media, which is now readily accessible on the Internet. The emergence of street gangs and unprecedented incidence of dating abuse and schoolyard slayings by young boys have now become a part of our lives."

Through MAWS, battered women and children have a chance to live. Through hot lines, emergency shelters and transitional housing, support groups, and the Men's Program, MAWS provides a range of direct services which help rebuild lives and create a violence-free future.

Says Garske: "We are committed to overcoming the root causes of domestic violence and abuse to provide safety and justice for all girls, women and men. We contend that domestic violence, for the most part, is grounded in men's violence against women. While it is true that women are sometimes violent in their relationships with both men and women, the fact is that 95 percent of domestic violence cases are attributable to men."

The no-nonsense Garske is committed to a broad-based movement of social change. "Root level change," she enthuses, "will affect men's lives by changing how power is associated with gender roles. We aim to free men of the destructive social conditioning which causes harm to themselves as well as to women. A radical uplifting of the role and value of women in our culture is also fundamental to our purpose. Only by raising the status of women can we really be free from violence."

In Marin, MAWS trains hundreds of law enforcement and medical agencies, schools, churches and community groups to improve numerous community-wide emergency, housing, health care, and legal systems for responding to domestic violence.

Statewide, MAWS drafts and helps pass legislation which increases the effectiveness of domestic violence intervention. Work also focuses on increasing the California Department of Health Services and California Office of Criminal Justice Planning funding for domestic violence programs and for assisting with statewide planning for effective use of the funds.

Nationally, MAWS worked to pass the Violence Against Women Act, which is part of the federal Crime Victims Bill. This legislation created new funds to carry out services for rape and domestic violence victims and to implement training programs with police departments and court officials to prosecute batterers.

"We are committed to overcoming the root causes of domestic violence..."

This is a rather remarkable social engineering feat and, more precisely, a miraculous act of sacrifice born of the vision of one woman, Donna Garske who, for the past 25 years, has stayed the course and helped nurture the tiny seed of her hope that has sprung an internationally acclaimed multi-service organization.

"Social justice movements," says Garske, "have taught us that individuals mobilized for change can alter the conditions, values, and norms of a community. We are committed to carrying out community mobilization strategies which can dismantle the embedded social belief systems that jeopardize women's safety and make them vulnerable to violence.

"During the past 25-plus years, we have acquired outstanding experience implementing a full continuum of domestic violence services and prevention strategies. We believe this experience has provided us with outstanding resources and the leadership capacity to effect broad-based social change. It is our vision that women may live in peace and freedom in a world where they do not encounter oppression because of their gender.

"We look forward to a day when all men and women can co-exist in cooperative ways based on values of safety, equality and respect."

And this is why Donna Garske seems so happy and free—she has created a tangible entity that has led to the safety, regeneration, survival, hope, redemption and restoration of sanity to untold thousands of innocent victims across the globe.

Mark Garwood

It's not exactly clear when bank presidents stopped looking less like Teddy Roosevelt and more like Tom Cruise, but Mark Garwood of Tamalpais Bank certainly fits the modern profile of young, vibrant, hip and no-nonsense executives.

It's more substance than looks, actually, since banking needs today have made a quantum leap into the 21st century, addressing the needs and aspirations of an entirely new world of consumers who are savvy, assertive, techno-sophisticated, and multi-generational.

A Palo Alto native who came to Marin with his family 14 years ago, Garwood has been married to Paulette for 23 years, and the couple has two children—son Brian who's a senior at Redwood High and daughter Monica, who is a freshman at Redwood High.

"Marin really feels like home to me," says Garwood in his downtown San Rafael office. "We live in Kent Woodlands, in the sunbelt. I love it there. There's a great view of the bay and Mt. Tam, so I wake up every day feeling like I am at a vacation destination. I love Marin, mainly because of the people. Yes, the climate is ideal, the environment is beautiful, but it's the type of people you encounter that gives Marin its special definition—people who have a great desire to give back to The County and to the community. It's this generosity of heart that makes Marin such a wonderful place to live."

During his 24-year-plus banking career, he has been a real estate investor and developer, and Tamalpais Bank affords him a happy marriage of the two careers. "One of the things I have been working on for a long time," he says, "is a workforce housing campaign. I started with Habitat for Humanity in 1991, followed by chairing the San Rafael Chamber's Workforce Housing Committee and the Marin Consortium for Workforce Housing. I work to improve the quality of life for the people of Marin. I helped bring together a major employers' housing group, and we have developed the Marin Workforce Housing Trust, of which I am the Chair. That's my passion, frankly, to effectuate some positive changes that would be healthy for The County.

"My view of Marin is that it is very upbeat. It is very positive, very alive. People are always thinking about the good in what they are trying to do, and they look for the good in others to help make this a better place. I have never been in a county that has been so dramatic about that. It just permeates, it's everywhere.

"People I bump into are always recognizing our workforce housing efforts. Although I gain great satisfaction from running a financial institution every day, it's the leadership positions that our company and I assume that *really* count for The County."

Tamalpais Bank is visible, indeed. It has partnered with the Marin Center for Non-Profit and Leadership Development for three years, organizing the Heart of Marin awards ceremony recognizing Excellence in Leadership, Excellence in Board Leadership, Volunteer of the Year, Youth Volunteer of the Year, "Achievement in Non-Profit Excellence," and the "Epic Award." Tamalpais Bank makes $5,000 grants to each one of these recipients at an annual celebration at the Embassy Suites Hotel, an Oscar-type party which Garwood admits is one of the most enjoyable parts of banking he's ever experienced.

As to how he would distinguish the bank from other similar local institutions, he quickly replies: "We have a more holistic approach to the customer relationship. We don't separate them into business and consumer customers. We make available to everyone all the expertise we possess in every relationship in order to help them achieve their goals and make their lives a little easier.

"We do all that in a very friendly, family-type environment that is not intimidating. It's not the old school, '70s look of banks that pits customers against people behind desks. A customer coming here has a very different visual, tactical experience—from the Internet Cafe to the Kids Zone to Online Banking to Gourmet Coffee, plus we also have Tamalpais University in all our branches where we teach educational seminars to our customers. We let non-profits use the university for their board and committee meetings.

"We don't hand people off. A customer has a banker personally assigned to him or her no matter who you are, regardless of demographics. We are relationship driven and we really are committed to making people's lives happier."

Garwood says the bank is also very big about educating its customers, so the bank offers classes as esoteric as Spanish for Travelers or investing for your future or learning how to obtain a business loan.

"It's this generosity of heart that makes Marin such a wonderful place to live."

"We also try our best," continues Garwood, "to make kids feel comfortable coming into the bank—all of our Kid Zone computers in every one of the branches have non-violent kid games on them. This allows the parents to discuss their affairs with their bankers in an undistracted atmosphere. The children simply don't want to leave.

"One of the things I am most proud of is our Community Outreach Program—how we give money back to non-profits. It works very simply. If you open an account at our company, you are asked to choose a particular non-profit that you would like the bank to support. We then make a donation to that organization based on your single deposit account balance. You can see how that can multiply very easily if others also name the same non-profit. Good word and good deeds spread like water ripples, so pretty soon both the bank and its customers are very actively and visibly constructing solid community ventures and a rich sense of community giving."

Talking with Mark Garwood is like taking a ride through the various little towns of Marin, a conversation that highlights each city's special needs and unique people, and, woven into the fabric, exactly how his bank can help foster better bonds between the citizenry and one of its banks. It's a far cry, indeed, from the stern visage of ancient Hollywood bankers eager to take your money with not much to offer in return.

In a very real sense, when you make a deposit at Tamalpais Bank, you are making a withdrawal for the good of Marin County.

Felecia Gaston

This native of Georgia-turned-Marinite for the past quarter of a century takes great pride in the day of her birth—December 1, 1955, the same moment in history that Rosa Parks, a brave black woman in Montgomery, Alabama, defied tradition and decades of segregation by refusing to let a white person take her seat on a bus.

Historians of civil rights in this country know that it would take decades more of relentless struggle to nudge the nation toward full inclusion, but the lonely, silent bravery of lovely Ms. Parks is considered to be a defining, shining event that would trigger the hearts of civil rights advocates all over the land.

Gaston was born outside of Atlanta, Georgia (at Ft. McPherson Army Base), so she, too, was no stranger to the evils of bigotry.

"In fact," she explains, "my biggest passion as a little girl in Georgia was dreaming of becoming a ballerina. I couldn't realize that dream, of course, because little black girls in Georgia were segregated from such aspirations."

Life and the good Lord move in mysterious ways, however, so imagine the serendipity involved when you consider that in 1990, in a faraway, infinitely more progressive land called California, Felecia Gaston founded Performing Stars of Marin, which ensures that children in low-income areas—like Marin City—can cherish, pursue and realize their dreams regardless of race or social status.

Steeped in the glorious gospel music of her parents' and grandparents' influence in the South, Felecia grew keenly aware of the powerful influence of both faith and music. She ascribes the inner joy she feels today to the tight bonds developed among her family members who would work hard together at home, worship and sing together in church, and share with each other dreams and plans so long denied them by the segregationists of the world.

And yet, Felecia still wanted to dance. . . and couldn't.

Her mother Roberta, who had been divorced shortly after Felecia's birth, remarried a man who took the family to Los Angeles on December 1, 1969. The area was still feeling the impact of the Watts race riots of 1965

—yet another meaningful event that would take root in Felecia's young life.

Gaston's hard-working parents wanted the best for their teenaged daughter, so they made sure she attended the Baptist Church in their neighborhood, and they also enrolled her in charm school. It wasn't yet ballet, but the foundation for confidence and solid self-esteem was being laid. While attending junior college in Los Angeles, Felecia went to work for the L.A. Police Department, where she worked many assignments including Detective and radio transmitter for L.A. Vice. It was during this stint that Gaston saw so close and firsthand how deep-rooted were the sins of racial segregation—children of race having their dreams dashed before they even sprouted, maladies like drug abuse and prostitution supplanting hope and ambition.

Realizing she had to do something at least for herself, Felecia used portions of her police salary to—finally—pay for ballet lessons. She was 24 years old.

In 1980, she moved to San Francisco, attending Cal State Hayward and San Francisco State, volunteering for the San Francisco International Film Festival, and generally immersing herself in the culturally rich diversity we all enjoy so much in Northern California. She took part-time jobs for the California Coastal Commission and the National Park Service. During the stint with the film festival, her best recollection and favorite moment was organizing a reception for famed black film star Cecily Tyson.

In 1984, Gaston was living in Marin City and fast becoming a visible community activist in that corner of The County. She loved the feel of the place, the clement temperatures that are a mix of sunshine and bay breeze. She enjoyed the tight sense of community shared by fellow Marin City residents. Always busy and ever mindful of creative ways to support herself, she authored and published a book titled "Gaston's Guide," a first-of-its kind listing of over 100 of the Bay Area's black-owned restaurants.

"It was during this time that I met Anne Rogers," recalls Gaston. "She was Executive Director of the Marin Community Food Bank. Even though she was 20 years older than me, we had a lot in common, great stories about growing up in the South. From this friendship grew a mutual desire to do something for the kids of Marin City. We were worried about their self-esteem, about their ability to handle life's tough challenges. We wanted to ensure that they had strong adult role models in their lives and ways to let their talents come forth."

Like manna from heaven, a gift from God, it so happened around this time that the Marin Ballet Center for Dance was offering a performance of "The Nutcracker Suite" as part of its community outreach program championed by Phyllis Thelen, Development Director for the Marin Ballet.

The performance was a hallmark event for the children of Marin City and their cultural/artistic aspirations. Seizing the moment and acting as their mentors, Thelen and Gaston swiftly set up a scholarship program for young Marin City residents. The program was wildly successful, and soon after, Gaston parlayed the enthusiasm into organizing Performing Stars of Marin, which took root in 1990 and still flourishes today as a magnificent vehicle for otherwise-disenfranchised young people to pursue their dreams and work them to fulfillment.

Steeped in the glorious gospel music of her parents' and grandparents' influence in the South, Felecia grew keenly aware of the powerful influence of both faith and music.

Ever the resourceful survivor, Felecia took a job with the Marin County Sheriff's Department as a Parking Enforcement Officer during the formative years of the Stars program. Her uniformed visibility in and around Marin City actually enhanced her reputation as a role model for youth.

Performing Stars of Marin is a multi-faceted organization that has evolved naturally and efficiently over the years—there is a Boys to Men program and a Girls to Ladies parallel that enables young people to march in drill teams and perform in local parades; a Social Skills outlet teaches kids how to discover positive attitudes within themselves and fosters ways to convert these attitudes into specific career choices; there is also a kaleidoscopic array of literary programs, music classes, photographic workshops, dance and art sessions that energize the community, trigger career goals for the youth, and keep students on a straight path away from the deleterious effects of drug abuse, crime and other forms of social alienation.

At the hub of this whirling wheel with many spokes is the solid core of Felecia Gaston, who is, in a very real sense, *the* star of the Performing Stars of Marin.

Bob Giacomini

His cousin Gary Giacomini—former Marin supervisor for whom Open Space lands are rightfully named—receives most of the press, favorable and not, but Bob Giacomini's life and work are equally identifiable with West Marin.

Son of preeminent Point Reyes Station rancher Waldo Giacomini, recently deceased 88-year-old patriarch of one of West Marin's most successful dairy families, Bob Giacomini has also been a dairyman—since 1959—who is currently the proud purveyor of Point Reyes Original Blue, the only farmstead blue cheese produced in the entire state of California.

"Our farm and its business, Point Reyes Farmstead Cheese Company, have a pretty bright future," says Bob, "because of our cheese. Blue cheese is a niche market. You can't just produce anything you want, like cheddar, and throw it out there on the market. We lucked out, because there was no other blue cheese out there."

The Point Reyes blue, which retails for $12.95 to $14.95 a pound, is crafted from fresh, unpasteurized milk taken from a herd of handsome Holsteins that graze the lush Marin hills. Fresh is the watchword here. On cheese-making days, milk taken from the 2 a.m. milking is pumped into processing tanks in the cheese barn at 5:30 a.m. The progression from milking machine to fledgling cheese takes barely four hours.

The family settled on blue cheese because there is no other classic blue being produced in California. They also were told by retailers and chefs that there is a shortage of high-quality, creamy, French/Danish style blue cheese nationwide. Besides, the family wanted something they would love to eat themselves—they are unabashed "foodies."

"The traditional ways of farming in West Marin," Bob Giacomini continues, "are dying out. To stay in business, you have to look at new ways of farming. There are other niches that people are exploring. In dairying, there's organic butter, ice cream or yogurt that people could explore. Grass fed beef is doing well, and there might be a way to grow fruits and vegetables. Some people are looking into olives, but I don't know if the climate in West Marin will support that."

The pale, creamy cheese is already the darling of white tablecloth restaurants and upscale retailers. The unique fog and moisture-laden breezes off Tomales Bay create the ideal microclimate for growing the mold and aging the cheese at the company's barns, just over the ridge from the bay.

Making Point Reyes Original Blue takes 21 days of intensive handling and another three to four months of storage in a 42-degree room. The result is a pale, blue-veined cheese, more creamy than crumbly, mildly salty, with deep flavors and aroma, reminiscent of France's Roquefort or Denmark's Danablu.

The product is one of California's very few true farmstead cheeses, meaning it is made strictly from milk produced by Giacomini's own herd. Farmstead cheeses are also free of artificial color and bleach. Only eight California cheese makers produce cheeses that qualify as farmstead. The only other blue-style farmstead cheese produced in California is not a true blue, but is a blue-veined triple cream cheese, made by Bravo Farms of Visalia.

The Giacomini ranch is home to 250 to 300 milking cows at a time, all born and raised on the 700-acre spread. In farm talk, this is called a "closed herd," which makes for healthy ranching, according to Bob Giacomini's youngest daughter, Jill Giacomini Basch, who helps market the cheese. "By not buying heifers from outside," she explains, "our cows aren't exposed to bacteria or viruses from elsewhere." She points out that consumers like the fact that the cheese is free of added hormones, even though the farm is not certified organic.

Still, the Giacominis branched out from traditional milk production to blue cheese partly because of economic reasons. Though Giacomini and the 30 or so other Marin dairy ranchers have been in the forefront of conservation—Bob was a director of the Marin Agricultural Land Trust (MALT)—they are also under pressure to reduce their herds. Many, including nearby oyster growers, see cows as the source of potentially harmful agricultural runoff into Tomales Bay and its ecologically sensitive oyster beds.

"There is always pressure for development in West Marin," explains Giacomini. "MALT has only acquired one-third of the farms out here, and while we have support from the Board of Supervisors, who knows what the future will hold? I'm still involved in civic issues, mostly local, and I'm trying to find time to play a little golf, too.

"To keep up our cash flow," Giacomini says, "we had to come up with a way to make more money from fewer cattle." He, his wife Dean and his four grown daughters put their heads together and came up with blue cheese.

The daughters bring different expertise to the venture. Oldest daughter Karen Giacomini Howard and third daughter, Lynn Giacomini Stray, both worked in marketing; second daughter Diana Giacomini works in commercial real estate; and youngest daughter Jill ran her own advertising business.

The farm can produce 400 wheels of cheese a day, adding up to a weekly total of 1,200 to 1,400 wheels—enough to supply an already impressive list of Bay Area restaurants and retail stores. Restaurant customers include Scala's Bistro, Jardiniére, Rose Pistola, One Market, Restaurant Lulu, JohnFrank and Eos in San Francisco; French Laundry, Auberge du Soleil and Domaine Chandon in the Napa Valley; Cafe Rouge and Citron in the East Bay.

The family wanted something they would love to eat themselves—they are unabashed "foodies."

Grocery customers include Real Food Co., Rainbow Grocery and Leonard's 2001 in San Francisco; Draeger's and Roberts of Woodside on the Peninsula; Whole Foods markets throughout the Bay Area; and the Cheese Shop in Carmel.

"With the national park out here," concludes Giacomini, "we are going to get more and more tourists. We already have 2.5 million visitors per year. More and more businesses in West Marin are looking towards the tourist trade. There are some advantages to us because we have our product distributed through B&Bs, who hand out small samples to their guests. The only downside to tourism is the crowded roads.

"My daughters have just published their own book," boasts Giacomini of the family's affair. "It is called 'The Blue Course.' It's all about blue cheese, and it has recipes and a history of the family and farm in it. We're selling it at farmers markets and at cheese shops."

Like everything else involved with family life on the Giacomini farm, even the cheese, so it seems, doesn't stand alone.

Gary Giacomini

All of us, in varying degrees, live and work hard to have people remember us when we are gone. Even the most modest of us have legacies.

Now, nobody has ever called Gary Giacomini modest, and it's probably a very safe bet to say that his legacy is intact. But the key to glimpsing Giacomini is to view the constant seesaw battle waging between his legacy and the style with which he forged it.

Giacomini would probably wince at the comparison, but Lyndon Johnson comes to mind. Johnson's most important legacy was signing the Civil Rights Act into law, making racism illegal in the United States. But mention of Lyndon Johnson also brings a whole raft of conflicting opinions about his personal style—politics by badgering, power grabs instead of leadership by consensus, a forceful personality turning ugly and threatening when cornered or angered.

The most important thing to say about Gary Giacomini the politician, absent any discussion of style, is to say that his name has become synonymous with the preservation of Marin County's precious and breathtaking open space. Nobody will ever question the unconditional toughness, ironclad devotion and brusque cajoling this man brought to the fight to keep Marin a miracle of nature to behold.

And maybe, in his mind, the battle to accomplish this was so vital that he risked friendship, reputation and good manners to get the task done. But as a Marin County Supervisor and a member of the California Coastal Commission, this native Marinite championed both the preservation of the coast and the delicate environmental/economic balance of West Marin.

This latter achievement was crowned by the establishment in 1980 of the Marin Agricultural Land Trust (MALT), which assured open space in West Marin on a permanent basis for over 150,000 acres eyed greedily by developers while assuring environmentally conscious agricultural and dairy types that their work would continue to feed the lifeline of the North Bay's economic trough.

Not to be overlooked, of course, is his work as a Marin Supervisor covering the needs of Marin's poor, homeless, the mentally and physically disabled, seniors and youth. He also stepped up boldly to defy efforts to allow massive clear-cut logging proposals on Mt. Tamalpais and in the Nicasio Redwoods.

Yet another success in his quiver of accomplishments was his help in securing desperately needed water for Marin residents and ranchers during the seemingly hopeless drought years of 1976 and 1977. Marin was bone-dry, the reservoirs in his West Marin district looked like parched lunar-scapes, and his constituents were not only restless, but fearful.

Joining forces with then-Marin Municipal Water Board General Manager Diet Stroeh, Giacomini made treks to Washington, D.C. to confer with his associates and colleagues in Congress, John L. Burton and Barbara Boxer, and eventually President Jimmy Carter's White House staff to secure the important federal seed money it would take to solve the drought.

Through the force of their personalities and political connections, Giacomini and Stroeh provided enough savvy, political imagination and cunning to create a highly unlikely yet eventually successful solution—placing a pipeline on the entire length of the Richmond-San Rafael Bridge that would allow water to flow to Marin from the less stressed aquatic systems of the East Bay.

"My political roots, connections and loyalty run deep," says Giacomini, "and I don't hesitate cashing in on them when they benefit the people of Marin. John Burton was a principal in these drought meetings, and when you're with people that you've worked for and supported and campaigned with in the past, you can cut right to the chase.

"The Burtons—John and his late brother, Phil, who was an eyelash shy of being Speaker of the House one year—are all about loyalty, and once you back up your word with them, your word is gold. I forget the details of how we secured emergency rush money for the pipeline project, but it was shortly after one of our meetings that we received a call from the White House saying that Jimmy Carter had set aside $10 million to help us with the pipeline."

Yet another more notorious legacy maker in Giacomini's resume is the truculent way he fought like a pit bull to preserve the intent and purity of Beryl Buck's massive will bestowing untold millions of dollars upon the residents of Marin. In the 1980's, some members of the San Francisco Foundation filed suit to secure some of Buck's funds for needy people throughout the Bay Area, not just Marin.

Their reasoning was that Marin, already renowned as a lucrative community not exactly hard strapped for cash, would do well to spread the inheritance around to areas that needed the money in a worse way.

Nobody will ever question the unconditional toughness, ironclad devotion and brusque cajoling this man brought to the fight to keep Marin a miracle of nature to behold.

This was a no-brainer for Giacomini, a political hot potato/softball thrown tantalizingly smack down the middle of the plate. To say he ripped the pitch out of the ballpark like Babe Ruth on steroids would be an understatement. He went ballistic, referring to San Francisco Foundation members as "grave-robbing bastards" determined to dishonor the last will and testament of this very serious-minded woman who was committed to helping her beloved fellow Marinites.

Primarily through the sheer force of his bombast and intimidating one-man stand against these would-be raiders, Giacomini (and Marin) prevailed. Today, the Buck Trust is a thriving, vibrant life source pumping a steady stream of dollars into the betterment of Marin people's lives, careers, aspirations, housing and employment and educational needs.

Oh—by the way—a significant *persona* was added to the Buck Trust's Board of Directors in 2003—one Gary Giacomini. What was that he was saying about deep political connections, roots and loyalties?

It's hard to believe that this fiery, always embattled, frequently frothing proponent of all things Marin is now considered an elder statesman among his younger constituents, but youth best beware—Giacomini is ever watchful from his law offices atop Wood Isle in Larkspur where he works for a high-powered law firm.

And God help anyone who dare mess with this unique character's legacy now that he is (mostly) retired from public life. He would bolt like Zeus from his hilltop perch if and when the occasion called for yet another Giacomini-esque clash with legacy.

Elissa Giambastiani

Some names become so intrinsically entwined with the businesses or organizations that employ them that it soon becomes difficult to distinguish one from the other.

Any mention of the San Rafael Chamber of Commerce, for example, immediately evokes a more than subliminal reference to the name Elissa Giambastiani. She has been with the Chamber since 1987, but it's hard to imagine her ever not being with that organization.

"Fear is a great motivator," laughs the affable President and CEO. "I remember my biggest fear in the early days of my Chamber experience was making a mistake, and it would be on the front page of the *Marin Independent Journal.*

"I was terrified of that happening, and resolved early on to always work very hard to know exactly what I was talking about, because, frankly, there would be nobody to cover for me except me."

She need not worry. When her name pops up—and it does so quite frequently—on the local scene the first thought is not of someone who makes mistakes, but rather of someone who is an expert and a doer, although she would scoff at the "expert" part.

"It's a wonderful job for a generalist," she explains,

"which is what I am—I know a little about a lot. It's a great thing for someone as curious as I am. Curiosity is really the key to whatever success I have, because if I am curious about something, I will do everything in my power to learn it and then to own it. Curiosity is also what makes every day so new and inviting."

The Minnesota native who lives now in the Terra Linda section of San Rafael—she and husband Ron have four children—came to the Bay Area in the mid-'60s, and soon landed a job with the Walter Landor firm in San Francisco, the colorful Emabarcadero-based company where she did market research and learned the fundamentals of business principles that would serve her so well later as a Chamber executive.

Just prior to the San Rafael Chamber post, Giambastiani worked as Marketing Director for the Marin Ballet, and if that job entailed juggling many things at once, it was nothing compared to what was to come her way as a Chamber executive.

"The late 1980s and early 1990s were a critical time for San Rafael," she explains. "The downtown area was dying, but we took part in a vigorous renaissance campaign in conjunction with the city that is still bearing fruit to this day."

Old San Rafael was crumbling. Business facades looked tired and uninspired. The City of San Rafael, once the vital hub of the entire county, was losing its identity. The situation begged for leadership on many different fronts, and Giambastiani stepped up to the task.

"It would be far too easy to take credit for what has happened in San Rafael," she says, "but the truth of the matter is that Marin business people are simply not given their due. They care so much about this place, and that gives me all the motivation I need to serve their needs. What you see now in downtown San Rafael—the revitalization of Fourth Street, the physical improvements that delight the eye and attract the shopper—is simply the result of the business community that refused to give up on this old town.

"It was easy for us to create committees—the Chamber installed a Government Affairs Committee, an Economic Development Committee, an Education Committee, a Housing Committee, an Environmental Committee, to name a few—but the real work came from the business owners who worked together to create a new San Rafael that is business friendly, physically attractive, and reflective of the diversity that makes up our population."

Giambastiani's stewardship at the San Rafael Chamber has overseen a membership drive that has grown from 650 in 1987 to 900 members now. Her leadership ability has resulted in the creation of alliances with Chambers in Napa, Santa Rosa, and Fairfield-Suisun, areas that are grappling with the same kinds of crises that have faced San Rafael in the past two decades.

Giambastiani, particularly sensitive to housing issues brought on by the escalating cost of living in Marin, worked hard to create a housing trust fund; she works closely with affordable housing experts

"It is pure joy, for example, to help coordinate the complex efforts of seemingly divergent groups, to create a consensus instead of discord."

throughout The County who are working tirelessly to come up with innovative solutions to workforce housing issues in this, the most expensive county in the State, to find permanent residence; and she was instrumental in the creation of Marin Consortium for Workforce Housing.

"What I'm most proud of in this arena," she states, "is that the San Rafael Chamber of Commerce was actually the first organization to take on housing as a business issue. As a matter of fact, we were the ones who coined the term 'workforce housing.'"

She has also used her position to give an effective voice to businesses who struggle with politically sensitive hot buttons like Worker's Compensation, legislative mandates, land use planning, healthcare, and environmental questions.

"I believe in clear and upfront communication," says Giambastiani, "whether it's dealing with a newspaper reporter, a city official or a Chamber member, so I've been able to shed a lot of attention on local economic issues. It is pure joy, for example, to help coordinate the complex efforts of seemingly divergent groups, to create a consensus instead of discord.

"The bottom line is that it's all about people. Whatever leadership skills I possess come from the ability I have to put people together as they work toward a common goal. It's really that simple. That's the joy I experience as a generalist. I keep learning new things every day, I never let ideology get in the way of success, and I watch wonderful things take place. And if you think San Rafael has come a long way, you haven't seen anything yet."

Marilyn and Sandy Greenblat

One of the privileges and honors involved in writing this book was the occasional invitation to spend time inside the home of one of our 100 profiles. We tried not to be intrusive, but it did help to see these Marinites in their own element. Artist Marilyn Greenblat and husband Sandy, a realtor/race car driver/community activist, live in a cozy home in East San Rafael just off of San Pedro Road. The living room is a nestled fireplace pod with an inspirational view of Mt. Tamalpais looming peacefully to the West. The home is graced with some of Marilyn's more breathtaking pieces of art. Outside, just off the driveway, is a separate structure a bit larger than an average garage which serves as Marilyn's studio. Inside is an explosion of her trademark Marin sunsets illuminating hillsides, pastures, knolls, canyons, rivulets, and other familiar local landscapes. The interview began in front of the fireplace just as a sunset-splotched dusk descended upon mighty Mt. Tam.

"I am a painter and Marin is a natural canvas," says Marilyn. "Here you have everything, whatever pleases you that day, it's just all around you. You have this diverse landscape—the rolling hills, the egrets, herons and many of nature's other beautiful creatures, the ocean—whatever you want, and that's what makes it so dynamic for me.

"To be able to capture all of that on canvas is a thrill of a lifetime. It's a privilege to be able to document the beauty of The County and then give it back to the people who also live here.

"We are both native San Franciscans. When we got married, we both wanted to get out of The City, and this was the place to come. It was a really easy decision. It's just so beautiful. We came to Tiburon in 1959. Unfortunately, coming from The City, we were used to the fog, and Tiburon wasn't far enough away from the fog. I was raised in the Richmond District, Sandy in the Sunset. So, we decided to move to sunnier

San Rafael in 1961.

"I started painting after we bought some Western art. I kept walking past it in the living room and telling myself I could do that. So I took some courses at College of Marin to see if I could draw; then I found a school up in Whidby Island in Washington State where I undertook an intense six-week course. I came back with a couple of good oil paintings and I have been painting ever since."

Marilyn is a landscape painter whose work has been showcased at the Marinscapes Show, at the Local Collectors Gallery in Kentfield, and at Marin Open Studios. She has a few collectors now and her art career has blossomed. Her work has been accepted and lauded by Oil Painters of America, Women Artists of the West, and the American Academy of Women Artists.

"These are shows where you are juried by your peers," says the modest artist, "so I feel pretty good about having made that step in my career. Then, when you get responses from people who buy your paintings and who tell you how much joy they receive from them every day, it's just priceless."

Husband Sandy chimes in: "Marilyn celebrates the wild and so do I. I'm out in it a lot—it was one of the first things that attracted me to Marin, that open space feeling, magnetic and fenceless. One of the things that disturbs me about Marin now is that's it's all fenced in, but I do feel that the basic character of The County is still here.

"I recall coming to Marin by ferry and then by train to visit a summer house some friends had in Larkspur. It was a cottage with a big screened-in porch. That was before World War II, and that's where my bond with this special place began.

"When Marilyn and I moved here, I commuted to The City for years. I worked for an import company. There was too much travel, so I quit in 1964. That's when I became self-employed and got involved in sports car racing. I knew Peter Adams who owned Honda of Marin, so I became a motorcycle dealer from 1964 to 1977 in San Rafael."

Greenblat was actually the personification of racing in Marin. He was instrumental in getting the motorcycles to run at the internationally renowned Laguna Seca race track—these were the Grand Prix bikes that attracted all the famous European racers who were hungry for an American track. Greenblat's intervention led to the birth of the American Federation of Motorcycles.

"When Motor Cross first came to America," says Sandy, "one of the five stops was at China Camp. We sponsored a lot of races out there. The guys were very dedicated—they'd work on their bikes in the morning and race in the afternoon. We started a school to teach kids how to race the bikes. It was quite a sight to see little kids aged four on mini-bikes learning all the moves from these seasoned professionals.

"But my biggest thrill was driving race cars. My favorite was the Corvette. I was involved in the early development days of the Corvette; the Northern California Corvette Association was born on our living room floor."

"Marin is a natural canvas... You have this diverse landscape—the rolling hills, the egrets, herons and many of nature's other beautiful creatures, the ocean—whatever you want, and that's what makes it so dynamic for me."

Greenblat gave up car racing in 1977 and started a new career in real estate, which led to his many community affiliations.

"I always believed that one man could make a difference," he says, "so in the '80s I got involved in community issues big time, speaking at City Council meetings, bemoaning the fact that so may businesses were leaving Marin and saying that we simply had to stop the bleeding.

"By the late '80s, something close to 1,100 jobs had gone away, so we knuckled down and, with the help of people like Al Boro, here we are in a new century and San Rafael is doing just fine, with a whole new look and a bright future."

Greenblat received the San Rafael Citizen of the Year Award in 2003 and was the first recipient of the San Rafael Chamber's Ann Weston Award for Community Service.

The Greenblats' son, Martin, is close to 40 years of age, works for Microsoft, and is married to a Brazilian woman, Maria Carolina. Sandy has a daughter from a first marriage named Jerris who lives in Southern California. Marilyn and Sandy have an adopted daughter, Tam Khuc ("Tammi"), born in Vietnam and educated here; she and her husband, Kevin Tran, are in the computer industry.

Roger Grossman

Roger Grossman just *looks* like a newspaperman, a strapping figure with a mellifluous voice and a clear-headed vision of good journalism.

Hired as the publisher of the *Marin Independent Journal* in 2001 (and now the paper's Chairman/CEO since Marty Rubino's appointment as current publisher), Grossman speaks with strength and simplicity. For a person who possesses the physical theatricality of a Shakespearean actor, he is a refreshingly frank, common sense-driven person with no pretense or affectation. Many newspaper publishers in both fiction and reality exude pomp and arrogance. Not Grossman.

What he has brought to the *Marin IJ* is exactly what the paper has needed and what Marin deserves—an accurate reflection of the community, an open-minded paper that nurtures diversity and divergence, and a dynamic conversation between editorial and reader that benefits and enhances both.

"Really, though," says Grossman, "it's the employees who have done it. I may have brought a different style of leadership and a can-do attitude in a county that begged for local news, but basically I have just stepped out of the way to let the talent flow."

When he came here from San Mateo, he says he checked his preconceptions at the door. "Sure, I knew Marin was a wealthy, well-educated county," he explains, "but preconceptions beyond that don't allow you the objectivity you need to publish an effective paper.

"I am very pro-active in new situations. I don't wait for the phone to ring. My first week here, I made a list of the top 20 community leaders and called them immediately. They were impressed. The tone I set was one of openness, conviviality, awareness and a willingness to listen and to lead, from both a personal and business standpoint. You can't do that if you hide behind the doors of the 'Ivory Tower.'

"I want to hear what people don't like in order to make needed improvements. One way we've accomplished this was to start the 'Community Observer' program, whereby from four to seven community leaders actually sit in on the news budget meetings and see how the paper evolves from planning to printing—they witness photo, graphic, advertising choices, the whole dynamic of how a paper comes to be.

"Another way we've revitalized community engagement is through a healthy give-and-take on the editorial pages. Under newsroom management's direction, we offer a lively presentation of all sorts of opposing viewpoints. Our 'Marin Voice' column provides readers a chance to write an editorial."

Under Grossman's leadership, what he calls the "five-legged stool" of Marin issues—transportation, health, workforce housing, education and the environment—have been showcased and spotlighted on a regular basis. Two of the most burning local issues—workforce housing and Marin's shocking breast cancer rate of incidence—were expertly wrapped in packages that received extensive national media attention. Using the *Marin IJ* as a model, in fact, there is even a national workforce housing committee in place.

As for the story about cancer afflicting Marin women in skyrocketing numbers, Grossman asks some tough questions: "Go across Highway 37, the cancer rate drops, it drops a lot. Go across the Golden Gate Bridge, the cancer rate drops, it drops a lot. We want to know why and we will find out why. My assistant lives on a block in Marin with 10 women. Seven of these women have breast cancer. Don't think for a minute we will drop our pursuit of this story."

Another key to Grossman's effectiveness is the public visibility he fosters with advertisers and community leaders. "I have never seen a locale," he says, "where a paper's major advertisers are also vital leaders: people like Larry Brackett of Frank Howard Allen, Bill Daniels of United Markets, Keith Ray of Marin Honda. I can't emphasize enough the importance of advertising, because, after all, with the cost of newsprint and related expenses, you really don't make a dime on circulation. It's all about advertising and the ways we work to create an attractive vehicle for the advertising to work effectively."

Grossman emphasizes the fact that Marin is the highest educated county in the nation. "So," he says, "not only the pages of the paper, but also the *ethos* of the paper needs to reflect that high standard. That's why our work is never done. We constantly experiment with new ways to reflect Marin—one of the best pieces we've had is the 'Marin 101' magazine, which has everything you can imagine in it, from restaurants and entertainment to lodging, recreation, business, natural splendor, the works. We will never stop continuing to enhance the product."

"There are a couple of ways to run a newspaper. You can micro-manage it and be all worried about misplaced commas and colons or you can set a tone, establish goals, and then get the hell out of the way. This second way is my style."

The only surprising thing about Grossman is that he is such a relative newcomer to Marin. That's how good a fit it is between him and The County. "There are a couple of ways to run a newspaper," he explains. "You can micro-manage it and be all worried about misplaced commas and colons or you can set a tone, establish goals, and then get the hell out of the way. This second way is my style. And in 13 years with my company, ANG Newspapers, I've never once been told what to do. My bosses understand that what I am about is developing leadership. After all, if you're the only one who is a leader, then you've got a problem."

Then there's the simple likeability factor. The man is easy to like, period. He is warm, curious, completely inofficious, humorous, positive and brave. The courage is a daily battle since he has been struggling with cancer for over three years. He gets plenty of strength from his wife Cheryl, who has beaten cancer twice herself and who is currently in a third round with the dread disease, and from his two teenaged sons, Elliott and Trent, who love their Dad dearly.

Grossman approaches his health battle with the same sense of sober determination and moral fiber that he brings to newspapering. If who we are is best revealed by the daunting challenges life serves us, then Roger Grossman is as robust on the inside as he is on the exterior.

Richard Habib

"Carpet Diem" is a perfect quip that sums up the playful business acumen and fun-loving-yet-soulful lifestyle of Richard Habib, owner of Alexander's Decorative Rugs of Mill Valley.

Despite an uncertain economy that is in continual flux, Richard has managed to stay afloat. He has maintained good relations with all his customers, and has remained open and in business while others around him have closed. His passion is dealing in rugs and textiles. He is a student of rug and textile history and artistry, and takes classes to learn even more.

Richard Habib exudes an irresistibly vibrant sense of life in all that he does. While rugs and textiles may be his passion in business, he has expanded his talents as an expertly engaging speaker, author, appraiser and auctioneer. And he is actively involved in the rug community nationally and internationally—he is well-known and respected.

Proving that there is more to the rug business than meets the eye, Habib also offers workshops to help clients attain success in both their business and personal lives. Collaborating with Habib in past workshop sessions has been Susan Berland, a Certified Professional Personal Coach who has spent nearly 20 years helping small business owners and entrepreneurs. Some of the workshop topics sponsored by Habib and facilitated by Berland include: "Overcoming Procrastination," "Having It All: Balancing Your Life and Your Work," "A Fresh Approach to Setting Goals," and "Values—Being True to Yourself."

"I am a certified appraiser," says Habib, "and I think there are only about two dozen auctioneers and licensed retailers in the state who are certified as appraisers. I found early on that I had a gift for it. I started doing rug and textile auctions in 1998 (I was certified in 1989), and I guess I've done about 60 by now, raising approximately $2 million for different non-profits.

"I recently did an auction for Blue Star Music Camps. The camps help give skills and self-esteem to young people who might otherwise never get a chance to go to camp. I auctioned off a guitar donated by Bob Weir of the Grateful Dead. Weir played the guitar, signed it, and it sold for $5,000. We also auctioned off guitars donated by Robert Cray, Bonnie Raitt and B.B. King, generating $30,000 for Blue Star.

"I've done auctions with Michael Pritchard, the comedian, with Joel Bartlett, the Channel 7 meteorologist, along with other Bay Area and international luminaries. And next I'm doing two auctions back-to-back within an hour of each other for Rainforest Action Network and Grace Cathedral. I support artists' studios in Mill Valley and the SPECTRUM group that gives a voice to young gay people in Marin. I help with fundraisers for some local political groups, animal rights "schools," the arts, incurable diseases, women's groups, and children's rights in Nepal. We hold events at my Rug Gallery in Mill Valley. I've also invested a lot of money into renovating my neighborhood on Miller Avenue—'Midtown Mill Valley.'

"When I'm not working on my business or helping in the community, I'm working out. I do about a thousand sit-ups and pushups every morning, martial arts, and I have been a marathon runner off and on for the last 20 years. My beautiful wife Sheila and daughter Rachel have been very supportive and understanding. I value my time with them very much. I'm not competitive with others, but I am with myself. I always feel that I can do better in my life, every single day raising my own bar."

While Habib's breadth and scope of life embraces far more than being a purveyor of import rugs and textiles, he's been in the business long enough to have honed a razor-sharp understanding of all its intricacies. Since 1976, he's been trading contemporary, antique and decorative rugs of quality and artistic merit. He possesses a broad and sophisticated knowledge of the world's finest rugs, and places customer service at the top of his list of industry standards.

His business is an all-inclusive enterprise, offering verbal appraisals on the premises; providing hand washing and conditioning for Oriental rugs and carpets; accepting on a consignment basis for clients fine rugs for sale or trade; and offering expert re-weaving, decorative textile art, and cost-effective maintenance for the delicate fringe and sides of his merchandise.

"I think my business is unique in the rug world. I refuse to be a salesman, but, rather, an advocate."

"I deal with all sorts of people at my rug gallery," continues Habib. "When people come in the door, you don't know who they are, and we treat everyone with the same respect. I practice my philosophy through my business. I treat all people with respect. I was instructed early in life that your teacher comes in many different forms. You never know whom you are going to meet.

"I think my business is unique in the rug world. I refuse to be a salesman, but, rather, an advocate. We don't have fake sales, there's no hard sell at business. I try to educate my customers about what they are buying and treat them with courtesy. We are the most awarded company in Marin County history. Our walls are full of plaques and awards—earned, not purchased, as some have done.

"Business has been tough the last three years with the economic situation. But I have the same sort of philosophy in my business—I support about six dozen community non-profits throughout the Bay Area, either by cash donations or rug donations or being an advisor. I sit on the boards of the Mill Valley Chamber of Commerce and the Marin Theater Company, plus I am on the advisory boards of several other non-profits."

Wayne Hansen

Wayne Hansen came to Marin from Pasadena in 1992 to join a small consulting group as a systems analyst.

"They folded," is Hansen's quick response about the group's whereabouts and a two-word explanation of why he is in this book as one of Marin's burgeoning new wine makers and not as a systems analyst.

With three partners—Skip Granger, Mike Miller, and Bruce Walker—Hansen began making wine at an amateur level.

"Our motivation," says Hansen, "comes from a shared, lifelong passion for wine and an increasing disdain for the over-priced and often mass-produced wines found in the market.

"In our first year," he continues, "we crushed several hundred pounds of grapes and produced about 50 cases of Zinfandel, Cabernet Sauvignon and Chardonnay in my basement. With my food background—the others had been in equipment leasing and leasing/corporate finance—it was destiny that I be elected wine maker."

Combining the best of both new and traditional methods, pooling their money, and renting a roll-up warehouse in Bel Marin Keys in 1999, the four vintners discovered, somewhat to their shock, that they were capable of making outstanding wine. They started getting really serious about their endeavor after the first sips—they signed up at U.C. Davis for classes, and sought voluminous advice from an assortment of very successful commercial wine makers. They became a bonded winery in that same year, 1999.

Hansen, 60 years old and divorced (his daughter Sallie and his granddaughter live in Vallejo with Sallie's husband), was discovering that, just perhaps, there really is such a thing as a Second Act in America.

"It started dawning on me," he says now, "that this thing just might fly. Our next step was coming up with a name—we whittled the short list down to about 200 ideas, but settled on Starry Night Winery because, frankly, it was the only one that received our complete agreement.

"I had a degree in Chemistry and had worked for Hunt/Wesson Foods, and I knew a little something about microbiology—analyzing ripe tomatoes, for example, before they become tomato sauce or ketchup—so we weren't too far astray studying how crushed grapes can turn into fine wine. Being a food technologist was a good living. Given the choice, though, between making a good tomato sauce or creating an excellent wine, well, you know the answer to that."

The group's philosophy of wine making begins with selecting the finest grapes available. Since excess handling can detract from the grapes' quality, Starry Night employs methods that have minimal impact on the fruit. One such method is to use gravity to move the grapes into the fermenters and destemmers.

"We have an absolutely *killer* Zinfandel," boasts Hansen, "and we ascribe this to the fact that we keep production of any one wine to below 1,000 cases. This gives us a very high-quality, hand-crafted wine that distinguishes us from many of our larger competitors who think that 'big is best.'

"Zinfandel really is our primary focus—it accounts for 40 percent of our production. It's not only a great wine, distinctly American, but also a terrific value compared to other varietals. In 2001, we became a member of the Zinfandel Advocates and Producers Organization (ZAP), which promotes Zinfandel around the globe."

The group behind Starry Night Winery also strives to produce the finest wines possible that accentuate the regions where the grapes are grown—Chardonnay and Zinfandel stem from the Russian River Valley; Zinfandel and Cabernet Sauvignon from Napa Valley; Mouvedre from Lake County; Sauvignon Blanc from Mendocino and Lake Counties; and Zinfandel, Syrah and other Rhone varietals from the Lodi appellation.

So—how do they grow their grapes in. . . *Novato?*

"That's the most asked question we get," laughs Hansen. "The answer is we don't grow any grapes in Novato. What we do is find the best grapes and growers that allow us to produce the finest wines. We have now worked with one of our growers for eight harvests, and two of our growers for five harvests."

On the business end, the bottom line is ripening like a finely manicured vine. Slowly and steadily, the yield in 1999 was 1,000 cases overall, 2,000 in Year 2000, and 5,000 cases in 2001. Sales, says Hansen, are finally catching up with production, a triumph for which he salutes his partners for their vigorously efficient sales, marketing and business techniques.

"Our motivation comes from a shared, lifelong passion for wine and an increasing disdain for the over-priced and often mass-produced wines found in the market."

"I think one of the keys to our success," says the affable Hansen, who refers to himself as the grunt man in the operation, "is that we very carefully nurture excellent working relationships with our growers. They are, after all, handling our babies, so we have great respect for their work."

Starry Night Winery offers a "Stellar Club" for new members to join. Offers include an automatic two or three-bottle shipment of current releases; four annual shipments delivered directly to the recipient; 20 percent off bottles for each delivery, which usually range in price from $50-$60, plus shipping; and, best of all, no cost to join.

Starry Night, although still a relatively young vintner, has managed to win several awards—namely, its 2001 Tom Feeney Zinfandel, 2001 Lodi Zinfandel, 2001 Russian River Valley Chardonnay, 2001 Adara, and the 2001 Russian River Old Vine Zinfandel.

In case you're wondering about start-up costs for beginning your own urban vineyard, the group had to come up with roughly $200,000 for its 2002 vintage, and that's money that needs to be fermented for a time before the numbers can be crunched (er, *crushed*).

Wayne Hansen is proud that he and his partners have found a niche; have discovered ways to keep the company streamlined, efficient and profitable; and, probably most importantly, are enjoying an avocation whose fruit can be, well, downright intoxicating.

Chris Hardman

Chris Hardman, 53, hitchhiked to Marin from L.A. in 1972, and has been so busy ever since, he hasn't had time to look back.

"I saw the Golden Gate Bridge," says the artistic director and founder of Antenna Theater, "and that's all it took. Who could ever leave this place?"

Antenna Theater is the showcase home for "Walkmanology," Hardman's invention that uses the portable audio player as an actual performance tool. If you are part of an Antenna "audients" (Hardman's coinage), you have been inside theatrical mazes, carnival-like environments, interactive installations, site-specific performances, radio programs, guided tours and even giant walk-through sculptures.

Hardman's work combines cutting-edge audio technology with interview-driven sound designs, puppetry, masked movement, 3-D projections, sensor-tripped animation, sculptural objects, features of the natural landscape, and prefabricated environments.

Prior to his landing in the Bay Area, Hardman had worked on New York's Coney Island as a painter dabbling in glow-in-the-dark carnival exhibits for the Bread and Puppet Theater.

His next stop was the San Francisco/Marin journey, where he worked for the Renaissance Faire, then, in 1980, started the Snake Theater in Sausalito, the precursor for Antenna Theater

He had recently flown to Europe to study museums. While walking through the austere buildings, he was struck by how "infuriatingly silent" they are. The idea popped into his head to create Walkman-driven productions. So, when he returned to Marin, he wrote a play, "High School," in which headset-wearing theatergoers actually got to play high school students. The performance was showcased at Tamalpais High School in Mill Valley, and thus was born Antenna Theater.

A hallmark production of Hardman's company was his 1988 "Alcatraz Cellhouse Tour," which employed actual voices of former inmates and guards to narrate the tour which was created for the National Park Service.

Weaving *avant garde* artistry with a shrewd nose for business, Hardman credits the progressively tolerant atmosphere of San Francisco and Marin for his ability to thrive doing what he does best.

Married to Sausalito politico and former member of the Marin Board of Supervisors, Annette Rose, the couple has one daughter, Trent.

Both actively engaged in Sausalito political affairs, Chris and Annette live on a houseboat (a 100-year-old converted tugboat called The Liberty), and they are vociferous proponents of waterfront preservation and other burning southern Marin issues.

One of his more recent breakthrough presentations was an event called "AllTime" at the Exploratorium in San Francisco in 2003. "AllTime" is Hardman's alternative system for what we conventionally call time and the historical calendar systems. The illustrated talk was an intriguing exploration into what we think we know about time and the possibility to dare looking at time in bold new ways.

What keeps Antenna Theater real instead of mindlessly experimental is Hardman's commitment to tackle controversy, taking on topics that are at once timely and relevant. In "Etiquette of the Undercaste," for example, audience participants played the parts of homeless people. And, in "Enola Alone" (a play on the name of the bomb-carrying U.S. plane Enola Gay), "audients" members wandered through an interactive maze which funneled into the bombardier section of a plane—thereby establishing, perhaps, the sheer horror of what it might have been like to be the conveyor of a nuclear explosion.

"I saw the Golden Gate Bridge and that's all it took. Who could ever leave this place?"

"Enola Alone," effectively chilling, was produced in 1994 to coincide with the 50th anniversary of the end of World War II and, of course, the dropping of the atomic bomb from the Enola Gay.

Antenna Theater's production company occupies leased space on the Golden Gate National Recreation Area's land on the Marin Headlands—thereby completing Hardman's circle, from Coney Island to Cronkhite Beach. Inspirational acreage floods the building with great big gulps of Pacific breezes that are alternately delivered on platters of sunshine or misty forks of fog, creating the exact sort of mysteriously auditory and evocative characteristics that are components of Hardman's artistry.

What Chris Hardman's daring sense of exploratory, sensory-laden theater has contributed to contemporary culture is significant, melding as it does compelling social messages, educational opportunities, and fully engaged "audients" involvement.

Robert Hass

During the Bill Clinton years—an era during which truth was far more frequent and much stranger than fiction—a quiet spoken Marinite injected a contribution to the Clinton legacy that was pure poetry.

Robert Hass (who lives with his wife, Brenda Hillman, in Inverness) held the distinction of being Poet Laureate of the United States of America in the years 1995, 1996 and 1997, a span of time sadly marked more for the cheesy prosecutorial shenanigans of Kenneth Starr than they were by the loftier yearnings of the heart normally voiced by famous previous Poet Laureates like Robert Frost.

Granted, the leader of the free world did bestow upon his intern a copy of Walt Whitman's "Leaves of Grass," but that was about the only remotely poetic gesture that surfaced during the whole unseemly affair.

The job of Poet Laureate is a bit obscure and there aren't any confining restrictions attached to the position as there might be, for example, to the position of Head of Homeland Security. Perhaps the most famous Poet Laureate was the aforementioned Robert Frost, best remembered for braving the cold whilst reciting poetry for John F. Kennedy's presidential inauguration in 1961. He will forever be framed in the gallery of our memories for wearing a heavy overcoat, layers of scarves, with mist and steam curling from his mouth at the recitation of every brittle stanza.

Robert Hass, a product of Marin schooling including Marin Catholic High School where he excelled on the debating team, lights up when asked about how one is picked for the unique position.

"It's actually a very interesting job," he says, enunciating the word "interesting" with far more passion than most people would. "I really got to know the Library of Congress and the neighborhood of Washington, D.C. very well. It was truly fascinating."

One might describe the position as being the Chief Executive of the soul of the country—presiding, as it were, over the nation's more internal aspirations.

Interestingly, the Poet Laureate is actually appointed by the Librarian of Congress, who in turn is appointed by the President. The original concept behind the job was to name someone who could be the poetry consultant to the Library of Congress. As a prolific poetry professor, as a gifted and widely respected poet and author of numerous tomes on the subject, Hass was a brilliant choice.

His two driving passions in life behind the poetry are children and the environment—and he strives to wed one with the other. In his volume "River of Words," which he produced with co-authors Pamela Michael and Thacher Hurd, is an effort to encourage kids to make art and poetry with water as an inspiration.

Full title is "River of Words: Images and Poetry in Praise of Water," and it includes contributions from children all over the world—the United States, China, the Ivory Coast, Thailand and the Ukraine. The volume is a vividly illustrated and passionately written collection of art and verse from these young, fertile minds filled with expressions of sheer joy and exultation, as well as sorrow and longing, all inspired by water.

Hass says that the book is clear evidence that children have the capacity to be intelligent, articulate, caring, creative, humorous, inventive, and, most importantly, passionate. Hass says the book creates a stinging pang in the hearts of overly busy adults for whom the natural world was once a font of boundless discovery.

Chimes in Hass contemporary Gary Snyder, himself an internationally acclaimed, Pulitzer Prize-winning poet: "These selections of the best of the best give us pleasure and hope."

Other titles by Hass include "A Roadside Dog," a collaboration with Nobel Laureate Czeslaw Milosz; "Essential Haiku"; "Addison Street: The Berkeley Poetry Walk"; "California: Views by Robert Adams of the Los Angeles Basin, 1978-1983," a collaboration with Robert Adams; "Into the Garden: A Wedding Anthology: Poetry and Prose on Love and Marriage"; "Sun Under Wood," Hass' fourth poetry collection which was published in the midst of his term as Poet Laureate.

Of this last book, one critic wrote: "What elevates Hass from preciousness is a powerful need to engage and indulge—to navigate—memories of his alcoholic mother and his own painful divorce. In this volume, Hass speaks with a clear, disturbing and urgent voice."

The Robert Hass book which has received the most, well, *praise*, is a volume titled "Praise." Wrote Peter Davison in *The Atlantic Monthly*: "His second book, 'Praise,' has an architectural grandeur that even his nearly flawless first volume, 'Field Guide,' did not aim at. Poem after poem sets limits for itself as stern as gravity: white on white, block on block of stone, frames around pictures."

His two driving passions in life behind the poetry are children and the environment—and he strives to wed one with the other.

Echoes Hayden Carruth in *Harper's*: "Hass writes in many shapes, moods, even styles. Yet everywhere one recognizes this reverence for the power of language, words in their full flight of syntax, what we—or our ancestors—used to call eloquence."

Some of the more fetching poems inside "Praise" include: "Meditation at Lagunitas," "Heroic Smile," "Against Boticelli," "The Yellow Bicycle," "Picking Blackberries With A Friend Who Has Been Reading Jacques Lacan," "Child Naming Flowers," "Not Going To New York: A Letter," and "The Beginning of September."

Hass' writing is stark, harrowing, often chilling, evocative, multi-diversified, always poignant, never predictable, and ever respectful of the magnificence of language where brevity is the soul of wit and poetry is the saving grace.

Hass loves the dance of words; like many great orchestra leaders, he merely steps aside to let the simplicity and the genius and the talent of the orchestra members flow.

One excerpt from "Praise" which may serve to tantalize the lover of poetry: "We asked the captain what course of action he proposed to take toward a beast so large, terrifying and unpredictable. He hesitated to answer, and then said judiciously, 'I think I shall praise it.'"

"Praise" has been hailed as one of the five best poetry books of the 20th century. Writes one critic: "This is Hass at his finest. There is not a disappointing poem in this book. All these poems deserve to be reread often, and serious poets should study this book to learn exactly how Hass creates his magic."

Carole Hayashino

Carole Hayashino is a rising star shining brightly on the Marin political/social activism scenery.

The San Rafael resident is a longtime civil rights advocate, a luminously articulate progressive who brings to the table a sense of fairness, a passion for social justice, and an eloquent voice for those too long disenfranchised from complete political engagement.

California Congressman Mike Honda, a fellow Japanese-American, raved about her candidacy when Hayashino ran for the Assembly from Marin and Sonoma (unsuccessfully but valiantly) in Year 2000: "Her passion for social justice," said Honda, "made her a perfect candidate. She has been right on the mark on all issues, and she has never wavered."

The daughter of Barbara and the late Henry Hayashino, Carole was born and raised in Stockton, then schooled at San Francisco State, where she earned a degree in sociology, and the University of San Francisco, where she received a Masters in educational administration.

Being in the politically foaming world of San Francisco politics in the '60s and '70s gave birth to her outspoken civil rights beliefs, deeply rooted in the Asian American Movement which she helped organize to rally against the displacement of Japantown residents struggling against redevelopment relocation.

A consensus-seeker and pacifist, Hayashino organized the first Bay Area Day of Remembrance in 1979, which put the spotlight on the signing of Executive Order 9066—the notorious presidential decree which activated the evacuation and internment of over 100,000 West Coast Japanese-Americans during World War II.

Part of this Day of Remembrance included a somber parade from Fort Mason in San Francisco to what used to be called the Tanforan Assembly Center, a euphemism for the herd-like gathering of unfairly feared Japanese-Americans sadly caught up as victims in the post-Pearl Harbor racially motivated hysteria.

In 1996, the Marin resident returned to her

alma mater San Francisco State as Director of he Office of University Development, a prestigious post that taps into her ability to organize people, resources and fundraising activities, funneling all into the web of the university's many school, library and athletic programs. A result-oriented person who brings a no-nonsense efficiency to her administrative abilities, Hayashino presided over an immediate 80% increase in her first year as solicitor of private gifts.

The following year, in a nifty twist of poetic justice, Hayashino brought back the "Concentration Camps, USA" class which she helped create years earlier as a student but which had long since been disbanded. Putting a cap on this accomplishment was her ability to convince the university administration to bestow honorary degrees upon former Japanese-American students whose educational goals and dreams were abruptly stripped because of the "years of infamy" surrounding the shameful concentration camp experience.

In an emotionally charged ceremony, the once-scarred students were academically honored at the university's 1998 graduation rites.

As Hayashino would later tell the *Nichi Bei Times*: "It meant a lot to me. My father was supposed to go to the University of the Pacific, but he had to go to camp. The internment forever changed his life."

As a member of the Marin County Human Rights Commission, she spearheaded a campaign to induce the Marin County Board of Supervisors to officially apologize for the actions of the Board during the internment tragedy when then-members of that Marin body issued a resolution supporting evacuation to concentration camps.

A fiery and tireless advocate not only for the rights of her own Japanese-American citizens, but also a savvy community organizer who knows how to rally all marginalized people back into the full share of the American dream, Hayashino draws heavily from the shameful experience her parents had to endure.

"My parents' loyalties were in question," she says pointedly. "Because they were seen as a threat, their constitutional rights were devalued. Let us now and forever renew our commitment to preserve and protect civil liberties for all."

In an elegant blend of a public servant coming together seamlessly with art, Hayshino parlayed her membership on the Commission for One California (a forum created to promote cultural understanding among diverse peoples) to render a hearty boost to the restoration and revival of "Farewell to Manzanar," a wonderful film produced by Mill Valley filmmaker John Korty. The movie, based on a 33-year-old book by Jeanne Wakatsuki and her husband James D. Houston, is a 28-year-old sensitive piece on what can go wrong when a nation is in the clutches of monumental stress.

Jeanne Wakatsuki was seven, the youngest of 10 siblings, when her family was rudely transplanted from their Santa Monica home to the barbed-wired confines of internment. Her book, and later Korty's film, offer stark reality and poignant history lessons. Hayashino's commitment to bring the film back into circulation is yet another triumph of her civic activism. Because of her, the film was restored to perfection and is now distributed to schools as an excellent educational vehicle.

Hayashino is a champion of the underdog and a voice of strength and hope for the powerless.

"This is still a very significant film," Hayashino told the *L.A. Times* upon its re-release in 1991. "It was the first widely seen movie by, about and starring Japanese-Americans. Its message is still very relevant. 'Farewell to Manzanar' is a reminder of how precious our civil liberties and rights are."

Hayashino—married to Kyle Tatsumoto and mother of Ali Kagawa and Kenso Kagawa—is a champion of the underdog and a voice of strength and hope for the powerless. She has been chair of the Marin Japanese American Citizens League and president of the Japanese Cultural and Community Center of Northern California.

Her 30-year career in civil rights earned her in 1990 a special appreciation from the U.S. Department of Justice's Civil Rights Division, and in 1994 she was awarded the Martin Luther King Humanitarian Award from the Marin County Human Rights Commission. The Japanese Cultural and Community Center of Northern California showcased her as its 1995 Community Leadership Award designee, and, the same year, she was presented the Community Ally Award from the Gay Asian Pacific American Alliance.

She brings to the ever-varying tapestry of Marin activism a richness of personal history and a wisdom that knows how to improve history's darker moments.

Bonnie Hayes

Marin and Bonnie Hayes go together like soothing lyrics and sexy music. She just oozes this sense of what The County has been about for the past 40 or so years. Surprisingly, she's lived here for a flash amount of that time.

"I've been in Marin about six years," says the singer/songwriter in that lazy, sensual voice which might pass for the famous Sleeping Lady that towers above us all. "I moved here from LA because I wanted a good community, some place that was family oriented to raise my daughter Lily. Actually, I spent my whole life in San Francisco before going to LA, so I'm a local. Right now I have a cozy little place in San Anselmo.

"It's the beauty and the perfectness of it all," she raves of Marin, "the open spaces, especially. I love the weather and the light. There's something about the light. I love the fact that the open spaces are held in such high regard.

"Marin is changing. It used to be so Bohemian here. We would hitchhike out here from San Francisco and hang out with the hippies. Now it's getting older and richer and that's not necessarily all good."

She still looks hot and edgy, bright-eyed and mischievous. More importantly, she's still creating, pressing forward in a career that began around 1980 with her band called The Punts, which later became Bonnie Hayes and the Wild Combo. Her first album, produced on Bondage Records in 1981, was "Good Clean Fun," featuring her popular single, "Shelly's Boyfriend." Her band at the time consisted of Kevin Hayes (drums), Paul Davis (guitar), and Hank Maninger (bass). Guitarist Bill Engel joined Bonnie's band for her second album, "Brave New Girl," which also featured Benny Reitveld on bass, Nick Milo on keyboard, and two new backup singers, Annie Stocking and Teresa Trull.

Her third album, "Empty Sky," was released on Beacon Records in 1996. It featured two songs that were later recorded by Bette Midler on her "Bette of Roses" CD in 2003. Hayes released her fourth CD, "Love in the Ruins," which she recorded with her current band featuring her brother, Kevin, bassist Darryl Anders, and guitarist (and fellow San Anselmo resident) Ted O'Connell.

Hayes is especially proud of the fact that Reitveld later joined Miles Davis and Carlos Santana, and Milo became a member of Tower of Power. One of her most heartfelt convictions is "keeping the music alive," and, says Hayes, "I'm really interested in changing things here in Marin. One thing I plan to do is open a music school. I'd like young people here in Marin to have a place to learn, to stay here instead of leaving.

"It worries me that there aren't a lot of young musicians here any more. They can't afford to live in Marin. As soon as they can, they all leave. There are still a lot of musicians here, of course, but they tend to be a lot older or very successful. My brother Kevin plays drums for Robert Cray and another brother is with Huey Lewis. I grew up with Huey and I'm friends with Bonnie Raitt and Maria Muldaur—but many musicians left for greener pastures in Los Angeles, New York City and Nashville.

"I do a lot of work here at my home studio. I make records for about $10,000 to $30,000, mostly for the independent movie scene. I use Pro Tools and digital tools and often play all the instruments myself, act as producer and hire engineers and musicians. I advise artists about the graphics and marketing of the records. I have about five businesses going at once.

"I also help young songwriters, semi-pro and professional musicians refine their writing to their commercial or artistic vision. I ask them 'Who do you want to sell your songs to?' and help them figure out how to write songs that will work for those artists. I work within the parameters of the business, help them calibrate their goals to achieve success. Sometimes you get people who just want to write for the joy of it, and that is the most fun!

"I'm doing a lot of teaching these days, primarily with San Francisco's Blue Bear School of American Music, which is a non-profit where I studied as a teenager in the '70s—along with Carlos Santana, Clarence Clemons, Bobby McFerrin and Bonnie Raitt (none of these people went to Blue Bear, but they have all supported the school)—and where I serve today as a board member as well as teaching songwriting and composition. I've also taught at the San Francisco Jazz Workshop and every summer at Blue Star, which is a national non-profit summer camp music program."

What makes Hayes ever-vital and forever young is the refreshing way she incorporates so many influences into her singing and writing, including jazz, rhythm 'n blues, pop, rock 'n roll. Starting out with The Punts, she was mirroring Blondie and the Go-Go's with lots of sassy and bright lyrics, then, as her experiences and heartbreak and self-effacing humor grew, so too did the breadth and embrace and maturity of her songwriting. One song that has become almost synonymous with Hayes' style and legacy is "Have A Heart," which has become one of Bonnie Raitt's most recognizable standards. Hayes has also written for artists Bette Midler, Robert Cray, Adam Ant, Booker T and the MG's, Cher, and David Crosby.

"I reject the idea that music either has to be smart or kickass—why not both?"

In the 1980's, while the Wild Combo was still playing together, Bonnie's band toured with fellow Marinite Huey Lewis on a nationwide jaunt. In 1990, Hayes joined the worldwide tour of Billy Idol, where she played keyboard and worked as a backup vocal arranger.

Not only has she become one of the most widely lauded songwriters in America, but she has also managed to evolve into a sharp businesswoman, as well, naming herself her own business manager and extending services to fellow artists for consulting and production services.

Major accolades have come to this bright Marin star, including this line from normally tough-crowd critic, the *San Francisco Chronicle*: "One of the Bay Area's best voices, and arguably its finest songwriter." And this description from the *Indianapolis Star*: "Somewhere between Alanis Morisette's anger and Tori Amos' ethereal weirdness lies Bonnie Hayes."

Bonnie Hayes is a throwback to the golden age of rock women, who left it all on the stage and still managed to find more for their friends and loved ones—*if* they didn't first burn out. Her uncompromising, leave-nothing-behind spirit is reflected in this typically brash Hayes comment: "I reject the idea that music either has to be smart or kickass—why not both?"

Barbara Heller

San Rafael City Council member Barbara Heller, Ohio born and Arizona raised, is a plain spoken, no-nonsense straight shooter. She and husband Norman, married in 1986 after her first marriage ended in divorce, have sunk deep roots in Marin. Serious-minded, community-aware and pro-actively engaged in San Rafael's ongoing emergence as the revitalized center of Marin County living, the couple has definitely made an impact in their adopted city.

Their daughters are Sarah, a University of Oregon graduate who runs triathlons and works in New York at J.P. Morgan and Leslie, a high school educator in Pleasanton. Norman, now retired after a retail career with GTE, is frequently teased by his wife Barbara that she is, flat-out, the more active of the two.

"I've worked on army bases in Israel for Volunteers for Israel," she says, "and I've gone to Afghanistan. I have a strong belief that if you are an elected leader, even a locally elected one, you bear certain responsibilities to take your vision globally, as well."

After graduating from college with a degree in business administration at Arizona State University, she got married, went through a divorce, then came to San Francisco to be with her family. By the time her girls were 7 and 8, Norman and she decided she didn't like the weather or schools in San Francisco, so she moved to San Rafael, where she has lived since 1978.

"I got involved with community issues when I retired from the State Bar of California in the late '80s," says Heller. "I was on the San Rafael City Planning Commission in 1991 when an opening came up for a city council seat. I was first elected to the council in 1993 and I'm still there, although I ran (unsuccessfully) for State Assembly in 2000."

A meat 'n potatoes type of politician with an ever watchful eye on budgetary and tax woes, Heller is an ardent believer in hard work and persistence. She's extremely proud of the fine new look of downtown San Rafael, which has arisen from the doldrums and now boasts a modern, soothing, California casual sort of ambience that has injected retail businesses with a rush of oxygen.

Always mindful of the need to shepherd, honor and preserve diversity as the life source of an ever-evolving multinational populace, Heller points proudly to the Canal District as an example of how hard work can help people maintain their communities and improve their lives.

"In the Canal District, the problem is that the density there was set long ago," she explains. "Our goals there are to improve the quality of life for people while maintaining living conditions. It's a really mixed area, with rich and poor people together. The Pickleweed Park Community Center is a vibrant place, probably the most used facility in The County. The soccer fields are always in use.

"The key issue for San Rafael these days, and for municipal governments everywhere, is financing. Basically, the state keeps taking away sources of money. We are required to provide the same services but with less money. My personal goals are 'quality of life' issues to give the community better parks, a new library, the maintenance of police and fire departments and to do so even though we are facing financial cutbacks.

"The best thing about living in Marin is the people, our open space, and the schools. Our open space lands are just fantastic. You can't compare any place to Marin. Our schools give our kids a wonderful start in life. One of my daughters has become an educator and the other is a business manager with J.P. Morgan. You can't do that without a proper education. The arts and theater in Marin are also terrific.

"A future problem is that San Rafael is close to being 'built out.' The city must have some commercial investment. Lucasfilm is about to move out of its buildings in the Canal District, and they have been a huge presence there. We really have to plan carefully in the future how we are going to replace their presence.

"The interesting thing about Marin is that The County is like an incubator. There are a lot of very smart people here. Companies are started here, then they grow up and they move out. For instance, an entrepreneur starts a company in a house in Sausalito, rents an office in San Rafael, and then moves up to Sonoma for more room.

"The best thing about living in Marin is the people, our open space, and the schools. Our open space lands are just fantastic. You can't compare any place to Marin. Our schools give our kids a wonderful start in life."

"Another problem is the aging of this community. Marin is starting to become a community of elderly people. That brings up transit and housing issues. What happens when people can't drive anymore? We have older folks living all alone in empty houses and they can't move because there is no place to go. We really need to attract younger families to Marin and to retain our service workers. But where are they going to live?

"The key is to plan today for tomorrow. Problems can always be solved if you can get people to connect. People are not trained in government and it is difficult to get people to understand how the system works. Term limits are a big problem in California, but generally people are not aware of how the system works. It can take 10 to twelve years to get a piece of legislation through, yet term limits say that state legislators have to leave after six years. You can't accomplish anything in that short amount of time. Lobbyists have become pretty much the history of the State of California.

"The real problem is that people have a distrust of bureaucracy. Polling shows that voters trust local governments but not senior levels. Here in San Rafael, if people have a problem, they can yell at me in the corner grocery store. People need someone in a leadership position to listen to them. You just have to give them time to explain their opinions."

Sha Sha Higby

One of the joys of doing a book like this is the free education it has afforded me and my associates. We read and write to expand our minds and our love and understanding of the world in which we live. This book has opened entirely new vistas for me, delving as I have into the previously unknown lives and careers of so many fascinating Marinites. Sha Sha Higby's world is truly fascinating. I am drawn to what and whom I don't know. Basically, I am a simple man. I love and care for my children, I live and die for the 49ers and Giants—and sometimes the Warriors—and I keep showing up for work day after day in hopes that one day I will do it all right.

Beneath my common man exterior, I guess the one distinctly "me" characteristic is an absolutely insatiable curiosity about this ever-unfolding drama we call life. I knew zip, nada, about Sha Sha Higby's world before I researched and interviewed her. And I certainly can't claim to be an expert after the process. But I am enormously grateful for the opportunity to discover the mysteries of life and the miracles that have taken place in the recesses of my mind just from asking questions of yet another truly remarkable Marinite.

Sha Sha Higby, who probably has the most lyrically fun name in this book, is a Bolinas resident who is carving for herself a very artistically esoteric niche in the culture of The County.

As an artist, Sha Sha is nationally recognized for her

evocative and haunting performances and for the exquisite and somewhat ephemeral body sculptures she creates to move within. Sha Sha teaches textile, mask-making, "*urushi*—Japanese lacquer," performance, headdress and costume construction workshops around the world. Participants in her classes cast multiple versions of a mask, then explore a different structural or textile technique for costume. They next combine these materials with movement in order to explore the creation of a theatrical image within an imaginary environment.

"I've been well grounded in all things Marin," laughs Higby, whose work exudes the flair of an international kaleidoscope. "I grew up in Tiburon, and my mother had a knitting business in Marin, so I had lots of color and design influences as a child. I went to school in San Francisco, so between Marin and The City, I had a lot of exposure to nature as a child that still comes out in my work."

So—to the uninitiated—why masks?

"Masks give you an endless source of pleasure in their creation," she answers. "There's theatrical imagery and the ability to transform yourself into a puppet character that comes alive to perform and entertain. When you think about it, the experience is mind-expanding—using your intuition, movement and poetry, you are employing a myriad of techniques in puppet construction that can grow into a three-dimensional costume.

"Then you can use the experience to create your own performance temple with an iconic image that comes alive as a structure, an archetypal spirit that you move within, if you will, in a performance-like ritual. I teach students to cast and mold, then re-cast, adding hands and extensions—then, inspired by the natural environment, the students decorate, preparing to enter another world: Wild, powerful, humorous, flamboyant."

Sha Sha Higby's universe is a trip. Simply let go of your preconceptions, misconceptions, or no conceptions at all, and let her speak to you about her work, her world, her life.

"As a child," she says, "I was fascinated by the peek boxes we used to make out of shoe boxes. You looked into the peephole and saw cutout layered landscapes portraying a silent wonderful paper world. I seek to do this today. I am allured by the theatrical quality of flipping through ancient palm leaf drawings from India, for example—they are visual line clusters of symbolic journeys through love, emotions, battles and life. So—one of my goals has been to make theater that is like turning through pages of a book of paintings. The stylized turning of the pages makes the intricate detail of each individual picture come to life. The slow shivery movements of each scene make the potential of the next scene even greater. A shattered piece of story seems even richer alone because it has the potential of being inserted into the whole."

"Masks give you an endless source of pleasure in their creation."

Higby creates ephemeral body sculptures. These painstakingly constructed costumes, interwoven with delicate props, are the foundation for haunting performances, inspired by Indonesian, Japanese, Indian and Western dance traditions. Her workshops are as plentiful as are the shards of her kaleidoscopic world—seemingly infinite. There is her golden foils and reactive metals demonstration—she teaches the application of gold leaf and foils to different surfaces, as well as simple patinas she uses in her work. She demonstrates heat coloration and anodizing of reactive metals.

There is a slide show demonstration whereby Sha Sha introduces the student to her approach to movement and theater as it originally came to her through sculpture, mask and costume. She approaches dance through the medium of sculpture—using the painterly manipulation of materials such as wood, silk, paper, lacquer, ceramics and gold leaf.

Any attempt to sum up Sha Sha Higby's work would be as futile as dicing liquid mercury, but, fittingly enough, Sha Sha herself has just the right touch: "My work strives to create a path where movement and stillness meet. Shreds of memory lace into a drama of a thousand intricate pieces, slowly moving, stirring our memory toward a sense of patience and timelessness.

"The air surrounding us is like many planes in space, assorted canvases of images. Every time we move about, the space around us is filled with drawings, colorful sketches and complex patterns. With these costume sculptures, I want to express and teach how we are the elegant complexity of the atmospheres about us. Emotions and thoughts cluster on the surface of our bodies and then break away, fly and float off. Each bundle of emotion becomes yet another entity in itself, splitting into many facets again, gathering and returning to its source."

Michael Hingson and Roselle

In the horrific aftermath of the Twin Towers' catastrophe of September 11, 2001, all of us have probably tried to visualize what it must have been like for the thousands of survivors scrambling down the crumbling staircases of the doomed skyscrapers.

We have imagined the chaos, the heart-stopping panic and fear, the profound sense of bewilderment and terror, the absolute horror of the moment.

Now imagine experiencing this vision of hell as a blind person.

That is precisely how Michael Hingson and his Guide Dog Roselle experienced this nation's worst domestic tragedy.

Roselle, a sweet-faced yellow Lab, was curled under the desk of Hingson, who was at the time the District Sales Manager for the computer firm, Quantum ATL.

"I heard a loud noise like a bump and then a lot of shaking," recalls the blind man who now resides in Marin's Bel Marin Keys. "It was worse than any earthquake I've ever experienced. The building started swaying, and the air was filled with smoke, fire, paper and the smell of kerosene."

Michael and Roselle were on the 78th floor of the first tower struck by terrorists and the hijacked airliner 18 floors above them.

"We knew the emergency exit procedures, and people did a very good job of following them," recalls Hingson, who credits the teamwork between himself and Roselle for calmly guiding them through the weaving office to begin the agonizingly long descent to New York City streets. Roselle would alternately lead the way, then jump behind her master, always thinking foremost of her prime mission to save her partner's life. In kind, Hingson would be the steadying voice in Roselle's ear, the fortifying hand on the dog's fur.

(What a lot of people don't realize in the relationship between guide dog and master is that there is a clearly intended *inter*dependence between both—that's what makes the bond so special.)

Somewhere around the 50th floor is when the second jetliner struck the other tower. It had become extremely difficult to breathe and both dog and blind man were near exhaustion. What encouraged them both were the reassuring words and helpful pats on the head they received from New York City firemen racing bravely toward their own somber demise like quiet angels in a scenario of Armageddon.

When they finally emerged from the doomed building, they had walked through the madness only about two blocks before the building began to collapse. "That is a sound that never goes away," says Michael. "It sounded like a metal and concrete waterfall."

The pair started to run for the subway. When they emerged from the subway, the second tower began to crumble, showering them with even more ash, smudge and debris. Roselle guided them to the home of a friend in mid-Manhattan, where they waited until the trains started to move again. By 7 p.m., they were able to go home to fall into the waiting arms of Michael's wife Karen.

Roselle is the fifth in a long line of four-legged blessings in Michael Hingson's life. In 1964, he received his first dog, a Golden Retriever named Squire who had been trained under Benny Larsen, a future Executive Director of Guide Dogs.

His next companion was Holland, another Golden Retriever who accompanied Hingson on his first date with wife Karen and who walked down the aisle with the couple on their wedding day. Holland was helpful in launching Hingson's business career and got him started in sales.

Golden Retriever Klondike was next in line, and accompanied Hingson on over half a million airline miles. Then Yellow Lab Linnie was by Hingson's side as the business grew and the family moved to the East Coast in 1996. Enter Roselle, a frisky-six-year-old who on August 1, 2000 helped his master celebrate the move into the World Trade Center.

In a courageous career move, Hingson decided after 9/11 that he would dedicate his life to making speeches and promotional events for Guide Dogs for the Blind.

Michael Hingson is a spellbinding speaker whose enthusiasm and vigor simply cannot be contained. Having experienced close-up and survived America's first homeland attack, his mission is to infuse his listeners with a sense of fearlessness and self-esteem. The twin pillars of his talks are trust and teamwork, and

"That is a sound that never goes away. It sounded like a metal and concrete waterfall."

it would be impossible to find anyone in this country who so convincingly owes his very life to those characteristics of survival.

Michael is absolutely passionate in delivering his inspirational talks, in which he unveils the underlying guiding philosophy of his organization's vision: "The human-animal bond is a mutually beneficial and dynamic relationship between people and other animals that is influenced by behaviors that are essential to the health and well-being of both. This includes, but is not limited to, emotional, psychological, and physical interactions of people, other animals, and the environment."

The values expressed by Guide Dogs for the Blind in Michael's speech making are clear, simple, profound and lifesaving:

"Kindness towards people and animals, and respect for their dignity and well-being. Innovation and openness to change. Accountability for our actions and our resources. Teamwork and good communications. Supportive and trusting work environment. Honesty, integrity and fairness. Professionalism balanced with humor."

Today, Michael lives a tranquil life at Bel Marin with his wife Karen, an accomplished quilter, and the two enjoy feeding the ducks and playing with Roselle. Time has passed since 9/11 and much healing has transpired throughout the nation. Thanks to heroes like Michael Hingson and Roselle, two amazing individuals who walked down the stairway of death to live another day, their acts of courage and blind faith serve as twin towers of bravery and illumination.

Wayne Hodgins

Autodesk has always been considered a somewhat forward-thinking Marin company, but what many might not know is that the internationally renowned firm has on fulltime payroll a professional futurist whose very title places him in the vanguard of forward thinkers everywhere.

Wayne Hodgins—a Canadian by birth but a Marinite since 1988—is actually a fast-forward futurist. This is not to make light of a very serious malady which afflicts him—Attention Deficit Disorder—but Hodgins would be the first to admit that his ailment is ironically, if somewhat painstakingly, tied to futurism. He describes ADD as the inability to pay attention to any one thing; even worse, he says it's the ability to pay attention to everything all at once.

For a man with a curious, whirlwind kind of mind, and a futurist to boot, it must not be easy to be Wayne Hodgins.

So—how does one get to be a futurist?

"I was in the education field," he says from an office atop the hill near Northgate that fields one of the company's squadron of buildings. "I was a teacher, a counselor, a principal and a superintendent. Initially I taught at high schools and the University of British Columbia, and then had the privilege to work for the Canadian government and international schools in Europe. As an educator working with children and young adults, you always have a futurist bent, and that's how I got involved with Autodesk.

"It's just natural to think about where your students are going to end up in the workforce. Since that's a few years down the road, you've got to wonder what that is going to be like and, more importantly, how am I not teaching them the irrelevant and the redundant now?

"Stay with me—you see, I believe that serendipity and synchronicity are strategies. I find in fact that serendipity is a normal state, not an exceptional one. Peter—would you have ever imagined you would be the author of this incredible *100 Faces of Marin* project? This is what I teach at Autdoesk. I have long been a Marshall McLuhan enthusiast, the brilliant man who coined the term 'global village.' Just recently, I received a call out of the blue from his daughter Mary, who had heard about me because I had been a recipient of the award named after her father.

"She called to ask for my help in setting up the Marshall McLuhan Foundation. This is something I am very excited about because it ties into some other work I was doing in creating a foundation. The interesting thing about McLuhan and people like him with that same level of genius is that they are way ahead of everyone, and the world doesn't catch up for some time. So Mary McLuhan calls me out of the blue—serendipity and synchronicity, twin strategies at work if you are open to them. Being a futurist—it's all about awareness.

"When people try to pin me down and ask me where I work, I am delighted not to have a good answer. If they ask me if I spend more time with business or education or government, my answer is yes! I sit on an airplane and I say to myself—Geez, I'm this schmuck from Canada who used to be a teacher, what am I doing on a plane going to give some advice to a king or a general or a CEO? How can I crisscross countries and have anything relevant to say?

"My answer is that whether it's playing the oboe or being a father or being a janitor or a CEO, it simply doesn't matter—focus should be on continuously improving that capacity to excel and perform.

"I love juxtapositions. To have in one sense this one speck on the globe which is Marin, then you go from that to the Cosmos—it's not aimless, it's not chaos, it is focused, I assure you. Tangible results come from it.

"I am very appreciative that Autodesk—Carol and my other management—allow me to hold this position. I've been with them for over 15 years now. I describe what I do as being a bit like a wine sommelier. If the objective is to have a great bottle of wine on your table, and if you are going to avoid the high-priced purchase option, then one avenue is to have a cellar. If you have a cellar, then you have to have a sommelier, someone who is gong to know which bottles of green wine to keep in the cellar for 10 or more years. Then you think to yourself—how would I ever evaluate the performance of this sommelier? So, my joke is—wait 10 years, it will be very clear one way or the other.

"I am the chagrin of the family when they get the inevitable question—what does your Dad or husband do? They say, oh, here we go again, we've got to explain it this time. I have a great family—I have a wife and two teenaged children. My wife keeps me grounded. My son is 17, and my daughter, who is 19, got accepted last year at Cal Poly in pre-Vet medicine. They enable me to do what I do.

"One of the things I talk about is how we are managing to learn more, learn faster. That's what I signed up for—my life goal is to make the world a better place upon my exiting than when I entered. What I get told by people a lot is these connections I make for them. There is nothing magical in what I do—I'm not clairvoyant, I'm not the predicting futurist guy. I can help you see your world and all these connections that happen. I describe serendipity as the discovery of something better while searching for something else. Serendipity is this wonderful quality—actually, the proper word is sagacity—to allow yourself plenty of latitude.

"One of the things I talk about is how we are managing to learn more, learn faster. That's what I signed up for—my life goal is to make the world a better place upon my exiting than when I entered."

"Therefore, the serendipitous thing is—you will end up in a different place than where you set out to go. But if that place is better, it's not wandering, it's not aimless, it's not fatalism. Think how powerful that is! I believe that is such a great equalizer on the planet. I practice serendipity all the time while traveling—my wife and I would ride our motorcycles across Europe and we would never make hotel or camping reservations, for example. That would be the anathema of serendipity. And we had the greatest adventures time after time for almost 15 years there, and continue to do so.

"Same with my presentations—I quite literally do not know what I'm going to say. I refuse to send in slides in advance of a talk. I'm not being flip and I can't really explain it other than there is something different about a 'live' performance. The fundamental reward is to see that spark, that sign of recognition from the audience. The real magic moments are that 'Aha!' Just like when I was a teacher. For me, I think I still am—my classroom just got a lot bigger!"

Mary Hughes

Mary Hughes is her actual name, but Marinites probably best know this '80s icon as Futon Mary. She is as much a part of Marin lore as are macramé classes, fern bars, bookcases made out of bricks and Galliano bottles, lava lamps, water beds, hot tubs and the music of Van Morrison wafting mournfully through the patchouli-soaked hills of Fairfax.

"I started in 1980," says Hughes inside her Santa Venetia home stuffed with what might be the world's most diverse collection of *Coca-Cola* memorabilia. "I worked for a woman in a loft in a Sausalito shipyard, and we had this ladder so steep that, to this day, from all that practice, I can walk down a ladder forwards carrying a bale of cotton. It's an acquired skill!

"I worked hard and handmade all the futons, tearing the cloth, sewing up the sack, and turning the cotton futon inside out through this very tricky maneuver. Then I sewed it shut with a five-foot seam and tufted with a 12-inch needle. *Voila*—a futon—and a stab in the thigh from the 12-inch needle."

To the uninitiated, a futon is a Japanese bed that came to America along with macrobiotic cooking. It signifies an all-natural lifestyle. Japanese homes were so compact that everyone would sleep in the same room, rolling up their futons during the day.

"Americans are bigger," says Futon Mary, "and have more living space, so American futons are thicker. Unfortunately, because of this, mildew would develop under the futon. So I can almost visualize how this happened—some guy throwing out his old futon, rolling a joint and thinking, 'Wow, man, if I put it on pallets, there won't be mildew.' That's how the first futon frame was made of two pallets."

Hughes says the early days were great fun, flying by the seat of her pants—futons were everywhere, all the rage. Gradually, they became a bigger piece of the market, and then mainline furniture companies wanted them, seizing a big chunk of the once-alternative lifestyle market.

Hughes, now in her third decade of selling futons, says that what has helped her survive in a highly competitive marketplace is her ability to adapt to change.

"When the futon industry was young, so was I, and I had a chance to make a difference" says the blunt-spoken businesswoman. "For instance, there's a little plastic lock on a futon frame now. That's because one day I had to deliver a futon to Sausalito. There was no place to park and I had to navigate four flights of narrow stairs to bring a futon to a living room that had a floor-to-ceiling plate glass window. The people wanted the futon right in front of the window. I thought—what if someone leans back really hard and goes through the window? What if someone has a bad dream or good sex and lands on their head four flights down?

"So I ran to my van and grabbed two pieces of wood and made a locking wedge on the futon frame. The improvement was refined within the industry with a wood wedge that would automatically lock the futon frame in place. Problem solved—no worries about lawsuits."

As many a small business person can attest, working for yourself can be brutal.

"Some mornings," says Hughes, "I would stand in the shower and cry, worrying about the chain stores with their half-off futon sales. It kills me how naive consumers can be. No matter how alluring the pitch, there is no free lunch—somebody somewhere somehow is paying for it, usually you, but it is so cleverly camouflaged, you just don't see it.

"My business concept has always been to give you the same deal I gave the guy before you. That way, everyone gets the same 'Best I can do.' It is simple, it is fair, and it works. I believe people don't want to be tricked, so I deal straight."

In 1989, like many ambitious entrepreneurs who can't resist expansion, Hughes branched out and opened a store in Oakdale, a small town past Manteca on the way to Yosemite. The appeal was retail space at twenty-five cents a square foot. She also opened a third store in Modesto for the same reason.

"But," she admits, "this scathingly brilliant idea fizzled. What I was attempting was to open two new markets and leapfrog the competition, but I ran out of energy. I was trying to run three stores 100 miles apart. People were ripping me off, and the commute was killing me. So, in 1995, I shut down the other stores and focused on San Rafael alone. I concentrated a lot of money in advertising and secured a warehouse here."

Through hard work, constant visibility and clever advertising (like standing on her roof to attract customers in one TV ad), Futon Mary has become a Marin household term—the "Liza" or "Barbra" of cotton-stuffed bedding.

"The notoriety is cool," she admits. "It''s fun to go somewhere and have people recognize me and buy me a drink. I've had so may good friends be so incredibly supportive, especially during the tough times like the '90s during the recession. For me, it's been music first, family always. The Mayflower Chorus did so much for me. I've always had this 'family' of friends. It's about the music. I love to sing, and I was really inspired by them. We were under the leadership of Larry Vargo who passed away in 1991—we would all hang together at the Mayflower Pub in San Rafael, and we were a core group of people who genuinely loved each other. They have always been there for me, and still are today."

Hughes, now in her third decade of selling futons, says that what has helped her survive in a highly competitive marketplace is her ability to adapt to change.

Although she's a proven survivor in a fringe market that has suffered blows from ruthless competitors and an always-daunting economy, Hughes is jaded about the current state of affairs.

"Some people in Marin," she declares, "are so pretentious. It seems people everywhere are ruder and more demanding. It really makes retail tough. Also, the business legislation sucks. Worker's Comp rates are off the charts. I hesitate to hire another employee."

In addition to singing with the Mayflower Chorus, Hughes has also tried her hand at stand-up comedy. When some friends asked if she, too, would "come out" like Ellen DeGeneres, she replied: "Don't need to. Do people see my ads and think I'm running this business with my husband? Hell no. The cool thing about Marin is that people let you be. I have always felt safe place being 'out.'"

Stuart Hyde

Stuart Hyde of Corte Madera is a person you may have encountered at the grocery store without recognition. He is the personification of the adage, "Looks are deceiving," for beneath this most affable, middle-class appearing individual burns the soul of a fiery revolutionary.

A little sense of history is in order. Fast backward to 1968—domestic America is in turmoil, Vietnam is in full rage, the long festering boil of institutional racism in the United States has been lanced.

San Francisco State University is one of the nation's many venues of both physical and philosophical outrage. The site of scores of demonstrations and riots—with no small thanks to the reactionary antics of image-savvy university president, S.I. Hayakawa, whose legacy consisted of pulling the plug on students' loudspeakers and free speech—San Francisco State was a microcosm of what was brewing on campuses and in communities around the nation.

Intricately enmeshed in battles for free speech was the emerging consciousness of communications, media and broadcasting as the key avenues whereby vital issues of the day could be processed and let loose upon the national "audience."

Stuart Hyde, in a masterful collision of social upheaval and academic timing, was the head of the now-famous Broadcast Communications Department at the school, a position he utilized brilliantly as a way to wed social consciousness with what soon emerged as the single most powerful influence in modern America: The Media.

A deeply emotional man with well-founded convictions about what is morally right, Hyde traces his racial activism to a chilling incident in a Birmingham, Alabama church in 1964 that shamed a nation yet crystallized forever Hyde's personal ethos.

"When that bomb exploded in 1964 and killed those precious black children," he says, his eyes shimmering with pain, "I was just devastated. I did not know what to do. I kept thinking—what can be done about what's going on in this country? There isn't anything I can do in the South. The only place I might be able to do something is here in the Bay Area, and the only place I might have some conceivable influence is in broadcasting.

"Broadcasting is an all-pervasive profession, so maybe we could do something about that. We all know that both radio and television in the Bay Area employ very few people of color, on or off camera, and I think we can change that. Not overnight, because 'crash courses' just doom students to low-paying, dead-end jobs. Our goal has to be a solid, four-year education, or our efforts will be worthless.

"I decided what we had to do is desegregate our faculty. When I brought it up to the department faculty, a person who wasn't with us very long said, 'That's reverse discrimination!' I replied, 'Don't give me that crap. We have never had a person of color teaching on this faculty and that's probably why we don't have any students of color.' We have to get a first-rate teacher, a role model.

"After a long search, we hired a brilliant man, Vic Webb, who'd clawed his way out of the Chicago ghetto. I told him he had two responsibilities—do a good job of teaching and be a great recruiter. Let it be known that our doors are open to people of every color. Word got out lightning fast. Pretty soon, all these wonderful students with long-range career plans and a four-year college education got into the field and gradually started moving up because of their competency.

"Remember—that started back in 1964, before there was either a term or a government program for Affirmative Action.

"Now, let's be clear—to just turn out students of color to get jobs to satisfy an FCC requirement is anathema to me. You have to turn out people who are good at what they do. So I think our department gives a first-rate education in Broadcast Communication to people of color who were once disenfranchised but who are now thorough professionals."

Hyde is a beloved figure in Bay Area media circles. Countless numbers of graduates have benefited from his writing and communications expertise, but all would offer testament that what has shaped his influence upon them is his sharply honed sense of social justice.

Hyde is impassioned yet realistic about the state of racism in America today: "I used to think," he muses, "that if we could only do such and such and solve this big problem. . . but I realized that big problems never get solved with big solutions but rather by individuals doing small things.

"As far as where we are now in regards to racism, I think we are on a very slippery slope and I think there is a danger in this country that isn't generally realized. I want to get up on the top of Mt. Tam and shout 'Wake up, America! Don't you see what's happening here?' I think what will happen in this country is an upsurge of racism and an upsurge in resentment by people of color because one by one we are having an assault on our environment, on women's rights, on civil liberties, and on just about anything that benefits people on the lower end of the economic scale.

A deeply emotional man with well-founded convictions about what is morally right, Hyde traces his racial activism to a chilling incident in a Birmingham, Alabama church.

"I am more frightened by the future of this country than I have ever been. It's not just Bush, but it's also Cheney and Ashcroft. Hillary Clinton was correct—there *is* a vast right-wing conspiracy. They've taken over school boards and radio stations in the South. Why the FCC didn't do something about it when we had eight years of Clinton, I just don't know."

In his own modest fashion, Hyde has made a significant difference in community relations. He taught radio and television performance for 11 years at San Quentin Prison, lugging his audio and video recorders in and out each week, and he proudly points out that his students made Public Service Announcements for The House (the hospitality center for visiting relatives) as well as an excellent series on drug abuse. Both campaigns were played widely on local stations.

Stuart (who's tailed constantly at home by his faithful dog Jezebel) is married to Allie Hyde, a noted Marin artist. They have three adult children: Stuart of Petaluma (buys and sells antiques and collectibles) who with his wife Gina has two children, Maxwell Stuart and Katie Rose; John of San Leandro (a Sustaining Manufacturing Engineer with KLA-Tencor in Milpitas) who is the father of Sophia; and Allison Elizabeth (supervises first and second year teachers in the San Mateo School District) who is married to Miguel Angel Rosales from Mexico City.

H.C. Jackson

In his 40 years of serving Marin County hardware customers, H.C. Jackson's reputation as an honest, hard-working, employee-friendly businessman has taken on legendary proportions.

Since the day he opened deep in the heart of Bret Harte, Jackson has manifested the wisdom of treating workers—"My fellow owners," he always calls them—with utmost respect. "I vowed from my first day as a new store owner," he says with conviction, "that I would never abuse people. You see, in my previous jobs, I learned a lot from watching owners doing bad things. I watched one disgruntled employee try to tear down a pallet of nails with a forklift! My life has been a commitment to doing just the opposite.

"I like to say I have one location and 65 owners. My co-owners, my friends, enjoy full benefits, profit-sharing, season tickets for 49er games, company dinners. My philosophy is extremely simple—treat people with respect and you will gain far more in the long run."

Once in a while, an ad will run in the local paper showing mug shots of Jackson's happy employee/owners. Under each picture is a short description specifying how many years each individual has worked in the hardware business. The average hovers around 30 years.

And, oh, H.C. serves breakfast and lunch to his staff every day from a $100,000 kitchen that is a gourmet's delight. As he told "The Best of Marin" magazine in 1991: "It's the Golden Rule. Treat people the way you want to be treated. Be honest. Be fair. It's as simple as that."

When you think about it, this is a perfect kind of business fit for mind-and-soul-conscious Marin—maybe the first-ever holistic hardware store in the land? Ironic, too, since

H.C., an Oklahoma-born and bred U.S. Navy veteran (a member of the elite submarine corps based in San Diego), has the look of a crusty seadog who is anything but touchy-feely.

But the man is always thinking of ways to improve his situation with his beloved co-owners. "Years ago, soon after we first started to turn a profit, I would treat everyone to weekend workshops at Harrah's Tahoe," he says. "Then someone pointed out to me that for just $5,000 more, we could stretch that weekend into a full week—in Hawaii! To show how grateful they were to me, the employee/owners promised that they would make up the extra expense by coming back to work more inspired than before the trip. Did they ever! Sales for the next six months following the Hawaii trip increased by $45,000."

When Jackson first came to Marin in 1953 following his Navy stint in San Diego, he was equipped only with an optimist's energy and an absolutely ironclad decision to succeed.

"Failure simply wasn't an option," he says today, his joyful eyes crinkling from years of continual success. "I started out with the J.B. Rice Company in San Rafael. It was a large wholesale company dealing in flooring and electrical work for clients in Vallejo, Santa Rosa, Ukiah. I was in training for a management position, and I was extremely ambitious. For extra pay, I did janitorial work.

"Then I went to work for a floor covering guy, L.C. Smith, who spotted my ambitious ways and liked what he saw. When I asked him why he was so interested in me, he told me it was because I would work for cheap. Then, faster than I could show my appreciation, he fired me after 10 years and half ownership in the company. I vowed then and there I would never treat my employees shabbily. The secret to life, I think, is to absorb the punches you are dealt, then get on with living and treating people in a better fashion."

Hard work, a loyal customer base, and years of treating his co-owners with dignity and respect have all dovetailed into a solidly successful business whose roots are so deep that the enterprise can successfully hold its own in the face of monster competitors like Home Depot.

What Jackson's Hardware offers its customers is, first of all, the same kind of esteem and warmth it extends to its employees. The place is a veritable cornucopia of everything under the sun, hardware-wise—bathroom and kitchen accessories, door knobs to robe hooks, lavatory faucets to towel bars, over 5,000 square feet of space dedicated to decorative plumbing and hardware showcasing.

The store is a literal emporium of tools—everything for both commercial and private accounts, the best products available with service guarantees included and on-hand employees trained to answer the tough questions. And, for outdoor-conscious Marin, Jackson's offers top-notch barbecues, outdoor furniture and heaters, grill accessories, and landscaping equipment.

H.C., who with his wife (former Marin Superior Court reporter Beverley Jackson) has five children, 10 grandchildren and three great-grandkids, is mindful of his younger clientele, as well. Jackson's boasts of a Kids Corner in the store furnished with unique Radio Flyer wagons, train sets, Klutz books and toys by Scientific American.

"The secret to life, I think, is to absorb the punches you are dealt, then get on with living and treating people in a better fashion."

Like so many of his successful Marin counterparts who have left an indelible imprint on The County, Jackson's goodwill spills over into community giving, as well. As one of the founding directors of the Bank of Marin, Jackson proudly and generously parlays his position there to sponsor and foster a multitude of Marin-enhancing programs and agencies.

"Community involvement is very important to me," he says, "and I encourage my family of employee/owners to get involved, also."

In today's corporate-minded business world where big box mentality has overwhelmed neighborhood merchants with homespun character, rarely does one man's personality shape and deepen an enterprise that bears his name. But H.C. Jackson's engaging personality is so closely interwoven into the texture of his hardware store—a venture that began with five people in 1965 and thrives today as a smoothly humming mega-business—that one is virtually indistinguishable from the other.

Whether it's nails or paint, screwdrivers or buzz saws, conviviality and companionship, conversation or consultation, if Jackson's Hardware doesn't have it, it simply doesn't exist. One might even say that the man and his store provide it all, including the kitchen sink.

Jerry Jampolsky, M.D. and Diane Cirincione, PhD.

A significant part of Marin County's magic is that the terrain has become the nurturing spawning ground of truly remarkable human beings whose unique talents blossom and thrive in this very special place.

If to be alive is to hurt, then psychiatrist Jerry Jampolsky and his wife Diane Cirincione have figured out a very compassionate way to convert that pain into an insightful search for life's meaning—that is, to heal.

Jerry recalls how the idea for its creation first came to him—"I was making my rounds on a pediatric oncology ward," he says, "and I overheard an eight-year-old boy ask his doctor what it is like to die. The doctor ignored the child and changed the subject.

"I discovered later this was the commonly accepted approach doctors took—ignore the young patients. Luckily for this particular boy, he turned to a person he trusted, the cleaning lady in the ward, and he received honest, direct answers from her.

"The incident made me wonder generally where kids could go to talk about such serious things as death, and I found that there was no safe place for them to talk."

Thus was born the Center for Attitudinal Healing, which has graced Marin and been a model around the entire globe with loving and specifically healing ways for people with a wide assortment of human suffering to attain inner peace and the strength and power to live with disease, conflict and fear. Attitudinal healing defines health as inner peace and healing as letting go of fear. It regards love as the most powerful healing force there is.

The Principles of Attitudinal Healing: 1.) The essence of our being is love. 2.) Health is inner peace. Healing is letting go of fear. 3.) Giving and receiving are the same. 4.) We can let go of the past and the future. 5.) Now is the only time there is and each instant is for giving. 6.) We can learn to love ourselves and others by forgiving rather than judging. 7.) We can become love finders rather than fault finders. 8.) We can choose and direct ourselves to be peaceful inside regardless of what is happening outside. 9.) We are students and teachers to each other. 10.) We can focus on the whole of life rather than the fragments. 11.) Since love is eternal, death need not be viewed as fearful. 12.) We can always perceive ourselves and others as either extending love or giving a call for help.

These are principles that have healed the souls and soothed the bodies of thousands of individuals suffering from life-threatening illnesses. The remarkable thing about the Center is that it utilizes an empathetic peer support model providing community support services free of charge and offering consultation, training, and education on a free basis.

"We keep things simple," says Jampolsky. "Volunteering at the Center offers the opportunity to work on your own healing through helping others, to be both student and teacher, and to give and receive unconditional love.

"Our clients and volunteers have shown that there is another way of looking at illness, another way of being with all the difficult circumstances that arise, and even a different way of approaching death and dying. It is really a different way of living, a way of being peaceful inside regardless of what is happening."

Since 1975, the Center has directly helped more than 38,000 people. Each year, 11,000 group visits are provided, supporting roughly 180 families with home and hospital visits, responding to over 1,000 crisis interventions, and filling 6,000 requests for information.

The Center was one of the first agencies in the Bay Area to respond to the AIDS epidemic, and it also established one of the first national AIDS hotline for children. The Adult Program, providing more than 7,000 interventions annually, addresses a variety of life situations, such as women with metastasized breast cancer, bereavement and grief issues, heart disease, and chronic or long-term illnesses.

The Children and Youth Program for life-threatened children is one of the first of its kind in the nation, offering support to children and teenagers facing catastrophic illness, and providing outreach assistance to parents and siblings. Children are urged to explore and express their innermost feelings, and they are encouraged to seek and believe in their own answers rather than look to outside facilitators for solutions. All direct services are free.

"It is really a different way of living, a way of being peaceful inside regardless of what is happening."

Financial support for all these programs comes from private contributions, foundations, income generating activities like workshops and special events, and grants. Primarily, individual contributions are what support the Center, and these are generated through the Membership Program. Direct donations and the Endowment Fund ensure that the services will be available in the future.

Diane Cirincione aptly sums up the Center's deep impact with what she calls a prescription for hope and freedom—"Attitudinal healing," she says, "is the realization that it is not other people, events, stressful experiences or circumstances outside ourselves that cause us to be in conflict or a state of upset. Rather, it is our own thoughts, feelings, attitudes and judgment about those things that actually cause us distress."

Unlocking the power of choice is what the Center is all about. They give no advice. The Center points out that at any moment we can choose love or fear, peace or conflict, to be a love finder or a fault finder, to be a love seeker or love giver, and to be a teacher of love rather than fear.

Chimes in Diane Cirincione in what has to be a universally underlying tenet of both mental and physical well-being: "Jerry and I have been doing this for almost 30 years, but it doesn't seem like work when what you do is your life's passion."

Cheryl Jennings

It would be accurate journalism to state that Cheryl Jennings is a fully engaged community activist who also just *happens* to be a television news anchor. Yes, she has held sway with ferocious tenacity over Bay Area airwaves for a quarter of a century, but what stirs her heart are the numerous community involvements, many of which have spilled over as stories in her Emmy Award-winning career at ABC7.

Consider this litany of public service engagement—longtime board member of the San Francisco Child Abuse Council; fund raiser for the Tenderloin after-school program for inner city children; moderator with the San Francisco League of Women Voters; a fund raiser for "Community Action Marin" which assists the poor, disadvantaged and disabled in Marin County; an honorary board member of LITA (Love Is The Answer), a Novato organization which provides volunteer visitors for senior citizens in nursing and retirement homes; honorary board member of a Rohnert Park program called Sunburst Projects which serves children and families with AIDS; an organizer for Camp Okizu, which sends cancer-stricken children to summer camp; a fund raiser with The Taylor Family Foundation in Livermore, which provides camp for children with life-threatening diseases.

How she finds time to co-anchor the 11 a.m. news with Kristen Sze and the 5 p.m. news desk with Dan Ashley every day in addition to hosting her community affairs show, "Beyond the Headlines," is a fair question, but Jennings is used to working non-stop without sleep.

"It's how I started in this business," she says. "In the '70s, it was almost unheard of to have a woman broadcasting the news. I had to start somewhere, so I went to work at KNBR radio where my first job was serving tea and sandwiches for the male reporters, and sharpening pencils. The advice I got early on was to get your skills in place, get your foot in the door, work as hard as you can, and be ready when the break comes.

"I got hired as a secretary, then made tapes to work on my voice skills. My voice was way too high, but I kept after it. I joined forces with Rosie Allen, who is now the Queen of Drive Time Radio in the Bay Area. We volunteered to work the weekend overnight shifts. I made $100 a week as a newsroom secretary; then my first big break came when KNBR reporter Juan Escobar helped me through my first on-air shift. He held my hand all the way through it. I even missed my sister's wedding to do this shift because I knew the opportunity would never come again if I let it go.

"Pretty soon, K-101 Radio hired me as a full-time reporter, then four months later as News Director. Channel 5 offered me a night time reporter's shift, so I would work at K-101 Radio from nine in the morning, then head over to KPIX when my shift was done at 5:30 p.m. and work until midnight. I simply didn't sleep. I knew I had to hang on for my life, because these were awful days for women."

Putting that last remark in context, readers should recall that women weren't really in leadership positions in those days, as they are now. Tokenism was rampant. As hard as it is to imagine these days, women simply had to seize upon whatever was offered them.

"I was determined to persevere. In 1979 Channel 7 hired me as a reporter, and I've been there ever since. I became a weekend co-anchor with Willie Monroe in 1986. I was promoted to the 5 p.m. newscast in 1988. And somewhere in there, I also became a co-anchor of the 11 a.m. newscast. I became the host of the community affairs program, 'Beyond the Headlines,' in 2003."

In 1986, she met her husband Rick Pettibone, a broker with Merrill Lynch in San Francisco, a quiet, unassuming man with news anchor looks himself who shares his wife's passion for community activism. Together they have taken into their home troubled children to mentor them back into secure, safe, goal-driven living.

Just prior to the start of Game Three of the 1989 World Series featuring the Giants and A's, the Loma Prieta earthquake struck the Bay Area. Jennings was just finishing the 4:30 news with Don Sanchez when the temblor started shaking the building furiously. She returned to her news desk and was the first ABC7 reporter on the air with live, late-breaking updates, leading the local coverage and ad-libbing virtually everything in this signature moment in Bay Area history. Her expert reporting contributed to the station's efforts, which resulted in ABC7 winning a prestigious Peabody Award for the extended quake series.

The eldest of seven children, Jennings is an Army brat who credits this wanderlust lifestyle for both her perseverance and her sense of curiosity. "Never give up" is the mantra of her life, because she fought for her very survival in a male-dominated profession, and it is this same mantra that drives every one of her public service activities. "I never say no to a young person who wants to visit me in the newsroom," she says, "and I believe strongly in the responsibility we all have to be mentors and role models."

Her own role models are Barbara Walters, Diane Sawyer, and Oprah Winfrey, and Bay Area residents are fortunate that Jennings has turned down opportunities to leave the region for similar high-visibility positions in larger markets. "There is no place like Marin," she says, "and I have no intention of ever leaving."

"I believe strongly in the responsibility we all have to be mentors and role models."

A pioneer journalist reporting on children's issues, women's rights and domestic violence, Cheryl has been recognized both locally and nationally for her active involvement. In 1980, she produced a documentary on sexual harassment of women in the work force, earning an award of merit from the National Commission on the Status of Women. She worked on a six-part series on the children of Kosovo, a project which brought her an Emmy nomination. She hosted a special on breast cancer called "Fighting Back." In 1996, she won two Emmys for a special report on a camp for children with AIDS and for a segment of a program aimed at teenagers called "Straight Talk N' Teens"—she credits fellow Marinites Carlos and Deborah Santana for being the inspiration behind this report. In 1998, she won another Emmy for her story on caring for aging parents.

More recently, in 2002, Cheryl received a national award from the American Women in Radio and Television. Called the Gracie Allen Award, it honors "superior quality and stellar portrayal of the changing roles and concerns of women." The report for which she was honored, "Behind Bars: Battered Women Who Kill Their Abusers," profiled women serving life terms for killing their abusive partners before a law was passed that allowed evidence of "battered woman's syndrome."

And, if you think Cheryl Jennings is even close to being done, stay tuned.

Tom Johnston

I guarantee that this page will stay in your mind longer than most of the other pages in this book—not author's vanity, by any means, but just because mere mention and memory of some of the Doobie Brothers' song titles will evoke exact moments in your love life, your younger years, and your most intense aspirations. It's the "Song Title Syndrome" (my appellation) which, sort of like irritating jingles only better, lodge themselves in your brain until something more driving and rhythmic comes along.

So—I dare you. It will be impossible to shake the vibes of titles like "Takin' It to the Streets," "Listen to the Music," "Minute by Minute," "People Gotta Love Again," "Black Water," "Jesus Is Alright With Me," "What A Fool Believes." Anyway, you get my drift. These guys are not only unforgettable, they are eternal.

What a truly amazing run it has been for Tom Johnston—the Doobie Brothers have been his life since their birth in 1970. Both he and fellow original member Patrick Simmons have been delivering a steady stream of quality folk, R&B rock and bluegrass. . . *since Ronald Reagan was in his first term as Governor of California.*

In the parlance of the day—*Phew!*

But the genuinely astonishing thing about the band's longevity is that they still play nearly 100 dates a year. Mick Jagger may be the hottest senior citizen in rock, but Johnston & company still make it feel like it's 1970 all over again.

The facts are staggering—one of the most popular American rock bands of all time, they have performed for nearly 40 million fans, and they've produced 14 albums which have sold more than 50 million copies. First formed in San Jose in 1970, their consistency was interrupted in 1982 when the band members split off to start solo careers, but in 1988 they reunited.

It may not be surprising to know that Johnston attributes a great deal of his success and seeming immortality to Marin—he first came here in 1966 from the Central Valley to see a performance of Quicksilver Messenger Service in Larkspur, and he says he's been enchanted with the area ever since.

"I had never been in Marin before, had never seen anything like it, and still haven't. For a kid from the Central Valley, this was like paradise."

Johnston, who lives in Novato with wife Diane and children Christopher and Lara, says Marin keeps his sanity intact in a whirlwind life that has seen more than anyone's share of airports and hotel rooms.

"There's something about Marin," continues the Visalia native who since 1973 has lived in Fairfax, Mill Valley, Tiburon, and now Novato. "The proximity to the sea, to Tahoe, to Sonoma; the fact that I can walk through the beautiful Marin hills with my dogs and feel such peace; the amazing air and climate; the good schools for my children; the friends and neighbors who don't treat us as anything special, so we can go about our lives like everyone else who does a lot of commuting and is involved in their kids' activities and busy school schedules."

The Doobie Brothers have always returned those favors in an equally classy way. Years ago they did fundraisers for Stanford Children's Hospital and the Vietnam vets—"We did this year after year," says Johnston, "and to see these kids in such dire situations, and their parents, it was really wrenching"—and now they perform for local favorite causes, like St. Mark's School in Terra Linda and children's AIDS projects, as well as continued work for Vietnam vets.

"I am especially fond of Bread 'n Roses," says Johnston of the longtime Mill Valley charitable organization that provides free top-notch entertainment to people confined or isolated in hospitals, juvenile halls, drug and rehab centers, prisons, and wards for the developmentally disabled and AIDS patients.

"Bread 'n Roses is special to me not only because of the great things they do for those in need," he adds, "but also because of my friendship with the late Mimi Farina. She was a very special lady who positively impacted not only my life, but also the lives of so many people in Marin and the Bay Area in general, and was a great example of what Marin County has to offer in quality, caring individuals. It was a blessing to have performed at their gala 25th anniversary a few years ago. Mimi came out and dazzled the crowd with her humor and warmth, even though she was quite ill, and she inspired the performances by many present and former Marin luminaries from the 'show biz' world who raised a huge sum of money to help Bread 'n Roses carry on with their valuable work."

In 2001 when the Doobie Brothers released what was then their first album in 10 years—"Sibling Rivalry" on Pyramid Records—Johnston spoke to music interviewer Michael Cimino about the various incarnations the group had experienced and survived over the years, and these were his views:

Asked if he thought their brand of music could change the world, he replied: "That's what I thought in 1970 through 1972. I don't hold that view anymore. I think you can have a small influence on a small sector of the population but I don't think you can change the world. The world right now is pretty unsettling, and I don't believe what I once did in my early 20s—that if all the leaders of the world got together and sat down and just listened to music (all forms) with everyone else, they'd figure out we're not all that different and solutions that would benefit us all could be reached through the common bond of humanity. A great Utopian dream, but very naive."

"I had never been in Marin before, had never seen anything like it, and still haven't. For a kid from the Central Valley, this was like paradise."

As for today's quality of music, he's similarly opinionated: "A lot of the music today has been influenced by the transformation of the record industry from being a business run by musically oriented professionals to soulless corporate giants run by lawyers and non-musical business people who are only interested in the monetary bottom line. Modern artists aren't looked at for a long-term investment, but for an immediate cash flow value which has really hurt the individuality of musical styles and furthered the premise that if you tell people it's great with enough hype behind it, they will buy it. The result is less than encouraging to those who want to be more than this week's pop phenom.

"And me—being an R&B, blues and rock oriented guy—I'm frustrated. I grew up listening to all the greats. It's frustrating, because they've always had the best music. But now there is no new Otis Redding, there's no Aretha Franklin, no Marvin Gaye, no Albert, Freddy or B.B. Kings, no Meters or Dr. Johns, no new James Brown, no Temptations. And in the rock world, there are no new Beatles, Cream, Hendrix, Traffic or Stevie Rays."

But, thank God, there is still, after all these years, the Doobie Brothers.

Pirkle Jones

When our crackerjack research team was on the prowl for compelling names to include in this edition of *100 Faces of Marin*, I never would have dreamed that this specific gem of a choice would have been discovered in the leafy sanctuary of the rarefied air of Mt. Tam's dreamy eucalyptus-and-redwood groves. In fact, when I was informed that the man who photographed the Black Panther Party lived in a gorgeous cabin-like retreat near Mt. Tam's summit, I honestly thought I was the butt of an April Fool's joke. Much to my surprise, the report was true. I simply had to include this man. You see, in my youth, in 1969, I lived for a summer at Sacred Heart Catholic Church in the Fillmore District of San Francisco, working with the poor and disenfranchised residents of The City's Western Addition. The pastor of the church, Father Gene Boyle, was one of my mentors; he opened the doors of the church hall to allow the Black Panthers access to run their Breakfast for Children program. Fr. Boyle, risking a great deal by the courage of his convictions, incurred the wrath of San Francisco Archbishop Joseph T. McGucken, San Francisco Mayor Joseph L. Alioto, and the membership of the House Un-American Activities Committee. It was all great fun; and so was meeting this wonderful man many years later on the slopes of Mt. Tam.

Pirkle Jones is a feisty photographer with a well-defined niche in the recent, tumultuous history of radical United States political activism. Quite modestly, he gives his late wife, Ruth-Marion Baruch, full credit for the fame.

"It was her idea to photograph the Panthers. Both of us were politically oriented as members of the Peace and Freedom Party, so it was a good fit for us. We collaborated on the book project, and it was a wonderful partnership.

"Our study of the Panthers is very precise—it's 1968, and we wanted to document the Black Panther Party. Those were crazy days. The CIA was watching what the Panthers were up to, and one day we got a knock on our door from an FBI guy—he wanted to talk to us about the Black Panther Party. I adamantly refused to let him inside our home. Ruth-Marion, in her sweet naiveté, was livid that he wasn't courteous enough to ask for an appointment first!

"Some of my other clients were puzzled by my client, the Black Panther Party, but I just viewed it as another commitment I wanted to keep. And I never tried to argue with my other clients about the volatile political issues. I was just doing my job.

"It was an extremely exciting time. It makes me tired to think back about it, in fact. We operated on pure adrenalin. We never expected the notoriety or attention it has given us."

Asked how he and his wife gained the trust of the Black Panthers, perhaps the most daunting obstacle, Pirkle's eyes shine brightly at the mention of his beloved wife's name, again.

"Ruth-Marion made the original contact with Eldridge and Kathleen Cleaver. Kathleen is such a brilliant woman, very sensitive to the Arts, and she recognized our work would be a significant contribution. Also, the Director of the DeYoung Museum at the time showed a lot of courage by promising the Black Panthers a full exhibition of the photos without even seeing them first or going to the Board—unheard of from a person in that position. That endeared us to the Panthers, as well."

The Black Panthers are much more than a footnote in the volcanic history of 1960s American radicalism. Born from the catharsis of an unpopular war in Vietnam meshing in an ugly fashion with race riots at home following the assassinations of Dr. Martin Luther King Jr. and Malcolm X, the Black Panthers were a party waiting to happen. Militant, defiant, ironclad in their resolve to *seize* power, not *ask* for it, the Black Panthers hatched many brilliant minds and lost an equal number of same.

"What happened to Huey Newton and Eldridge Cleaver," reminisces Pirkle Jones, "was that they were eventual victims of the whole environment. There's a film out on Huey—he was so drugged up and everything, I could hardly stand to look at it. He and Eldridge both died far too young and, sadly, mentally ill. Kathleen Cleaver, by a stroke of luck, was able to survive all the insanity and continue on. She's a lawyer and professor, teaching constitutional law and Black History at Emory, Yale and Harvard. A graduate with a degree in law, she travels around the country teaching Black History."

Pirkle Jones is a feisty photographer with a well-defined niche in the recent, tumultuous history of radical United States political activism.

Any act following such an exhilarating and dangerous photo shoot would be a letdown for most people, but Pirkle and Ruth-Marion always found joy in whatever they tackled together.

"I studied with Ansel Adams," says Jones, "at the California School of Fine Arts—now called the San Francisco Art Institute—and then I ended up teaching photography there for 28 years." (Ansel Adams was a great inspiration and Jones was his assistant for three years.) "Then I collaborated with Dorothea Lange on a story about the disappearance of Berryessa Valley, which deals with the destruction of a beautiful geographic paradise in order to create Lake Berryessa. I was also good friends with Imogen Cunningham, another famous photographer who sported pillbox hats and quite an acid tongue."

Ruth-Marion and Pirkle collaborated on a project about the town of Walnut Grove in the Delta in 1961.

Jones, a native of Louisiana, spends his time atop Mt. Tam, organizing exhibitions and the photography archive established with Ruth-Marion Baruch—written materials in the University Library special collections at U.C. Santa Cruz. The Santa Barbara Museum of Art presented his retrospect in 2001.

After his work on Gate 5, Sausalito and the Marin City Flea Market, he turned to Nature and created the Mount Tamalpais Series. "The pictures are beautiful," says Jones.

Mt. Tam thus joins the body of work of this restless little guy whose lasting legacy will always be his evocative photography of the Black Panther Party.

Rich Keaton

Studying Rich Keaton's face and hairstyle—and this is meant as a high compliment, Rich—is like visiting the 1950s. He oozes Frankie Avalon crooning to Annette Funicello about starry nights, ruby lips, kisses sweeter than wine.

What could be wrong with that? The Fifties, now that we've been traumatized by terror and paralyzed with fear, just may be the last halcyon epoch in this nation's ever-changing history—especially growing up in Marin, as did Keaton, where every night on Fourth Street was a mating ritual.

"I watched George Lucas make 'American Graffiti' on Fourth Street in San Rafael, which is also where I lived, by the way," recalls Keaton in a vivid example of art imitating life. "We lived a couple hundred feet off of Fourth Street, close to George's Pool Hall on a street called Cijos.

"My childhood was filled with all sorts of American apple pie events—the parades going up and down the street with the Spanish Dons, long before the Nave Patrola became a parade staple. Walking from block to block and greeting nearly everyone in sight—we all knew each others' families and paused long enough to inquire about friends and relatives.

"We all knew each other, we all trusted each other. There was this wonderful feeling of camaraderie and admiration—we all knew what the other families were doing, where they went on vacation, and we genuinely cared for each other. Marin simply had this amazing atmosphere—there was a keen sense of civility and fun. Life was so simple then—hope was always in the air, a new adventure waiting around every corner."

The Keaton family name is one of the most recognizable names in Marin County.

"Frank Keaton recently passed away," says Rich Keaton. "He was my uncle and owned Keaton's Mortuary in San Rafael. He was the baby in the family and was the big World War II hero at Normandy. My father, Bill Keaton, was the oldest of five children, three boys and two girls. In the early 1900s, my grandfather, J. Ray Keaton, was quite prominent in County politics and was very active in the Republican Party.

"The other half of my family on my grandmother's side comes out of the Russian River and Guerneville. One of my great uncles was Bert Guerne, hence Guerneville. Then there's Harold Keaton, a solid salt-of-the-earth type guy who lived in Loma Verde and was always on the golf course.

"In my family, I am the youngest. My sister is Margaret Viola and she lives in Novato. My brother is William 'Buzz' Keaton. He lives in San Rafael and has something like 30 grandchildren from seven kids of his own. I was in the Sheriff's Office along with my brother Buzz. My father and mother would always listen to the police calls on the radio, and many times we were working in Marin City together in the 1960s when there were a lot of gunfights and altercations.

"One night, my mother was watching Johnny Carson on TV while listening to the police radio, and she heard that Buzz got shot in Tiburon. He was bar-hopping with a couple of his friends celebrating a going-away party, and he walked into the men's room and ran into a guy whom he had once arrested. The guy reached under Buzz' sweater and grabbed his gun, which fired, just missing a major artery. Buzz still has the bullet inside. The only reason he survived is that he had played so many sports and was so strong from his years as an athlete.

"When I was a kid, I got my first ticket. I had a 1951 metallic green Chevy. I was coming home from a basketball game in San Francisco with my girlfriend Winnie Isetta, and I was doing 50 on the Golden Gate Bridge. I knew I was going to catch hell for it. I had to wake up my father to tell him the news. Half asleep, he told me to put my keys on the bureau in his room, and they stayed there for one month. I had to hitchhike to Marin Catholic every day.

"Then I had to go to court—Judge Harold Haley, a distant relative, was the biggest, meanest looking guy in the world. But he espies my father and yells out—'Hey Bill—what are you doing here?' My father points to me, and Haley tells me to approach the bench, and says, 'I don't think there is a sentence I can impose upon you that would outweigh what your parents have already done.' So, he gave me a suspended sentence. It ended with the judge and my father talking about the family.

"My father met my mother Olivia in 1929. Her maiden name was Allen. She came from a broken family and they drove all the way from Silver Springs, Maryland to San Rafael in a Model T Ford. My mother was the power behind the throne.

"The highlight of my career in Marin law enforcement had to be when I arrested serial killer David Carpenter, the infamous Trailside Killer."

"My father was a career Navy man, gone a lot. I was born four weeks after Pearl Harbor. My father was at Pearl Harbor on the USS Nevada directly next to the Arizona. He had just disembarked and was on a transport back to Eureka when the Japanese hit Pearl. His ship was destroyed. My father lived until 1972 when he died of cancer.

"When I was going to Marin Catholic, I worked at United Markets. I started as a box boy and worked my way up. I really loved that business, the interaction with people. Everybody went there. When graduation time came, I had the grades to go to St. Mary's, but I wanted to serve in the military. I joined the Army Reserves, but after active duty came straight back to United Markets where I worked as Assistant Manager. I was being groomed to be Manager, but I got smitten to enter law enforcement.

"The highlight of my career in Marin law enforcement had to be when I arrested serial killer David Carpenter, the infamous Trailside Killer. I arrested many other murderers, too, and they all got convicted.

"After 34 years in the department, I became a Private Investigator, which is what I am still doing."

Keaton and his wife Nancy, married in 1983, are Bernese Mountain Dog fanatics. She used to be a nurse at Marin General Hospital, and that's how she met Rich, who blushes when he says, "She's the best perk I ever had as a cop."

Dora Knell

When observers outside Marin think about the people of our county, most thoughts are directed to the flashy side of Marin residents—the famous, the wealthy, those super laden with what seems to be an overabundance of good looks, great fortune, and a vast array of material belongings.

A major intent and focus of this book has been to cast a strong ray of light upon those who are less heralded yet equally fascinating. When you examine the fiber and character of a particular region, it is especially revealing to peer beneath the veneer and study those who might be considered "grinders" or "true believers," that is, those who have a conviction that hard work, belief in Democracy, freedom of expression, adherence to strong virtue are the core values that guide and solidify a society. These don't seek the limelight, but their absence from the scene would make ours a less luminous county.

Meet Dora Knell—born in Sonoma in 1924, mother of seven children, editor and publisher for 30 years, community activist, feminist, President/Democratic Women of Marin for two four-year terms, Housing Chair/County Family & Children's Advisory Committee for four years, Civil Grand Jury, Democratic Central Committee member for 18 years, President/Democratic Women of Marin for a four-year term.

In her own words:

"I was raised in Guerneville but moved to Santa Rosa where I graduated from high school and junior college. I was the first woman elected student body president of the college. After World War II, I married my high school sweetheart while he was attending USC in Los Angeles. Our first child was born before he graduated. All of our children were born in the L.A. area.

"He became vice president of a publishing company and we moved to Chicago for a while, but in 1973 we moved back to Marin, where my husband was raised. Two of my boys graduated from San Rafael High School. I have four daughters and three sons. My youngest son,

Derek, came into my printing company as a pressman in his teens. He bought me out. He came in to the company as a pressman as a teen. He became a partner in five years. My oldest son, Greg, came into the business as a sales manager.

"I founded my printing business in 1978 and located it in the Canal District. Lucasfilms wanted our space and bought us out, so we moved to Novato and the name was changed to Graphic Arts Management. Our original name was The Copy Desk, which is a newspaper term, but we were never a copy company. My husband and I founded a publishing company, ETRI Publications. We published books in the educational field. My husband died in 1986, the year of our most successful book, 'California Controversies,' which included stories about issues such as the internment of Japanese during the war and the Bear Flag Rebellion. I retired in 1989 and sold the publishing company. Derek is now the sole owner of the printing company. In my retirement, I manage my own properties as Eldora California Properties.

"I guess I got my start as a political activist from my father. He was originally from Denmark, which was a Socialist country at the time. He was a union organizer in the '30s. I grew up in a political household and worked for the Democratic Party as a teenager. My first paycheck came from CIO, the big union. I was a typist. I stayed a Democrat my whole life, because I support the party's goals. Many of the things we take for granted today, like pensions, were considered Socialist then.

"I was Chair of the Transportation Committee for the Democratic Central Committee. Right now I am writing a history of Pickleweed Park in San Rafael, which was originally scheduled for development by the city. City policies allowed over-development of the Canal. There were powerful interests responsible for turning the Canal into an industrial zone then. I was against it.

"People poured in because of the low rents, and there was crime and prostitution. There were no immigrants in the Canal then. My husband and I bought a small apartment building in the Canal. We've always rented to families. Today I have Mexican, Asian and Vietnamese families living there."

As for her vocal activism, a trait she says is essential to a healthy Democracy:

"I fought against taking the railways out of service. The railroad used to go all the way through Marin down to Larkspur Landing. I think the plan to run SMART Rail from Sonoma to Marin in the future is a great idea. We need it to take congestion off the roads. The objection is that it will bring development, but the original County Plan was to bring any development towards the eastern corridor.

"I just wrote a letter to the *IJ* about the St. Vincent's and Silveira properties. My point is that it's wrong for the City of San Rafael to sit on the sidelines and watch. Perhaps San Rafael needs a history lesson. At one time San Rafael could have annexed Larkspur Landing and obtained that tax base. I think the City Council is short sighted. I understand the desire to save Open Space, but some development is needed. The way that Hamilton and Ignacio are growing, Novato could annex these lands, and then what happens?

"The healthiness of this country requires that we do speak out."

"I think certain city councils want to avoid controversy. But you know, we live in a controversial county and we are in conflict all the time. There is money to be made by development of the St. Vincent lands and the city needs the tax base. You could have a little village there, with shops and a hotel. That's better than nothing, which is what is there now."

And her overall philosophy:

"Conflict is the essence of Democracy. Compromise is the usual solution. We have two main parties in this country and we usually end up in the middle. Once in a while we get a party on the extreme and you see what happens then. I enjoy politics because of the conflict and because political action usually means we end up with something we can all live with. Barbara Boxer and Nancy Pelosi are good personal friends of mine. We need women in politics.

"I am also a feminist. Women of my generation remember when we had few opportunities for involvement in public life. The healthiness of this country requires that we *do* speak out. I don't understand the distrust of people like Hillary Clinton, just because she is strong. She has been unfairly portrayed as a Socialist. The truth is she was a Goldwater girl, originally a Republican, and quite conservative. I knew her as a young girl and I think she is great. Men don't like her because men tend to vote Republican and women tend to vote Democrat, but she is not the wild-eyed radical that the media portray her to be. We need all the women we can get to run for public office."

Michael Krasny

Progressives in America have fantasized for years about hoisting one of their own to combat ever-combative conservative talk show host Rush Limbaugh with someone mature, informed, non-judgmental, fair, compassionate, intelligent and balanced.

Marin County's Michael Krasny comes to mind, although pitting him directly against America's conservative voice might be demeaning, since Krasny is. . . mature, informed, non-judgmental, fair, compassionate, intelligent and balanced.

Then again, Krasny himself might surprise listeners with this, his own self-assessment: "While I would describe my personal politics as neo-progressive, I have, on occasion, voted Republican. I was never the liberal I was painted. I have a compassionate heart, I like to think, but I am also critical of the center. I'm not one of those predictable liberals. I keep my politics out of the programming."

The Cleveland-born educator/communicator—he was trained to be a scholar and somehow also ended up in broadcasting—came from a working class family, and he has never forgotten his roots. In fact, somewhat fortuitously, when he first came to the Bay Area to teach English at San Francisco State, it was shortly following the Black student-led strike on that campus. Briefly, during that increasingly volatile time, he taught a course in African American literature, and became a contributor to *Mother Jones* magazine.

"I moved to Marin in 1970," says Krasny. "I moved to the Bay Area from the mid-West and people told us that Marin was a beautiful area with a great climate, all of which has turned out to be true. Since moving here, I've lived in several places, including San Anselmo, Ross and

San Rafael, but we've been in Greenbrae for awhile now."

"We" refers to his wife of 35 years, Leslie, an attorney and U.C. Hastings Law School graduate. The couple has two daughters, Alexa and Lauren. There's a Labrador retriever in the family, also, who keeps the talking Krasny a walking Krasny, as well, tugging her master for as long as four miles a day on jaunts around Greenbrae.

A college professor since 1970, Krasny is best known for his measured and informative interviews and commentaries on local radio and TV stations— "People often ask me," he says, "whether I enjoy the classroom more than the radio or the radio more than the classroom, and I really enjoy them equally. It's a difficult choice that fortunately I have never had to make.

"My first opportunity to be on air as a radio host was in 1981. KTIM in San Rafael was a small alternative radio station broadcasting in both AM and FM. The station was located right above the *Marin IJ* offices, when the newspaper was located in San Rafael. I did a show once a week called 'Beyond the Hot Tub.' I interviewed people from all over Marin—artists and writers and musicians—to showcase the great level of talent living and working here. It was called 'Beyond the Hot Tub' because NBC had done a special called 'I Want It All Now,' which was about Marin and portrayed The County as a bunch of hedonists sitting around in hot tubs drinking wine. Yes, that's where former President George Bush got the expression 'Marin hot tubbers.'

"Since then, yes, I do follow Marin community issues and I do get involved, mostly as a speaker. I've spoken to groups as diverse as fire and police and Rotary clubs, Marin mayors and Marin lawyers. I do these talks on a *pro bono* basis. It gives me an opportunity to speak out and stay involved in the community.

"KTIM was a very cutting edge station, and longtime Marin insiders will remember it very well. I got to meet some fantastic talent, and touring musicians like the Plasmatics and Bob Marley. It was a lot of fun. It was basically a Marin audience, but if you were lucky, you could pick the signal up over in Berkeley.

"I met Ronn Owens through my stint at KTIM. We were both at a rally for John Anderson, who was running for President at the time. Ronn had heard my show on KTIM and recommended me for a job at KGO."

Krasny's list of newsmakers interviewed is far too numerous to mention in full, but a general scattering of famous names would include former President Jimmy Carter, Noam Chomsky, Newt Gingrich, Rosa Parks, Robert Redford, Salman Rushdie, Gloria Steinem, and Archbishop Desmond Tutu.

It is KQED's "Forum" show that is really Krasny's best niche, where his insightful and information-laden interviews and exposes are given appropriate audience.

It was definitely a mixed blessing, then, when he was fired from an earlier post at KGO radio—laughably, recalls former colleague Ronn Owens of KGO (the Bay Area's "dean" of talk show hosts). "I thought Krasny was excellent. What happened," says Owens, "is that the program director wanted someone who was less intelligent."

"I have a compassionate heart, I like to think, but I am also critical of the center. I'm not one of those predictable liberals. I keep my politics out of the programming."

But on "Forum," Krasny follows his sharpest instincts and his formidable storehouse of knowledge, attributes which have helped make the show one of the most listened-to public radio programs in the country, according to recent ratings.

None other than former San Francisco State Professor Stuart Hyde (Professor Emeritus in Broadcasting and Electronic Communication Arts) has said of the Marin mic man: "The host's ability to tackle an issue from different angles and his easy way with his guests help make 'Forum' discussions lively and interesting. Unlike some show hosts—Larry King, for one—Michael engages in a conversation rather than a question and answer session. He never holds forth, professing to have the final word on every topic."

As accomplished as his radio-TV career has been, he takes special pride in his academic contributions, having taught the likes of poet Reginald Lockett, journalist Adair Lara, a drama student named Annette Bening, and Ed Bullins, one of theatre's most accomplished playwrights. Krasny says he is equally proud of the hundreds of students who learned the basics of composition in his English classes.

Deb Kraus

In pet-friendly Marin, Second Chance Rescue is a perfect fit for people seeking a canine companion and for dogs and puppies craving happy homes.

SCR founder Deb Kraus, a Southern California native, moved here in 1990, and it didn't take her long to realize there was a crying need for matching endangered dogs with caring people.

"We're a non-profit that rescues dogs and puppies from high-kill shelters," says Kraus, "and we place them in loving, permanent homes. Since we started doing this in 1993, we have saved the lives of over 5,000 deserving dogs. Since the late '90s, our rate of rescue is about 500-600 dogs a year.

"I had been in marketing in The City when I first came here," she recalls, "but I simply had to follow my heart, not my pocketbook. Everywhere I looked, the problem was prolific. There were too many animals being born every day and just not enough homes. My mind was constantly at work thinking of ways to help solve this problem."

The obsession and hard work are paying off. SCR has a great reputation in the North Bay; the local animal shelters appreciate and benefit from SCR's services; Kraus' dedication is making a healthy impact on the dog population.

"Our 'dogma,' if you will," adds Kraus, "is simple—the reason dogs and puppies have to be rescued in the first place is that there are too many of them and not enough homes, so the first thing we need to do is prevent them from being born. Every animal we rescue is spayed or neutered before we place them in their new homes. We work all the time to educate the public on the importance of spaying and neutering."

Kraus says she never dreamed her early days of chaos and striving to get organized would result in what is today a fairly streamlined and smoothly running outfit.

"But," she says with conviction, "I discovered early on that if you believe in something strongly enough and just jump into the fray and start doing what you need to do, the creative process kicks in and results begin to appear almost miraculously."

Speaking of miracles, SCR depends entirely on individual donations and dedicated volunteers. You may qualify to be a foster parent without even realizing it. As for donations, the organization has a Wish List that details specific supplies that are needed—dog crates, kennels, wire exercise pens, baby gates, "dogloos" and doghouses, dog toys and chewies, brushes, nail clippers, dog beds, collars, leashes, or even office supplies and your used and no longer wanted car or truck. If you are already a dog owner, pay attention to the fact that when you purchase dog food, you may also purchase a certificate that will afford a free bag of dog food for an SCR dog.

High on the organization's Wish List are debit/gift cards to handle trips to Kinko's, Shell gas stations, Staples and PetCo.

As for cash giving, a mere $10 pays for a shot; $50 pays to spay a puppy; and $200 covers the entire expense for a single rescue dog. You may also check with your company to see if a matching-fund program exists. There is a Phoenix Fund, too, which accepts donations for animals requiring veterinary care or surgery. And, in a light-hearted vein, SCR has embarked (sorry) on several fund raising events during the year, like their Barking Lot Sale and the Canine Wine and Dine gala.

SCR is structured so that rescued dogs and puppies first go to a foster home on an interim basis. While there, the animals receive basic health care, grooming, exercise, plenty of affection and socializing tools to get them ready for their permanent adoptive families.

The adoption process is equally thorough and sustaining. SCR carefully screens and interviews the potential new adopters to ensure that a correct match is being made. The interview involves questions about work situation, desired activity levels, and the overall atmosphere of the new home. One reason dogs end up in shelters is that faulty matches may have been previously made, so SCR is meticulously careful about placement.

Deb Kraus proudly boasts that she is the mother of three four-legged children (all shelter rescues)—Tonto, 14, an Australian Shepherd mix; Maggie, 9, a deaf-but-lovable mutt, and Biggie, 5, a BHD (Big Hairy Dog) of unknown pedigree but of certain boundless affection.

"Rescuing deserving dogs from shelters," continues Kraus, "fostering and then adopting them out, is a true labor of love. It really is a wonderful way to attack the root of the overpopulation problem and to do something about the needless killing of so many innocent animals.

"Our program is truly all-inclusive. In addition to meeting the immediate crisis involving at-risk animals, we also educate the public about what it means to be an adopter. So many people just blindly buy a puppy because it's trendy or because their kids have been bugging them about getting one. But so many people don't think about the commitment—sharing your home with a new dog requires lots of time, affection, exercise and money.

"Rescuing deserving dogs from shelters, fostering and then adopting them out, is a true labor of love."

"Furthermore, dogs have distinct personalities. They feel both physical pain and emotional trauma; they experience loneliness; and they develop bonds with their human keepers. It's quite a commitment, and we help people see this as such.

"This is why we use the word 'guardian' rather than 'owner.' Being a guardian to a companion animal specifies the nature of the responsibility toward the pet, denoting that you are aware of the lifelong relationship with your new friend and the terms that go with this bonding experience. That's why we really question the potential guardians, asking them about unforeseen issues like chewed furniture and neighborhood restrictions, whether other people are available to care for the pet when the family is away from home, and whether or not realities like time and affordability are in place.

"Our bottom line is this, and it's a vital one—we are not trying to make it difficult for people to bring a new canine companion into their homes. It's just that if the previous so-called guardians had asked themselves the same questions at the outset, it may have prevented these dogs from being abandoned at shelters in the first place."

Heidi Kuhn

Heidi Thomas Kuhn was born at Marin General Hospital on January 6, 1958. That is the day of the Epiphany, so she says that "the work I do now is the faith of following the stars to Bethlehem."

That work is Roots of Peace, one of many humanitarian ventures she has undertaken in a lifetime of philanthropy and global activism. She founded Roots of Peace in 1997 as a way to carry on the work of Princess Diana who was devoted to eradicating 70 million land mines scattered across and around 70 countries worldwide.

Kuhn attributes her selfless world view to one of her first mentors—Marin County's legendary Sister Patricia of the Dominican Garden School. "Everything I believe and practice in life today," says Kuhn, "I learned from Sister Patricia in kindergarten. She taught me how to play fair and how to live with honesty and integrity, It's really that simple.

"I have always held dear to my heart the vision of the United Nations that first sprouted under the towering redwood trees in Muir Woods in 1945 following the atrocities of World War II. Franklin Delano Roosevelt had the original U.N. delegates gather under what he dubbed the 'temples of peace,' and that brilliant bit of Marin history is a defining moment in my life.

"Today, that United Nations vision of peace echoes stronger than ever. Roots of Peace, turning mines into vines, is just a small way that I can give to the world the lesson of peace that was ingrained in me in the county of my birth."

A 1979 U.C. Berkeley graduate in Political Economics in Industrial Societies, Heidi started a business career in Marin but soon grew restless and started to travel.

For over 25 years, Kuhn has been married to her college sweetheart, Gary, a Marin son whose father was Mayor of Tiburon, an influential man who came up with the concept of putting a bike trail through the town and installing a first-class library.

"I am capable and empowered to do my work," says Kuhn, "because of the support of my family. Family roots allow you the confidence to go forth in the world and plant seeds of peace.

"The very name, Roots of Peace, was chosen because of the profound admiration we have for our grandparents and great grandparents, who showed us the deep respect they have for the soil—how Marin was founded by Italian, Portuguese settlers, the immigrants of China Camp, and all others who came here to create the American dream.

"It hurts and frustrates me no end when I hear people refer to Canal residents as 'those illegal aliens,' because those who truly know the history of this rich county know that it was built by courageous immigrants. I am so proud that my husband Gary was instrumental in putting together funds from Bank of Marin and Burger King to allow the Hispanic kids of the Canal to play soccer. They learn to celebrate a win and how to console a loss so that by the time they get to San Rafael High School, they will have appreciated cultural diversity in its truest sense."

"Family roots allow you the confidence to go forth in the world and plant seeds of peace."

The Kuhns have four children—Brooks, 21, Tucker, 19, Kyleigh, 17, and what Heidi refers to as a "miracle baby," Christian, 9, who was born in 1995 following a bout with cancer Heidi had suffered a few years earlier, something she had thought would end any chances for additional childbirth.

"My uncle was president of ABC television, a real character, and he told me I'd be great on TV, but that I needed to go somewhere remote and gain some experience. So—naturally!—we went to Alaska and I became the weather anchor. During these broadcasts, I got an idea to get a business license and start something called the Alaska News Link.

"A few weeks later, the Exxon Valdez oil spill occurred, so I went to Governor Steve Cooper and earned a contract to satellite all the news from Alaska reporting the worst oil spill in U.S. history. I was the uplink, the camera crew was based at Prince William Sound, and we had a video editing center in the basement of the Governor's office.

"It was an incredible time to be up there, so close to Russia. Another story the world didn't know about because the media weren't marketing it was the melting of the Ice Curtain that separated our two countries—it happened a year before the Iron Curtain fell. Then, when the Berlin Wall fell, Alaska News Link got the worldwide exclusive—ABC, CBS, NBC were all kicked out. I got the first sound bite in Moscow and an exclusive interview with a spokesman for Premier Gorbachev."

Where Heidi is in today's hyper-volatile world of terrorism and war is at the helm of Roots of Peace, steadfastly and bravely continuing the work of turning mines into vines.

For a Marin woman steeped in the love of soil and the higher regions of humanitarianism, it is noble work, indeed.

Celia Kupersmith

If life is timing, one might say that Celia Kupersmith's touch is precariously elegant.

It's one thing to exult in being named General Manager of the Golden Gate Bridge, Highway and Transportation District; and it's quite another, shortly thereafter, to stand guard over what would soon become one of the nation's most vulnerable terrorist targets.

An affable, open, fair-minded and joyful person, Kupersmith has been at the helm of the Golden Gate Bridge since April 1, 1999—bridge district board members recruited her from the far less glamorous Regional Transportation Commission of Washoe County in Reno—but it was no April Fools' joke that interrupted her in a phone conversation the morning of September 11, 2001 when she was attending a bridge conference in Boston.

Like everyone else in America on that fateful morning of sorrow, she found the closest TV and watched in utter shock and amazement as New York's Twin Towers collapsed in a catastrophic heap of massive debris and human destruction.

With a phone wedged to her ear, she calmly voiced instructions to bridge personnel awaiting her orders on the West Coast. "Looking back, I am very proud of the fact that our security procedures went so smoothly," she recalls. "Our emergency checklist had long been institutionalized, and even though hell was breaking loose all around the nation, our well-trained bridge employees executed the evacuation drills, dispatching emergency boats and coordinating seamlessly with the Coast Guard on all that we needed to do. But still, I couldn't help but feel frustrated, stranded as I was on the East Coast."

Kupersmith had been absolutely elated when she landed this job—"I enjoyed every phone call I received from all sorts of media, and their first question was always the same, asking me how I felt being in charge of not only a local transportation link, but also a national landmark and world icon.

"Now, after 9/11, the media would call, but this time their first question would be how it felt being in charge of America's most obvious next target—it was at once eerie but fortifying. I felt a steely new resolve in rising to this challenge. I had come to love the Golden Gate Bridge in an almost personal way, so this took on the intensified devotion of a mother's love toward a child."

The Golden Gate Bridge is vastly more than a dramatic way to get from Marin to San Francisco—the *idea* of the bridge has come to represent people's hopes and aspirations, and, in far too many cases, their final sense of failure. Kupersmith refers to her structure as "performance art—not only do you see people constantly driving and walking the bridge but also caressing and embracing it, storing God knows how many feelings and memories for when they return to their home states. So my job takes on the added dimension of preserving a masterpiece."

And what a majestic bit of masterpiece the Golden Gate Bridge is, indeed. Dissecting it as a mere structure would be a disservice to the artistry of its creator, Joseph Strauss, who envisioned the bridge as a gracefully monstrous violin whose twanging cables would create string-like plaintive wails in the foggy mist of the lonely Pacific. But it's simply impossible to ignore some of the bridge's mind-boggling personal stats—its weight is 78,500 tons; the two cables which create the suspension contain 80,000 miles of wire, enough to circle the globe three times; the span is designed to sway 27 feet in each direction; it consumes 4,000 gallons of "International Orange" paint per year; its steel sections in each tower are fastened with 600,000 rivets; 23 miles of ladders climb their way through the twin towers; the bridge is 9,151 feet long, which makes it the fourth longest suspension span in the world, behind only the Akashi-Kaikyo Bridge in Japan, the Verrazano-Narrows Bridge in New York and the Humber Bridge in England.

Oh—and perhaps the most significant personal stat concerning the Golden Gate Bridge: Nowhere on Earth is there a more perfect spot to witness the evening sunset than at mid span on a Spring evening while wrapped in the embrace of your windswept lover.

Little wonder, then, that our very own international treasure is probably the most photographed manmade marvel in the world, and even less wonder why its chief guardian, Celia Kupersmith, is on such a determined course to preserve this miracle from dangers of all kinds.

Her role forbids her, of course, from divulging too many details due to the security threshold, but she alludes to an even darker period of doom a few weeks after 9/11 when she was informed by State police that terrorist chatter had revealed an imminent plot to blow up the beloved structure. That's when a joint decision by then-Governor Gray Davis and Kupersmith's staff led to the positioning of six National Guardsmen standing vigil over the bridge 24/7, their presence made more visible and intimidating by the presence of military Hummers and Jeeps.

"Now, after 9/11, the media would call, but this time their first question would be how it felt being in charge of America's most obvious next target—it was at once eerie but fortifying. I felt a steely new resolve in rising to this challenge."

Again, Kupersmith cannot say much about the finer details of security and vigilance, but she says it's amazing how closely monitored and documented are every action and movement on the bridge's pavement, sidewalks, and substructures—"Nothing gets past us; the cameras are everywhere."

Lest you think it's a breeze to land the job of Golden Gate Bridge Director, a job that's as hard to wrest from its holder as is the much-envied slot of toll taker, Kupersmith had to out-shine 16 other finalists selected from around the nation. Her first contract expired in 2004, but she has signed on for another span that will keep her riveted in her position through 2009. She's an ebullient, clear-headed leader whose positive approach and boundless enthusiasm no doubt led to her selection.

Celia has been married to John Kupersmith for 17 years; he is now a reference librarian at UC Berkeley. He is also a member of the Marin County Library Commission and an advisory board member and contributor to "Librarians Index to the Internet." The couple lives in San Rafael; Celia is especially proud of her daughter from a previous marriage, Echo Hall, a graduate of the California Culinary Academy in San Francisco.

Tony Lazzarini

Tony Lazzarini is celebrating his 21st year as a Marinite, but the transplanted San Franciscan says he feels like a Marin native. "I originally came to Mill Valley in 1983 for a house warming party for my good friend Mark Bissiri. He had just bought a house above Tam High School. Homes back then were barely affordable for a single person. It was peaceful, surrounded by trees and nature. It was the perfect place for a budding author/playwright. I was managing an import auto repair shop in The City and living on the Peninsula. He offered to rent me the bottom part of his home for less than I was currently paying. It was a great deal for both of us, and the fact I was single also gave Mark and me an opportunity to explore the Marin County nightlife. Mark now has a family and still lives in the same house. My wife Arlene and I purchased our current house about two years ago.

"I love this place," he says, gesturing on his Greenbrae boat dock to Mt. Tam on the west and the sparkling bay to the east. "When you break it down—that is, California is the best location to live in America, the Bay Area is the finest living in the state—it is a simple conclusion that Marin is, therefore, the most desirable spot to live on earth."

Lazzarini's family has colorful roots—his ancestors worked as crab fishermen and restaurateurs in San Francisco's bustling waterfront, and his mother was a popular pioneer waitress at Scoma's at Fishermen's Wharf.

In 1966, Lazzarini began two tours of duty in Vietnam. He served as a helicopter door gunner on a UH-1D (Huey) helicopter. "The pilots were protected by heavy metal, bullet-proof seating," he chuckles, "and we just sort of hung out the door with our M-60 machine gun. We were referred to as 'God's own lunatics' by combat reporter Joseph Galloway, co-author of 'We Were Soldiers Once, and Young.'"

Upon his return home after the Vietnam stint, Lazzarini worked in public relations for PSA, the now defunct airline company best known for its L.A.-San Francisco routes. Following this came a 10-year stint with IBM in San Mateo as a Customer Engineer, but, always an outdoorsy-type adventurer, he yearned for the type of speed and action he experienced in Vietnam.

So in 1971, Lazzarini got into auto racing. He received his racing credentials from SCCA and later his professional racing license from IMSA.

Today he races a 1968 American Motors AMX in Vintage and Historic racing events at such California tracks as Laguna Seca, Thunderhill Raceway and Sears Point (now known as Infineon Raceway).

A true auto enthusiast, he keeps a fully operational mini-automotive shop at his Marin home.

In 1983, based largely on his growing love of Marin during his frequent jaunts to Sears Point, he moved to Mill Valley to attempt yet another dimension in his multi-talented career ventures—screenwriter and author.

In 1985, he was widely heralded throughout Marin as the recipient of the Best New Family Production for his musical Christmas play titled, "Tale of the Toy Soldier."

And, more recently, 2003 saw the release of his second book, "Highest Traditions," a sensitive, compelling account of his Vietnam tours.

Lazzarini, like so many restless souls and aspiring writers, has interspersed his day jobs with frequent bartending gigs throughout his adult life. "I was never one for the corporate desk job," he laughs, "so bartending has afforded me the chance to have daytime hours free for writing and exploring while, at the same time, introducing me to a fascinating array of new people and experiences. Like many a bartender can attest, your job changes every time the door opens." Lazzarini has been a popular mixologist at a host of Marin taverns, including Piatti, the Silver Peso, The Blue Rock Inn, Zack's, Rancho Nicasio, TJ.'s on the Boulevard, the Avalon, and, more currently, the Wild Fox in Novato.

A civic-minded individual who believes wholeheartedly in the return-to-the-community concept of a full life, Lazzarini is a frequent participant in local charities and worthy causes, including Big Brothers/ Big Sisters, the Bay Area Discovery Museum, and Hospice of Marin.

Lazzarini shares his Greenbrae digs with his wife of six years, Arlene, a businesswoman for 20 years in San Francisco. Lazzarini proudly underscores the fact that his wife is the "best editor and pre-production organizer I know."

The prize-winning playwright ("Tale of the Toy Soldier") and award-winning author ("Never Trust A Man In Curlers") gained greatly from his wife's editorial skills during the writing of "Highest Traditions."

"I wanted to write the story of the missions I had flown and the men who flew with me. Telling people what we went through in Vietnam helps them to better understand the veterans of that war. To me, killing the enemy was secondary to getting our own guys back."

"When you break it down—that is, California is the best location to live in America, the Bay Area is the finest living in the state—it is a simple conclusion that Marin is, therefore, the most desirable spot to live on earth."

Lazzarini, like so many of his fellow Americans, had originally signed on for only 12 months' worth of active combat duty, but he extended that commitment to nearly two years, flying over 250 missions and receiving 12 Air Medals, three for Valor. His writing is riveting, spellbinding, including this excerpt from the book:

"Everyone knows that at twenty you are invincible. Soldiers bleeding, downed Hueys, smoldering ashes whipping around a helicopter caught in the violent turbulence of its rotor blades. Shoot anything that moves. We had the sixth sense that protected only the chosen few. The unlucky could be remembered for a short while. New people, new ships, new missions, the next mission, that's all there was. Get ready, stay prepared, stay loose, and smoke 'em when you got 'em. You are known for what you do. There is no hiding, lying or cheating. Bullshit carries no weight. Your word, your action, your machine gun is who you are. Period."

"Highest Traditions" has received awards for "Best Military Non-Fiction of 2003" and "Best Memoir 2003."

Michael Lipskin

To say that Michael Lipskin is a character is something of a gross understatement—sort of like referring to Grouch Marx as a funny fellow.

In life, there are these rare kinds of people for whom things just happen in raucous, boldly stroked ways. Michael Lipskin is one of them. He even looks like someone that life holds up as a visual aid for "off the charts funny and talented."

The raconteur/pianist—who would probably best like to be called a master at Stride jazz piano—first came to Marin in 1971 to work with the Jefferson Airplane. He had been employed by RCA (the Airplane's label at the time), so he became a Marin roommate of Marty Balin, the band's co-lead singer (who sang torrid face-to-face rock with fiery *femme* Grace Slick).

"I was supposed to form a band with Balin," says the West Marin resident (who currently lives in a remote cabin-like structure in the Nicasio woods), "but that didn't work out, so I got an apartment in San Francisco and just hung out. One of the things I always loved about The City is that you'd go to a place like Mooney's Irish Pub on Upper Grant and find celebrities who would be hanging out with prostitutes and dope pushers at the bar. Then you'd have some guy who worked as an accountant at the Transamerica Building, and they'd all be talking to each other."

But he digresses. Michael Lipskin is, in fact, one fast-yakking, quip-wielding, rim-shot-hopeful walking/talking digression. He'd love this comparison to the Julie Andrews' character of Maria in "The Sound of Music"—*How do you hold a moonbeam in your hand?* That's Michael. He's like trying to clench mercury.

"I've been playing Stride jazz piano for 30 years," continues the esoteric ivory performer, "so when Jim Dunbar (a well-known San Francisco media veteran) introduced me to Ed Moose, who owned the Very San Francisco Washington Square Bar & Grill, Ed hired me to play the piano at the Washbag and I did so for 16 years. Then I went with him to his new place a block away, Moose's, and I've been playing there for the past 12 years.

"In San Francisco," continues Mr. Digression, "there was this melding—no occupational or class distinction—that I find fascinating, being a New Yorker (by origin) where bars have some sort of social demarcation. But when I came here in the '70s, I must admit there wasn't as much of a Yuppie crowd which I find to be just simply oblivious to other people and who are rather inconsiderate. Their lack of culture is in direct proportion to their awareness of other people.

"I was a record producer for 17 years, 13 of them at RCA, and I worked with all sorts of engineers and big-name recording artists. I got to know all the jazz greats. I grew up with these musicians and got to know some of them, like Duke Ellington, Count Basie and Benny Goodman. I've been up to Bohemian Grove and gotten drunk with Alexander ('I'm in charge here now') Haig. I've also met former Secretary of State George Schultz while playing piano at Moose's—he's very intelligent.

"On occasion in supper clubs, I've read *The Wall Street Journal* and played piano at the same time. The club owners don't always like it, but I can do it—they think you are not giving enough attention to the audience. One time I was reading the *Journal*, and the club's assistant manager asked me why I was reading and playing. I replied that if the customers can talk while I play, I can read while they talk. I got fired the next day. I guess he didn't like my attitude."

As entertaining and peripatetic as Lipskin's banter is, he takes his music very seriously. He is widely heralded as one of only a very few contemporary jazz pianists who can play Harlem Stride in the genuine style of Fats Waller, James P. Johnson, Duke Ellington and Art Tatum. Lipskin also creates new pieces in this cool genre, and they can be heard on his recordings with Buskirk Productions and Downtown Records. He has played Carnegie Hall, Davies Symphony Hall, the Newport Jazz Festival, and he has appeared in the jazz documentary film, "A Great Day in Harlem," which was nominated for an Academy Award.

"From time to time, I play fancy parties for well-heeled San Franciscans—one was for Gordon Getty hosted at Marion Davies Lewis' house during renovation of the Gettys' home. I've performed on yachts on the bay. I'm a musician, yes, but my idols are old Jewish comics. I love Groucho Marx and Mel Brooks. I got to meet Mel but I didn't say a word to him—I was tongue tied." Now there's a first.

The irrepressible Lipskin was a dear friend of the late *San Francisco Chronicle* columnist John L. Wasserman—"We'd hang out and he let me write several jazz columns for the paper, and he gave me plugs all the time. He had this salon, and one night Clint Eastwood, Bill Evans, Cal Tjader, Joan Baez and Henny Youngman were all there. Everybody was ignoring Henny, but I went right over and just sat at his feet, just interviewing him. He started opening up about Milton Berle and George Jessel—all that great stuff.

"I'm a musician, yes, but my idols are old Jewish comics. I love Groucho Marx and Mel Brooks."

"I also knew Ralph Gleason (one of the most widely respected music critics in Bay Area history)," continues Lipskin in his trademark staccato-like chatter. "At RCA, I was in the position of hiring these people like Gleason as writers. I'd see Ralph at the Monterey Festivals.

"When I first came here," he recalls, "I didn't have much money, so I supplemented my piano tip jars with a career as a lawyer. I put myself through USF Law School from 1984 through 1988. One of the cottage industries in Marin is divorce, you know," he adds with a mischievous twinkle in his eye, "and rich neighbors suing each other over boundary encroachments.

"I don't have any kids, but for the last few years I have been doing volunteer work at Nicasio School, teaching English and Science to third, fourth and fifth graders. It's just wonderful and Nicasio School is amazing. That's one thing about Marin that is incredible—you have these one-room K-through-8 schools with less than 60 students, and then you have the big stuff and the fancy stuff down in Mill Valley and San Rafael.

"But you come out here in the country of Marin and you have one-room school houses that have been around since the turn of the century. That's probably the greatest thing about this wonderful county—its diversity."

Tom Marshall

Tom Marshall, a quiet spoken resident of Kent Woodlands, is the force behind the renovation of Inn Marin, which used to be the Alvarado Inn across the freeway from Hamilton Air Force Base in Novato. The hotel—which features its new restaurant, Rickey's—was once considered a garden spot by the brave men and women stationed at Hamilton who served our country during World War II, Korea and Vietnam.

In recent years, the Alvarado had declined—its bar had become home to such entertainment acts as female mud wrestling and wet t-shirt contests—so it took a bold leap of faith and much courage for Marshall to restore the place to its former glory. From all reports, he has succeeded.

"From 1961 on to the '80s, I was very busy running hotels I had in San Francisco and Los Angeles and elsewhere," says Marshall inside the spacious and cozy Kent Woodlands home he shares with his artist wife Helen. "So, Marin was really a bedroom for me. I knew Marin physically, but I didn't really get to know the people as I do now with a business here.

"We had hotels in San Francisco, Los Angeles, Oakland and Fresno. Our office was in the Continental Hotel on Powell Street in San Francisco. Shortly after we acquired that property, Hilton built their big hotel on the next block. I had an office there for seven years and then I moved into the Flood Building.

"My first hotel in San Francisco was The Lombard, which was on Geary Street, a 100-room property. We then acquired The Continental (on Ellis near

Powell) which at that time was a very beat-up place. We would renovate the hotels and do two things—rent to regular customers, but also reserve rooms for elderly people for as low as $100 a month on the 'American Plan.'

"It was an idea that worked. A lot of people with older hotel properties would come to see how they could save their old hotels. Ten to 15 years later, the government decided they should do something for the elderly, and we had a parade of government types checking out what we did.

"When I graduated from Cornell, I came out to California. I traveled up and down the state looking for a job. My father arranged an interview with Conrad Hilton in Beverly Hills—a very gracious man. I spent the entire afternoon with him and he said later in the day, 'I'd like to set you up in one of the Statler hotels.' The Statler Company was building a hotel in downtown Los Angeles, and he said, 'I'll call Jimmie McCabe who is running the hotel, and we will get you set up.' It was a great compliment coming from this famous hotel man, but I decided to strike out on my own, so I leased a hotel in Dana Point. This was successful but I realized I needed more experience, and I went to work as a manager for a San Francisco hotel company.

"I was there for five years. In the meantime, I told them I could not survive on the salary they paid me and they suggested I do something on the side. I thought that was a strange response, so I started looking around for a hotel for myself. That's how I found the Lombard Hotel. I got together with another Cornell University Hotel School graduate, and we purchased it together. A year or two after that, we acquired The Continental and, subsequently, other hotels throughout California.

"Helen and I bought a home in Forest Hills in San Francisco. We lived there for three years but it was so foggy. We'd summer on the Russian River, and I told Helen I wanted to buy a house in Marin. We found a Realtor and we found this place. I walked in and said, 'This is for me.' The house was built in 1930. Roger Kent built it when he was first married. He called it his honeymoon cottage.

"A lot of our social life was though the hotel business. We belonged to the Hotel Association and met all kinds of people across the social spectrum. We made friends with people in San Francisco and Marin. We joined the Meadow Club when we moved here and knew many people who already belonged. Yet, I really didn't know that many people in Marin. It wasn't until we had the idea about Inn Marin—every hotel manager's dream is to own an inn—that we got involved with Marin and started meeting the locals.

"When our two young boys, John and Robert, decided they wanted to be in the hotel business, I said come back to Marin and we'll get together and do something. By then I had sold all my hotels.

"So John came back in 1993 (he's a Cornell Hotel School graduate). We looked all over the Bay Area for a property and finally settled on the old Alvarado Inn—it has five acres and we were going to rebuild the entire thing. However, due to some business/political issues, we lost some time; then the financial climate changed and would have forced us to do some risky things. So, we ended up renovating the Inn, instead. By then, son Robert, who attended the hotel school at UNLV, had joined us in this project. The outdoor fountain on the property is something I designed and had built. It is my pride and joy. My wife Helen painted all the artwork in the hotel.

"We've owned Inn Marin for five years, and we've opened Rickey's restaurant there. The big plus of the Inn is that we've really gotten to know the people of Marin and we now have a real feeling for the place.

"I am the Chairman of the Board; son John is President and General Manager. Son Robert is Head of Operations. Our daughter Pamela lives in Eugene, Oregon. Our son David, a landscape contractor, also lives in Marin. There is also a United States Chief Justice in our family—John Marshall, five generations back. His landmark decisions helped establish the separation of powers—namely, executive, legislative and judicial branches in the United States government.

"The charm of the hotel business," concludes Marshall, "is that it is a people business. However, as you get more involved with the entrepreneurial day-to-day tasks of running a business, you get away from the people aspect. You don't have time to be with the guests—you rely more and more on the front line employees. Nevertheless, it is a great experience to run a hotel such as ours in the same county where we live."

"The big plus of the Inn is that we've really gotten to know the people of Marin and we now have a real feeling for the place."

Brendan Moylan

Larkspur Landing has always been one of the biggest mystery retail spots in Marin County. Situated in a cozy corner of Greenbrae/Larkspur, the Landing boasts an absolutely ideal locale for both Marinites and San Franciscans alike. A major Golden Gate Transit ferry terminal whisks both leisure travelers and business people to The City and from The County. . . and vice versa. A nexus of surface arteries, freeways, bike paths and hiking trails crisscross through the area like a finely spun spider web.

An outright breathtaking view of Mt. Tam looms god-like to the West, historical sites like San Quentin and the old quarry/brickyard cobble the landscape together snugly, and the oft-maligned shopping center serves as an anchor to a first-rate hotel, several thriving business complexes and the Airporter shuttle terminal.

And yet, the mall itself has always been something of a risk and a liability. Scoma's succeeded there for a few good years, then eventually failed; A Clean Well-Lighted Place for Books was a wonderful community centerpiece for many years, yet vacated the premises; Yet Wah and the Good Earth put in their respective tenures; and the requisite cluster of pick-up bars/steak 'n seafood restaurants have come and gone like the brisk breezes one encounters on the ferryboats.

The area begs for permanence and stability—strides have been made with a successfully developed condo community brilliantly embedded against the hillsides; the Farmers' Market has revitalized the Larkspur Landing parking lot on Saturday mornings; and an upscale feel has been injected into the ambience with a newly constructed Bed, Bathroom & Beyond outlet which has replaced a series of failed supermarket ventures.

But baffling questions have always haunted Larkspur Landing, and nobody has ever really pinpointed the precise reasons for the somewhat mediocre allure of the place—nobody except Brendan Moylan, that is.

A fast-talking, fearless and restless native San Franciscan from the Sunset District, Moylan opened the Marin Brewing Company on April Fool's Day (how's that for a Larkspur Landing calendar designation?) in 1989. Fifteen years and countless barrels of pub-brewed suds later, *that* venue continues to operate with great popularity and success.

Marketing-savvy Moylan (who also opened Moylan's in Novato in 1995) made the Brewing Company not only a hip watering spot for trendy young Marin people, but also a kid-friendly atmosphere boasting backyard-like outside tables and a gaily splashing fountain where both children and dogs can frolic, bark and giggle. He has brought vibrancy and a sense of family/community to a somewhat downbeat piece of retail property.

His latest spin-off a few kegs away from the brew abbey is Southern Marin's newest addition to the surge in tony, upscale fine dining—Noonan's. Elegantly lit, dramatically styled and smoothly decorated, Noonan's centerpiece is a seemingly football-field length bar that boasts the largest collection of esoteric liquor brands this side of Al Capone's imagination on nearby Alcatraz. How big is the bar and the height of the shelves that house the hooch? Well, let's just say a bartender scooted up a ladder to fetch an obscure quart of Jamaican rum one fine evening, and nobody has seen him again.

Noonan's—the name is a tribute to Moylan's father-in-law and wife Eileen whose family name is Noonan—is still evolving its way through foodie critique circles, but there's no question that the bar has become a lightning rod for young singles on the make, business folks seeking an ideal location for mutual meetings, and out-of-towners staying at the nearby Courtyard Marriott or wandering off the closely berthed ferry vessels. (In this day of sobriety awareness and designated driving, what better way to end an evening at Larkspur Landing than to stroll onto a ferryboat, which is also virtually a bar that drives you home?)

Moylan is thoroughly Irish. The middle of seven children from St. Cecilia's Parish in The City, Brendan and his wife Eileen moved to Novato when the Marin Brewing Company opened in 1989. They have a son, Sean, and a daughter, Chelsea, both Marin Catholic students and both, one presumes, very popular when it comes to Parent Career Day at the Kentfield high school.

The brash 43-year-old brewmeister—whose fast chatter is exceeded only by his deeply opinionated views on everything from beer to Bahia (if things seem dull at Noonan's one night, strike up a chat with him about the Bahia Lagoon controversy in his hometown of Novato)—is ironclad and undeterred about any kind of hex looming above the Larkspur Landing business tenants.

"I consider myself a hands-on businessman who just happens to be in the restaurant business" is how he explains his fast-paced, successful floating among his three Marin eateries, "and frankly, I don't have time to worry about or figure out what is wrong with Larkspur Landing."

In Moylan's world, that's because there's *nothing* wrong with Larkspur Landing.

His sparkling new restaurant—designed so seamlessly by Eric Ingstrom Design Group and architect Tim Dixon—looks like it has been the gemstone of the mall far longer than the mere months it has occupied the acreage. And, if he and his crew can work out the always-inevitable opening-act food flaws, they will undoubtedly succeed in drawing even more free-spending throngs to the sporadically damaged Landing.

Marketing-savvy Moylan made the Brewing Company not only a hip watering spot for trendy young Marin people, but also a kid-friendly atmosphere.

The Moylans are busy people, indeed: Brendan's wife Eileen spends a lot of her time with her five horses—"Moylan's Morgans"—which is her passion in life, while her husband and his General Manager Glen Philipps orchestrate the 250 employees under Moylan's tutelage, struggling as they are (like most restaurateurs these days) with pressing Workers' Compensation issues and the rising costs of energy, among other challenges. He's fairly certain that his expansion plans have reached a final destination, but in a business built around yeast and foam and the bustling bravado of a feisty Irishman, one should take that statement with a pinch of salt.

The restless and unpredictable mini-mogul received his degree in Accounting from St. Mary's College in Moraga, and he recalls his father eagerly asking him if he was going to do the family taxes after graduation. When he explained to his father that his most pressing ambition was to be a beer salesman, "the poor guy was very distraught; his jaw dropped."

Note to Moylan Senior—the kid is doing just fine. Raise a glass.

Leslie Murphy

Leslie Murphy is one of those people upon whom you truly hope and wish success. There's just something about the way she has her priorities in order—family first, then the family *at* work, then work itself.

At awards banquets honoring local businesses for Best This and Best That, audience members don't usually witness the workforce accompanying the owner to the stage to accept her plaque, *a la* cast members of "The West Wing" approaching the Emmy stage in a phalanx of euphoria.

But a few years ago at the Novato Chamber of Commerce dinner honoring local businesses for excellence, a veritable entourage of employee groupies lifted and floated Leslie Murphy off her feet and toward the stage to receive her Chamber designation on behalf of her company, W. Bradley Electric, Inc. (WBE).

Even the most hardened cynic witnessing such an event would have to admit that employee morale at *this* business was clearly running high and strong.

In personal style, Murphy is quiet-spoken, humble, and evidently somewhat in awe of the success of her company, and she is always quick to credit her workers as the reason.

"I learned every facet of the business as a young girl," she explains, "so I genuinely appreciate each position of employment. After college, I drove trucks in the summer, then office jobs at the business, and worked hard to learn all I could about electrical work. Of course, I had to pass a contractor's license, so I'm not just merely a white-collar CEO."

Leslie and her brother Jim Bradley bought out their father Bill a few years ago, which brought early retirement to the senior Bradley. He had founded the business literally out of a shed in the family backyard. (Leslie's mother Claudia died about 12 years ago.) The brother/sister corporate team oversees a firm that employs a couple of hundred workers servicing their clients directly from a fully equipped fleet of about 100 vehicles.

"I was born in San Francisco, on Silver Street," she says, "which is near the Cow Palace. But I moved to Marin 35 years ago as a kid and I was raised in Novato, so I think I can say I am from Marin. I was raised in the San Marin neighborhood, when it was first being built. I've been here almost my whole life."

Married to Mike Murphy, an electrician with the family business, the couple has two young boys, Sean and Kyle.

"There's no place like Marin, that's for sure," raves Murphy. "We have a young family, and I think the best thing about Marin is the school system. Our family is really happy about the schools our kids attend. They are great. The other best thing about Marin is the amount of Open Space. It's terrific.

"I think our biggest challenge in Marin is to keep the schools at the same level as they are now. The funding for our schools has to come from somewhere, but I don't know where. My kids are nine and eleven, so they will be in school for a while. The people at their Novato school are working hard at raising money. We need to find new ways of supporting our schools."

An avid community booster, Murphy is on the board of the Human Needs Center—"If I win the lottery," she promises, "the Center will be in luck. We have a big children's needs issue in Marin. There are a lot of low-income families living here. We need more support for low-income families. I think the lottery for housing at Hamilton was a great idea, and we definitely need more of those kinds of developments."

For 27 years, WBE has completed projects in single-building, high-rise, industrial, and campus environments. Though the concentration of its business is in the Bay Area, WBE does serve branch and district facilities throughout northern California.

Specializing in tenant improvements, the company is proficient in new construction, underground, traffic signal/street lighting, and fire/life safety systems.

While the trucks and vans are visible all over the North Bay, one of the company's more significant clients was San Domenico School in San Anselmo, where a few years ago WBE handled all the ground-up construction of the athletic center in conjunction with Cahill Construction.

How Marin grows determines how business develops, so Murphy is vigilant about taking the temperature of The County—"Being an electrical contractor," she states, "I have to say I am pleased with the growth in Marin. I think that, in northern Marin, things have generally been well planned. Overall, the changes here have been limited or controlled. Southern Marin hasn't changed that much, but northern Marin has grown a lot, and I think that the planners have done a great job.

"Of course the biggest change in Marin," she continues, mouthing an all-too-familiar local mantra, "has been the traffic. A lot of our employees live in Sonoma, and they certainly know the traffic has gotten worse. The planning for the growth in traffic hasn't been well done. I think the City of Novato has done a good job in general planning, but the traffic is a mess. Our office employees would benefit from having some sort of public rail installed between Sonoma and Marin, but our installation guys are out on the road all the time and—since there's only one guy in the truck—they can't use the car pool lane. The traffic is really bad."

Murphy is quiet-spoken, humble, and evidently somewhat in awe of the success of her company, and she is always quick to credit her workers as the reason.

A sophisticated part of WBE's ever-evolving business is WBE Telcom, which is one of the largest voice and data cabling contractors in northern California. Keeping pace for the past 18 years with the rapid changes inherent in this field, WBE Telcom strives to provide its employees with ongoing instruction and training to stay current (so to speak) on new technologies as they emerge.

WBE Audio Visual is another aspect of the multi-faceted business, serving northern California clients in the corporate, educational, retail and entertainment worlds to be a turnkey provider for all commercial and residential audio-visual needs. This is the newest division of the 27-year-old firm.

Rounding out WBE's services is the Security Control Systems division, which designs, installs, tests, and maintains access control systems, intercoms, CCTV, and life safety and fire control systems.

Quite a daunting corporate structure, especially in the complex world of electrical networking, but Leslie Murphy shrugs off the seeming hugeness of her work—"I have a passion for this business," she says matter-of-factly, "and I have a team of very happy employees. That combination makes for a smoothly running company."

Cynthia Murray

One of the best computer equipment salespersons in America decided to drop out in the late 1980s to stay home with her kids after experiencing childcare nightmares. Dropping out from the corporate world allowed Cynthia Murray to drop in to the political world. Marin County acquired the service of one of the hardest working, smartest, most dedicated politicians in local history. Cynthia is a product of New Jersey who earned the aforementioned high-tech praise from the owner of one of Silicon Valley's most successful computer firms. But alas, the East Coast's loss was Marin's gain. And what a bonus for Marin, indeed—Murray is viewed widely as one of the most accomplished, promising and astute public servants on the horizon.

If political *gravitas* were measured solely on the basis of how many boards and commissions one serves, Murray would be *maxima gravitas*. But it's the quality of service that counts, not the quantity of appointments. Murray's name is listed on the margin of so many Marin, San Francisco and Greater Bay Area public service letterheads that it would be ludicrous to list them all. Suffice it to say, there are at least 37 official civic and governmental organizations that include her name. But what's truly impressive is that she brings heart, information, dedication, leadership and decisiveness to each community calling. Whether it's Marin County Employees' Retirement Association Board, Bay Area Economic Forum, North Bay Watershed Association, or her elected position as 5th District Marin County Supervisor, Murray has crafted a political career that has been marked by a fearless sense of voicing her opinion backed up by a proven record of doing her homework and follow-up execution. She is a force to be recognized around The County. Most refreshingly, she takes her job, not herself, very seriously.

It is not a simple task to be a highly visible elected official. People feel they own a piece of you outside the official halls of power. Shopping at the grocery, relaxing at a favorite bistro, or simply strolling the avenues of Novato, Murray is constantly approached by people wielding their own intensely personal take on things political. She listens intently, absorbs the input with care, then thanks the resident for sharing ideas, grinning warmly with the winning smile that is more squinty wisdom than it is false friendliness.

She views her job as a work in progress, bringing both balance and moderation to a profession that has been scarred by ideologues and extremists.

The oldest of seven kids, she came to Marin in 1978 as part of a two week vacation. "When the plane was coming in for a landing, I had the strangest feeling that I was coming home, even though I had never been to the Bay Area before," she says. Murray never looked back, making Sausalito her new home. Over the years, Murray sampled many Marin cities and towns — living in Mill Valley, Greenbrae, San Anselmo, and San Rafael – before settling in Novato in 1988.

A graduate of Rutgers University, New Jersey, she was interested in politics in college, but put that on the back burner as she pursued her career. After a stint working in sales and marketing for several high-tech companies, Cynthia successfully ran for a seat on the Novato City Council in 1991, where she served diligently for seven years. Following that baptism of political fire, she ran for the Board of Supervisors in 1998. She won that hotly contested race, and notably, when she ran for her second term, she was unopposed. Cynthia is currently in the midst of her second term.

"There is such wonderful creativity in Marin," she enthuses, "that it's simply a joy to serve the people here. Marinites are, for the most part, better educated than in most other areas of the state and the nation, so it's not as parochial an area to serve. My background and schooling are perfect tools to address the challenges we have, like finding solutions to the transportation and affordable housing crises, working for a healthy economy and healthy environment, and seeking answers about the extraordinary rates of breast and prostate cancer."

Murray laughs while she praises Marin people for being especially vocal, and says there's no sense of timidity when it comes to airing their private views in public. "The folks here bring participatory democracy to a new level," she smiles, "and, if I weren't already dedicated to taking their pulse, they would certainly let me know what the temperature is at all times."

She serves on the Golden Gate Bridge Board, so she is intensely enmeshed in the constantly daunting problem of keeping traffic and transit flowing throughout the North Bay. Serving at a time when unparalleled cuts in transit service are making her job highly frustrating, Murray is seeking alternative ways to increase mobility, including a possible development of a ferry terminal site at Port Sonoma that would serve North Marin and Southern Sonoma commuters, and link with the proposed new rail service.

"There is such wonderful creativity in Marin that it's simply a joy to serve the people here."

Murray is also sensitive to the needs of Marin seniors, driving the creation of a Senior Strategic Plan for Marin County. One of the needs identified in the plan is providing transportation to seniors who no longer drive but want to live independently in their own homes for as long as possible. Cynthia started a demonstration shuttle project called EZRider to show how that could be accomplished.

A strong advocate of education, she serves as a member of the Schools to Career Partnership, working to bring in student interns and job shadows to the Civic Center to learn about careers in public service.

Demonstrating her independence and fearlessness, Murray led the fight in 2003 to oppose a proposed Indian casino in the middle of land slated for wetlands restoration. Standing up to the tribe and Senator Barbara Boxer, Murray rallied the community to fight off the proposal. The efforts were successful, and Murray's star as a true representative of her constituents took on new luster.

Cynthia has two teenaged children and is married to real estate developer, Dan Aguilar, who is busy with his own successful career. He cringes when people mistakenly refer to him as "Mr. Murray." While the couple may have different last names, they share a common view of working for a better community and giving each other the support to achieve their dreams. Cynthia says, "What I have been able to accomplish is due to the support of my family and community— success is always a team effort."

Joe Nation

Ah, to be young, gifted, handsome, bright, father to beautiful and brilliant twin girls, bearer of a name that sounds like an all-American action hero, and a state legislator with limitless potential from the most scenic and wealthy county in the State of California—life doesn't get much sweeter, does it?

The man is Marin-Sonoma 6th District Assemblyman Joe Nation. The twin girls are Kristen and Alexandra ("Lexi") Nation, who spend quality time with their Dad and Mom, Linda, in their beautiful home atop Bret Harte, and the political future is a plum some experts say is Joe's for the taking.

The only possible thing wrong with this picture is that Joe Nation is a genuinely very affable and friendly guy, qualities that are exemplary in real life yet sometimes anathema in the grimy, ruthless world of political ambition.

"I constantly have to dispel the notion that I didn't work for what I have," laughs Nation, whose sunny looks unfortunately connote silver flatware. "I was born to hard working parents—Joe, a seismologist, and Doris Nation, a high school librarian—in Richardson, Texas. I sold newspapers as a kid, bagged groceries, worked as a busboy at Denny's, Bonanza and Steak 'n Ale, and later, after college, I worked hard as a Pan Am flight attendant."

A graduate of the University of Colorado (Economics), Georgetown University (Foreign Service), RAND Graduate School (Public Policy Analysis), and Stanford (a post-doctoral fellowship), Nation spent a few years as a Professor of Economics at the University of San Francisco, teaching microeconomics, macroeconomics, public policy and public finance.

His adviser at Georgetown was one Madeleine Albright, who would later serve her country as U.N. Ambassador and Secretary of State under Bill Clinton. Nation says that when Albright worked with former Democratic vice presidential nominee Geraldine Ferraro (the nation's first-ever female Veep candidate), Albright asked Nation to write reports for Ferraro on public policy matters.

Spiraling upward from this came a consulting contract with former Nixon Secretary of State Henry Kissinger, who said to Nation upon receiving material the future Marinite had prepared on U.S./Russian and Soviet perspectives of security matters: "You have an unusual name."

A clear-thinking, open-minded man with a positive outlook on life, Nation jumped into the political current with a successful bid for a seat on the Marin Municipal Water District Board in 1992, a position that would help shape his skills as a communicator and community leader. MMWD is the heartbeat of Marin, a pulsing, sprawling district that serves 190,000 customers on a budget of $45 million.

Nation served two terms as MMWD Board President before springboarding into the State Assembly after a successful campaign in Year 2000. Demonstrating his sense of inclusion and civic engagement in an era when the State Legislature has turned mean, rancorous and ideological, Nation quickly instituted a series of "Pancake Breakfasts," hometown forums in which constituents are able to meet their assemblyman up close and personal. The more formal "Java with Joe" coffee clatches also afford Nation a chance to invite other statewide elected officials, Supreme Court Justices, and heads of state agencies and departments to come to Marin to offer their special insights into the art of governance.

Nation's star rose so quickly and brightly in the first term of his legislative run that he came seriously close to winning the Speakership of the Assembly, a post that would have given considerable cache to both this young leader and the counties he represents. New Speaker Fabian Nunez appointed Nation to head the Office of Policy Planning and Research, a significant role that researches, shepherds, and recommends expert short and long-term solutions to key policy issues California will be facing in the near future.

Nation was exuberant about the appointment. Offering an inside glimpse into how life at the Capitol can be an exercise in frustration for a newcomer, he explains: "This position has been a longtime goal of mine. When I was first elected to the Assembly, I was seriously concerned about the inability to draw upon existing expertise in developing strategies to address complex issues.

"I'm excited about the opportunity Speaker Nunez has given me to assist the Assembly in getting the best possible information to aid in our decision-making on issues that are critical to the state."

Nation's office provides the State Assembly detailed and objective analyses, drawing upon experts from a widely diverse pool of respected resources, including the Public Policy Institute of California, the University of California Policy Seminar, the Center for Continuing Study of the California Economy, Claremont Colleges, and Stanford University.

"I constantly have to dispel the notion that I didn't work for what I have."

Some of Nation's more notable legislation goes to the heart of today's cutting-edge social and political hot-button issues: his "No Child Left Behind" bill, reaffirming the commitment to high standards for optimum student performance, passed the Assembly by a vote of 71-1; his diligence in protecting children under the age of 14 from being exposed to harmful cancer-causing radiation from the use of tanning beds was another Assembly victory; Nation's Assembly Bill 2224 resulted in the establishment of the Sonoma-Marin Area Rail Transit District (SMART) that would eventually provide passenger train service between Cloverdale and San Rafael along the Northwest Pacific Railroad corridor which parallels Highway 101; his progressive-minded AB 2777 ensured county employees of Marin to enjoy domestic partner survivor benefits; and his environmentally sound/fiscally viable political philosophy secured ample state funding to fight Sudden Oak Death, a blight that threatens thousands of oak trees and plants in Marin.

The substantive trend of Nation's legislation pays specific interest to housing, transportation, education, health, and clean water needs of his constituents. He is a champion of legislation that preserves environmental integrity while fostering healthy economic growth. Child care development programs are close to his heart, as are bills that close tax loopholes for heavy, gas-guzzling vehicles.

Encountering Joe Nation, one can't help but wonder about the significance of his career as a flight attendant. After all, if you can handle rowdy, needy passengers on international flights, representing constituent needs in the State Legislature must seem like a stroll in Samuel P. Taylor Park.

Rich Nave

When I wrote a column for the *Marin IJ* in the mid-1980s, I wrote a silly piece one day mocking the sport of bowling. There weren't a lot of terrorists around in those years and it was a slow news day, so I decided, playfully, to make fun of those galleries of fans you used to see on TV during Saturday afternoon bowling tournaments. The people looked so very stiff and self-serious, you'd think they were attending a funeral, not a sporting event. Then I mocked the bowlers themselves, and the announcers, with all their quirks and idiosyncrasies.

You would not have believed the turmoil it caused in Marin. You would have thought I had joined the Taliban. Protesters came to the newspaper demanding my ouster. Boxes of angry mail were dumped on my desk every morning; editors received irate phone calls; a nationwide petition from something called the American Bowling Congress was mailed to the paper's publisher basically 86'ing me from the nation's bowling alleys (I am not kidding), and it was signed by 5,000 avid—and now infuriated—bowlers.

Rich Nave: For what it's worth now, 20 years later—I think you're a great guy. I used to love bringing my sons to Nave Lanes in Novato for Saturday morning bowling excursions (they especially loved the grilled cheese sandwiches), and I meticulously kept their bowling averages and watched their scores grow for years in my personal journal. I had really sweet memories around the sport of bowling, and even managed a nifty 165-170 average myself. Read me loudly and clearly: It was all a joke on a very slow news day somehow gone horribly awry. I threw a gutter ball. Ya gotta believe me, Rich.

Rich Nave is a nearly 75-year-old native son legend of Marin. Member of a pioneer Marin family and born in the old San Rafael Cottage Hospital, Rich is one of two surviving Nave brothers. Brother Bob is four years his senior, and a third brother, Bill, died in 1994.

It would be difficult to find a man with deeper Marin roots than Rich Nave, and it would be even more difficult to find someone who so happily returns so much of his good fortune back to the community.

A graduate of St. Raphael's Grammar School, San Rafael High School, and the College of Marin (the *troika* of Old Marin educational laurels), Rich went to Seoul, Korea as a Marine Sergeant in 1950 and served his country valiantly. He also holds a General Secondary teaching credential from San Francisco State University, where he is a member of that school's Football Hall of Fame.

When he came back from the Korean War, he vowed he would never leave Marin for any extended spell again.

"I have been here my whole life," he smiles warmly, "and I'm not about to change my good luck now. I lived here when there were maybe only 6,000 people in all of San Rafael and 3,000 residents in Novato. This was our own little paradise—we hunted, we fished, we ranched. The special flavor of Marin is incomparable—the weather is absolutely perfect and great for my health."

Formerly a San Rafael city councilman, he is an active partner in Nave Enterprises, the umbrella business that operated and managed Nave Lanes and still leases out and manages the Nave Shopping Center, work which keeps him "very much active with no thought of retirement."

(Incidentally, Nave Lanes was razed several months ago to make room for retail space. The bowling alley's architecture was *very* 1960 and designed to—sort of—resemble Frank Lloyd Wright's famous Marin Civic Center a few miles south on Highway 101 in San Rafael.)

Rich has been married to wife Dolly Nave since 1955, and they have eight children—Bruce, Kathryn, Richard Jr., Patricia, Sherilyn, Paul, Thomas, and Louis.

(Son Paul's name is recognizable as the man who is, perhaps, one of Marin County's all-time best boxers. Also, in the fiasco that was the California election process in the wake of Governor Gray Davis' recall from office, Paul Nave was an officially declared candidate for California Governor. Some other guy with more muscles won.)

Dolly Nave is a recognizable Marin name in her own right, having been named 1988 San Rafael Citizen of the Year by the San Rafael Chamber of Commerce for her tireless efforts to upgrade, modernize and thoroughly refurbish Albert Park. Marin old-timers and San Rafael history buffs will recall that "Albert's Field" was once The County's answer to Seals Stadium in San Francisco, which for so many years prior to the

It would be difficult to find a man with deeper Marin roots than Rich Nave, and it would be even more difficult to find someone who so happily returns so much of his good fortune back to the community.

Giants' arrival in 1958 was the closest venue any Bay Area residents ever got to professional baseball. "Albert's Field" played host to years of semi-pro ball before falling into disrepair—that's when Dolly Nave decided to organize the forces to restore the recreation area to its pristine glory days, and better.

Dolly had moved to Marin from San Antonio, Texas, when she was 11 years old, because her Air Force father had been stationed at Hamilton during the Korean War. Her family lived in Fairfax, so, while schooling at both Tamalpais and San Rafael High Schools, she worked as a waitress at Deer Park Villa near her home. She had met Rich in high school when she was at Tam and he was at San Rafael, and they had attended the same inter-school committee meeting.

Dolly said of her husband Rich in the 1990 issue of *Best of Marin* magazine: "I love children, and Rich is very good that way, too. He's very fatherly and a lot of fun, and always has an upbeat attitude."

Rich Nave really is a great guy. He is a past president of the Novato Chamber of Commerce, the Marin County Chamber of Commerce and Visitors Bureau, and the Marin Property Owners Association. He is a current member of the Marin County Airport Land Use Commission and the Novato Rotary, and a lifetime member of the Marin County High School Athletic Hall of Fame.

He is probably best known in Marin as the "Colonel" in the Nave Patrola—brother Bob is the "General"—which is a World War I comic marching group that patriotically and playfully makes appearances on significant holidays in cities around Marin.

Caral and Martin Newman

They look like a cover photo from an F. Scott Fitzgerald paperback. But Caral and Martin Newman are more mellow than either Zelda or the Great Gatsby. Their respect and love for each other has kept their marriage on a shining hill—much like, quite literally, the Sausalito hillside where they reside just north of the Waldo Tunnel which affords a spellbinding view of the twinkling San Francisco skyline.

Maybe it's the seemingly diverse chemistry that makes them opposite yet hopelessly attracted. Caral Newman is a MoTown girl from Detroit; Martin is a well-polished, expertly spoken Sussex Brit who exudes the high tea class and finery in all things: not a detriment for both his former acting and voiceover careers and his personal presence in the restaurant business. Both Caral and Martin possess high-fiber minds and lightning quick senses of humor.

"I'm originally from Detroit," says Caral, curled up on a sofa with a view everyone in Marin wants. "I went to Michigan State and majored in Football 101. I got bored early, though, and decided to go to Boston University, where I switched majors from theater and drama to speech pathology. It's a far cry from what I'm doing now, but the common thread is communication—I was an actual speech pathologist and I taught a caseload from pre-school to adults afflicted by strokes who had completely lost their speech content."

What she is doing now is a line of top-notch city-related accessories, silk scarves and ties being the initial launch. Communication skills vaulted her into the ear range of San Francisco Mayor Willie Brown, who loved her multi-scene depiction of The City on silk so much that he commissioned her to be the official scarf maker for The City and County of San Francisco.

Embellishing upon his commission just a bit, she designed a City Scarf with his name on it—Willie's, that is—and Da Mayor gave it away to visiting dignitaries Sophia Loren, Madam Sadat, Hillary Clinton, and others. Caral sells the city accessory lines at Federated Stores, museums, boutiques, gift shops, and a wide assortment of venues.

Martin Newman, chiming in from the background like a savvy husband who gives his wife first voice, says: "My parents moved from the South of England to Canada—to Vancouver, which is where I began as a stage actor. They wanted to be closer to the United States and all their cousins and relatives. A lot of my family has disbanded all over the world: South Africa, India, Australia, the United States and Canada."

If Martin's face and name are familiar to Bay Area restaurant lovers, you might recognize him as one of the founding owners of Scott's Seafood restaurant, which in its heyday was the premier "sea-foodie" gathering place among local culinary luminaries and common folk alike.

The first Scott's was at Lombard and Scott in The City, and many other locations soon followed on the West Coast. Says Mr. Newman in typically deadpan fashion: "Scott's Seafood was something else. It's amazing what comes about through necessity. At the time, my business partner and I had The Coachman on Nob Hill where we served meat dishes and other English delicacies. Don't laugh—the food was really good. It was a terrific hangout for the likes of Chief Justice Earl Warren, Sir John Mills, Rita Hayworth, Jane Russell, Eric Idol, John Lennon, Alistair Cooke, and doggie bags full of Crockers, Newsoms, Fleishackers, and other place names. In 1973, because of the oil crisis, the price went through the roof. So, we had to do something. It was fish. We just took off like a skyrocket. Some people who came for lunch would wait for dinner to be seated!

"Scott's became part of the new trend in the restaurant scene where you could actually see the people through the windows dining in restaurants rather than hiding in dimly lit caverns. This was the opening up, if you will, of food in the community. It was convivial. It's fascinating now to observe how those traits have been utilized in many, many restaurants—the open kitchen, the honesty in what's been prepared, the very upbeat, positive, fresh approach to food in general. If you look at some of the really hot and famous places these days, in fact, you can see very clearly the influence we had on the scene."

Caral and Martin met, fittingly and Fitzgeraldly enough, at San Francisco's Huntington Hotel, at the Big Four restaurant.

"I was waiting to be interviewed for a newspaper story about Scott's sponsoring a classic car rally—I'm an Aston Martin nut," remembers Martin, "and the reporter did not show up. Left to my own devices, I espied Caral as she walked in with a friend, who I think was setting her up with a blind date. Her friend walked up to me and told me I looked like one of her husbands. I suppose this got Caral's attention. At any rate, I took them both out to dinner at the Big Four after the blind date had been brushed aside. We didn't reconnect until six moths later."

"Scott's became part of the new trend in the restaurant scene where you could actually see the people through the windows dining in restaurants rather than hiding in dimly lit caverns."

Caral cuts in swiftly: "I was moving houses and my doorbell rang. I was holding my appointment book and when the bell sounded, I dropped the book, and Martin's card fell to the floor. Now, I am not in the habit of calling men, but I was curious to know what had happened to him. So I called him up. Timing is everything, because he had just broken up with someone and so had I. We went to Tadich Grill for lunch at 3 p.m. and left at 10 p.m. We were the first-ever wedding at the Sherman House on Green Street, now one of Ann Getty's abodes."

Gazing out the window toward the fog rolling past and over the Waldo Tunnel, Martin waxes philosophical: "It's wonderful to be where one is, despite the challenges, and to be able to say these are the things I have done and these are the observations I have made. These are the people I have encountered; these are the people I've played with. I love the adventure of life. I yearn to keep the curiosity and zest for life alive, and I believe strongly that the key to staying vital is to ask questions all the time. That is very important."

As if on cue, the Newmans clasp hands tenderly and stare longingly toward the San Francisco sunset.

Don Novello
(a.k.a. Father Guido Sarducci)

He bought the cape 30 years ago in a San Rafael St. Vincent de Paul thrift shop for seven dollars and fifty cents.

The cape still defines Novello every bit as much as the swoosh says Nike.

This delightfully madcap Marin comedian is a county icon. Even to use the term "comedian" falls far short of the mark. He's an engaging, gentle, sweet, hyper-curious blend of muse, magician, maestro of mirth. Like the holy man he portrays in his Fr. Guido garb, Novello pokes and probes his targets with love and compassion. Meanness and scorched-earth shock comedy are for scores of other less enlightened, far less successful stand-up acts.

While he's an offbeat veteran of American underground subculture, his resume is heavily laden with mainstream marquee milestone appearances, as well—numerous Letterman gigs, seemingly countless "Saturday Night Live" stints, Johnny Carson "Tonight Show" knee-slappers, guest shots on "Nash Bridges," "Midnight Caller," "It's Garry Shandling's Show," "Married With Children," and even weightier special roles in movies like "The Godfather; Part III," "Jack," "Just One Night," "Tucker," "New York Stories," and "Casper."

But the launch pad spawning ground for this 60-year-old Ohio native has to be "The Smothers Brothers Comedy Hour," the ground breaking and sadly short-lived theater of irreverence that was a little too fearless for corporate TV in the early '70s. These were the still-tempestuous days of post-Vietnam antiwar frenzy, and network executives were skittish about unleashing anti-establishment sentiment upon a war-weary nation.

Comic David Steinberg introduced Novello to show hosts Tommy and Dick Smothers, and soon afterwards Fr. Guido Sarducci became a staple of the program's never predictable range of humor. The sorrowfully poignant chain-smoking priest with the Italian accent lobbed provocative thoughts upon an American audience desperately trying to make sense out of Watergate, Vietnam and Dick Nixon.

"Tommy Smothers was the first person on national TV to criticize the Vietnam War," recalls Novello, who also credits the comedian for being his mentor. It was a bittersweet sign of the times that the "Smothers Brothers Comedy Hour" finally collapsed under the weight of political paranoia and business cowardice, but the impact Fr. Guido made on the nation's consciousness was an indelible stamp. The line that blurs between Novello and Sarducci is a phenomenon quite like the Brando/Godfather linkage. To hear Novello's voice today evokes instant echoes that hearken to Fr. Guido's early years.

Overlaying his more public career moves in the past three decades is the *persona* of Lazlo Toth, a pen name Novello has been using to write outrageously confrontational letters to worldwide leaders, politicians, corporate chieftains and religious luminaries.

The letters are Novello's way of somewhat maniacally getting under the skin of self-important big shots, and one can only imagine the delight Novello takes in visualizing the recipients reading these outrageously crafted tomes. Both the letters and the responses have been published in the books "The Lazlo Letters," "Citizen Lazlo!" and "From Bush to Bush: The Lazlo Toth Letters."

One such letter was penned to Defense Secretary Don Rumsfeld, which read:

"Dear Don Rumsfelt (sic):

"I had a dream I saw Osama bin Laden, sitting on a mattress, underneath a big rock. I don't think you have to be born in Vienna to interpret the dream as meaning that he's gone to the mattresses, and the 'rock' represents the grand mosque at Mecca. If I were you, I'd send a squad of special forces into Mecca to check it out. What can you loose (sic)?

"Bombs away!

"Lazlo Toth."

Given the somewhat rambling and wacky nature of the Defense Secretary's post-Iraqi War press conferences, it's probably a safe bet he took this letter quite seriously.

Toth wrote another letter to Saddam Hussein, which reads in part:

"You know, with all your money, you'll be able to hire the best American attorneys. And you could have the trial transferred out of the Middle East, maybe to someplace like Modesto. That'd be a good place. They could be called your Impossible Dream Team, and you could say you have bipolar disorder. It's a great excuse, and they could get you off, probably, with 30 days at the Betty Ford clinic."

Grins Novello: "I got the letter back—return to sender, not deliverable."

Who knew rat holes have no mailboxes?

Novello, a longtime Fairfax resident who has fit into the local landscape seamlessly and without celebrity status, joined California's gubernatorial sweepstakes in 2003 as a candidate for the state's highest office, but

Like the holy man he portrays in his Fr. Guido garb, Novello pokes and probes his targets with love and compassion.

he had to withdraw for lack of a sufficient number of valid signatures. The fact that a former bodybuilder turned action hero named Arnold Schwarzenegger won the Governor's contest is yet another example of the blurred line between reality and satire in Don Novello's world. If new Governor Arnold had any sense of irony, you'd think the least he could've done was appoint Fr. Guido Sarducci as Chaplain to the State Senate?

In an equally recent display of the comic's endurance and bottomless pit of inspiration, Novello was the light bulb illuminating the brilliant idea of bringing Portuguese water dogs to McCovey Cove behind right field at Pac Bell Park. This is the "splashdown" territory owned almost exclusively by Barry Bonds' prolific home run prowess, and Novello thought it would be a perfect touch of San Francisco panache to have doggies racing toward soggy home run balls bobbing in chilly bay waters.

Giants' owner Peter MacGowan loved the notion, and today this "Only in San Francisco" quirk of genius is broadcast nationwide whenever the Portuguese posse of water dogs puts in a weekend appearance at the nation's finest baseball yard. It should never be forgotten that this instant cult classic moment came from the fabulously fertile mind of Marin County's own Don Novello.

Part Don Quixote with a sardonic twist of Robin Williams, perhaps, this man is mostly Don Novello: kind, inquisitive, probing, genuinely caring, jesting and inspiring—yet another reason to celebrate the shards of light emanating from the kaleidoscopic allure of Marin's vast pool of talent.

Adriano Orsi

Adriano Orsi, the passionately vibrant offspring of one of San Francisco's most luminous restaurant families, is convinced there's an invisible barrier separating his first-class Novato dining room from the very restaurant-savvy denizens of Southern Marin.

"It's crazy," he chuckles in his trademark chirpy voice that is part Joe Pesci, part Soprano. "I get customers from Walnut Creek, Los Altos Hills, Capitola. I even get folks who fly up from Los Angeles and Palm Springs just to eat at my place, but for residents of Mill Valley and Larkspur, Novato may as well be located in Oregon."

What a loss for them, too, because Ristorante Orsi—located on the historic, almost sacred site of the legendary Galli's in Ignacio—is truly one of the top three fine dining eateries in all of Marin County. Combining as it does classically Italian fare with impeccable service and cheerful ambience, Orsi is a culinary jewel nestled beneath oak trees in a suburban section of the County just west of Highway 101 between Hamilton Air Force Base and the Marin Golf & Country Club. (Now that geographic specificity should narrow down the directions for Southern Marinites who view Novato as South Ukiah!)

Adriano is one of two sons of Oreste and Anna Orsi, Italian immigrants who came to the San Francisco Bay Area equipped with no money but with a passion for cooking. Oreste Orsi had schooled at the renowned Villa d' Este on Lake Como, and when he arrived in San Francisco, his first job as chef was at Bimbo's 365 Club on Columbus Avenue in The City. (The bartender at the time was a kid named Johnny Burton, who is finishing his term as President of the California State Senate, and who bragged openly that he was the best bartender in town and Oreste was the best chef.)

Oreste and Anna lived in Westlake in South San Francisco, where she cooked at a little deli named Armanino's (whose sauces later gave prominence to the Armanino food products line), and where the couple raised their sons, Adriano and Loreno. Oreste's cooking skills soon became legendary in The City by the Bay, so he left Bimbo's to open his own restaurant, Oreste's, at 365 Jones Street. The place caught on immediately, and by 1962, Mr. Orsi wanted to expand, so he sold his interest in Oreste's, and moved uptown to 375 Bush and opened Orsi's, which soon became the place to be seen.

In those banner days of San Francisco dining, one could count the cream of restaurants on two hands—Doro's, Jack's, Ernie's, Orsi's, Blue Fox, Le Trianon, La Burgnone, Trader Vic's, Fleur de Lys, Sam's. Orsi's was arguably in the top three—this is where San Francisco's raw power deals were made, where politicos and entertainers alike were whisked into their seats through a secret entrance, and where young busboys should never, ever greet a woman by assuming she was the wife of the man whose arm she graced. Ask Adriano Orsi the lesson behind that yarn. Also ask him about the time the triad of American gangster families—Gambino, Gallo, Colombo—shared a table one day in the '70s, breaking bread, slugging back Burgundy, and making peace while an accordionist made $50 per song drowning out the FBI bugs in attendance.

Adriano started as dishwasher, worked his way up to busboy and waiter, then captain and maitre d'. "I love every bit of this business," he says, "and I miss with all my heart those fine days of San Francisco night life that are gone forever. People actually dressed up to go out to dinner, and they were treated like royalty."

The dress code may be a bit more relaxed at Ristorante Orsi in Ignacio, but the lessons Adriano learned from his chef father are deeply embedded in the younger Orsi's heart. This place is a veritable shrine to the elder Orsi—Adriano's brother Loreno is the head chef, his wife Ferol works as hostess, and their children Orianna and Giovanni work the dining room. They opened doors here in 1996 following a very successful and festive restaurant stint in Kenwood, where the family ran the Golden Bear Lodge, a gorgeously woodsy setting on Sonoma Creek that celebrated trademark Orsi cooking and a wide collection of over 500 vintage wines.

Adriano is fiercely proud of the way he has maintained his father's knowledge of food preparation—the spices, sauces, soups, salads, entrees and desserts are mouth-watering delicious. The choices of veal, steaks, chops, fresh seafood, pasta, and tomato dishes grown from Adriano's private garden (at the family home in San Rafael) of over 300 tomato varietals are to die for. . . even if your name isn't Gambino, Gallo or Colombo. Adhering to the mystique and aura of chef wisdom, Adriano is close-mouthed about the secrets passed on to him by his father, but it has to do with the special alchemy created by spices, herbs, conviviality, excellence in food preparation, and rather large dollops of personality and flair.

Throw in a pinch of absolute adherence to traditionally prepared Italian dishes and a complete aversion to faddish foods and chefs who think they know everything, and you get a pretty good feel of what to expect at Ristorante Orsi. On spring, summer and autumn evenings, nothing competes with the outside patio with lights strung between oak trees and calm, soft, welcome breezes mingling with background tunes by Sinatra and Pavarotti.

Adriano is close-mouthed about the secrets passed on to him by his father, but it has to do with the special alchemy created by spices, herbs, conviviality, excellence in food preparation, and rather large dollops of personality and flair.

Adriano is the first to admit that his business is the craziest one to maintain on Earth—with monumental challenges around Worker's Compensation, stiff drunk driving laws, soaring beef prices, non-smoking regulations, and the scaled-down expenditures by families and businesses in an uncertain economy—but he would not trade it in for anything. "It's my testament to my father's life," he says proudly. "He was, at the top of his game, one of the top three chefs in America, and, even though he spoke only broken English, he was one of the most beloved San Franciscans of his day—his funeral procession in 1979 when he died at the age of 64 was 10 miles long. That's loyalty, and that's the kind of loyalty and commitment I bring to Orsi in Ignacio."

Now if he can just get maps into the hands of foodies in Larkspur, Mill Valley and Sausalito. . .

(Sadly, Ristorante Orsi in Ignacio closed on July 18, 2004, just prior to final publication plans for this book. We have chosen to include his profile despite the unfortunate closure, because the irrepressible Adriano Orsi has said that he will find a new location, keep the size and staff small, and offer the same excellent food and service that have become Orsi trademarks. We wish him and his family all the best.)

Kevin and Leslie Patterson

The Renaissance Pleasure Faire has been part of the fabric of Marin life, it seems, since the day Drake landed at Drake's Landing. The first time I attended one, I remember feeling utterly amazed that so many people were so completely into this then-novel and extremely wild and colorful carnival of ribaldry.

I owe the Renaissance Pleasure Faire gratitude for being an ideal outlet of play for my two sons when they were young and when their imaginations were so fertile. I vividly recall them being invited onstage for a knife-juggling exhibit, and I can still see the delight and awe and shimmer in their young eyes.

The Patterson family has been synonymous with the Renaissance Pleasure Faire at least since 1967. Hundreds of thousands of Faire-goers both local and international have ventured into the Forest in Marin to share a love of the period and the spirit of participation that has been the hallmark of the Faire. This Faire has made an enormous impact on the Marin landscape and in the lives and memories of culture-lovers everywhere who live to celebrate this glorious era of jousting and jolly-making, pewter mugs overflowing with ale and roasted turkey legs.

Kevin Patterson remembers the Renaissance Pleasure Faire as if it were his own childhood, mainly because it was. His parents, Ron and Phyllis Patterson, created the original Renaissance Faire in the country. Kevin, at the ripe age of three, was the bell ringer in the Call of the Faire procession at the very first Renaissance Faire in Los Angeles in 1963.

Four years later, when he was an even riper blade of seven—"My first memories of Marin," he recalls fondly, "are stepping out of an old Buick station wagon into the Magical Forest. The entire village embraced me.

"At first, I didn't want to wear tights," he laughs, "but pretty soon I fell into the concept easily, which is basically learning how to interact with strangers in a playful fashion."

That's really nailing the essence of the Renaissance Pleasure Faire on the head—leaving everyday concerns of self-importance behind for a few enchanted moments of make-believe, fearless celebration of life, and fanciful mind-expansion into a long-lost era that raised human gallantry, frailty, heroism, and romanticism to new heights of divine folly and glory.

"The really impressive thing about the Renaissance Pleasure Faire," says Kevin Patterson, "is that people of all ages came, and are coming still, from all walks of life. The media, of course, were instantly tantalized, so their frenzy fed the Faire's early attraction."

Actually, many people don't remember the first site of the Faire being at China Camp, but that locale's remoteness and Black Point's superior access to the highway made the transfer an easy choice.

The success of the Renaissance Pleasure Faire was simple—Faire-goers actually *became* the participants. This wasn't a Halloween pageant or a Hookers' Ball—the people who gave the Faire its life and flair did not see themselves as acting. They were—and are—simply *being*. Kevin Patterson is swift to point out that it is the visiting participants in their unrestrained freedom of expression and joy that consistently give the Faire its very soul.

The authenticity didn't stop there. All of the handmade items and crafts showcased, worn and utilized on the grounds were made out of natural materials. The crafts were high-quality.

"And," says Kevin Patterson, "the Renaissance theme gave the faire a richly creative artistic direction. People just blossomed with that kind of backdrop. They couldn't wait to celebrate this special epoch each year. Think about it—'A Chorus Line' made an impressive 22-year run on Broadway. The Pattersons' Renaissance Faires are now celebrating their 41st consecutive year. And there are now 100 similar faires coast to coast, creating all those livelihoods and all that joy. Our little family celebration has become a cottage industry nationwide."

The wonderful event is held these days at Stafford Lake County Park in Novato—Black Point with its perfectly set forests and trails and hiding spots for blackguards and maidens alike is now a fancy golf course—and Stafford Lake Park is proving itself to be just as conducive to the imagination and geographic setting that evokes clear Renaissance imagery.

Kevin Patterson first regaled his wife Leslie at the Renaissance Pleasure Faire's Tournament of Horses, where Leslie was an actress and Kevin performed as Master of Ceremonies. Legend has it that she asked to borrow his cape on a foggy morning in 1985. They have been together ever since, got married in 1990, and hope someday to pass the magic cape on to one of their sons (Andrew or Michael) for future acts of chivalry at the family's Faire.

Since his inaugural appearance as bell-ringer,

"At first, I didn't want to wear tights," he laughs, "but pretty soon I fell into the concept easily, which is basically learning how to interact with strangers in a playful fashion."

Kevin has worked in every phase of event production from Horse Guard to General Manager. Leslie, in turn, worked as Performing Arts Director for the Renaissance Pleasure Faires at Black Point and in southern California for 15 years, and is now co-producer with Kevin. She has also directed theatrical production for many special events, including the Old California Shindig, Old San Francisco, and the ongoing Great Dickens Christmas Fair now in its 26th year.

Kevin's younger brother, Brian Patterson, is an expert puppet master (Punch 'n Judy-type genre) who has been flown by clients all over the world for exhibits and performances. His parents, Faire founders Ron and Phyllis, still live in Marin.

Kevin and Leslie Patterson started As You Like It Productions, based in Novato, in 1995, with the aim of creating events with historical and theatrical flair for corporate, government and private clients. In 1999, the company began to produce its own events by reviving a Bay Area favorite—the Great Dickens Christmas Fair—at the San Francisco Cow Palace.

Their vision for the future has already taken root with the continued Faire tradition at Stafford Lake, now called the Heart of the Forest Renaissance Faire. They also plan to construct an authentic Elizabethan Great Hall for year-round educational programs and private gatherings, and are searching for the perfect Brigadoon-like valley in West Marin.

Nobody asked me, but in the Shakespearean spirit of "letting the world slip"—a fantasy perfected by the Faire—how about also bringing back the Faire Maiden Kissing Booths?

Dr. Tom Peters

When Dr. Tom Peters was chosen seven years ago to be the new President and CEO of the Marin Community Foundation, he brought a wealth of public service experience to an affluent county.

A quiet-spoken man given to refreshing outbursts of suddenly raucous laughter and banter, Dr. Peters looks back at his 25 years in the rough 'n tumble public arena with a bemused sense of amazed detachment. He seems like such a low-profile sort of man to have been so actively engaged in social chaos, but just recall San Francisco in the '70s and '80s.

That's when Peters served in The City's Public Health Department, two decades marked by catastrophic violence and cataclysmic disease.

"The 1970s were an extremely violent time for San Francisco," he recalls, "and I was in a highly visible position in the Health Department. I sat face to face with Dan White minutes after he turned himself in for murdering Mayor George Moscone and Supervisor Harvey Milk. I was the attending clinician, and I had to conduct a preliminary examination.

"Same thing happened after Sara Jane Moore was arrested for shooting at President Jerry Ford outside the St. Francis Hotel. Then we had the Jonestown tragedy, with so many San Franciscans poisoned to death by madman Jim Jones. I was, of course, a frequent visitor at the San Francisco County Jail, where a stream of violent crimes had both led prisoners to those confines and continued after their imprisonment—a lot of drug-related crimes, Hells' Angels violence, that sort of thing. My memory of the '70s is a vision of fearful uncertainty.

"The dawn of the '80s brought a new epoch to the scene—the genesis of HIV/AIDS. I had taken over as Chief of Staff for the San Francisco Health Department by then, and this is what I was about to confront—the onslaught of a worldwide pandemic. It all started in our offices in 1981 with four names written on a blackboard. These were young men who were dying of a totally baffling and scary and unknown illness. We'd call health chiefs elsewhere and compare notes—there were similar cases in Los Angeles and several in New York. Think about that—a handful of known cases in 1981, and today it is an international menace. Amazing."

Peters found himself once again at the core of what he calls the "red hot flaming politics of both San Francisco and the international scene." It was a time of relentless media glare and heart-rending pain and suffering. Fear and near panic ruled the day. Young men were dying in throngs. Peters vividly remembers the surreal element of what were once-sedate medical conferences. "Suddenly, with the whole world watching," he says, "we'd have news conferences jam-packed with 400 media from around the globe. My boss once had to wear a bullet-proof vest because the emotions and threats ran so high and out of control. These were crazy times—remember that more San Francisco men in those days died than all the local fatalities from World War I, World War II, Korea and Vietnam combined. It was a combination of a totally fascinating and incredible and fearful experience."

Somehow, we all got through it and are still getting through it, albeit severely damaged and extremely wary and cautious. For Peters, taking the helm of the Marin Community Foundation may have seemed like a genteel, bucolic event following two decades of turmoil, but this is a man of decision who courts action.

Sitting in the dramatically stark and spacious confines of the Foundation's home at Hamilton—a converted Air Force hangar now strung together with spider webbed steel, metallic walkways and theatrically lit wall art—Peters appears as a pillar of strength, a man whose fiber has been hammered and fire-walled into precisely the kind of leader the Foundation has needed to shepherd its myriad channels of giving.

Ironclad in his resolve to honor and enact the wishes of Mrs. Beryl Buck, whose fortune has mushroomed into the largest foundation in the state and the fourth largest in the nation, Peters reaffirms his newest mission—"We are wholeheartedly devoted to guarding the intent of her will, to enhance the lives of the people of Marin. She was a high-minded woman who had deep concerns about education, health, the environment, religious issues, ethics, housing, matters of conscience, the arts.

"Not many people know this, but she wrote eloquently, expressing her concern over the inability of the middle class to maintain health coverage. In this, she was far ahead of her time. The poor had government programs, the wealthy could afford their own, but she anguished over hard working Marinites' lack of health coverage affordability. I think she'd be amazed if she saw how actively engaged we are today in not only protecting her will, but enacting it."

Peters, who is passionately concerned about leaving a legacy of community contribution, sees his stewardship of the Marin Community Foundation as a natural expansion of his previous health career—"This affords me a wider range of expression in community service," he explains. He is also quick to point out that the Foundation, unlike the common perception, is not confined to the Buck family trust. It is actually a coalition of 300 Marin families who have joined with the Buck inheritance to create what is one of the most formidable foundations in the nation. Percentage-wise and on a per capita basis, if Los Angeles had a situation similar to Marin's, the L.A. foundation would have to be worth $32 billion. Peters credits the Bucks for their vision and lofty-minded spirit, and Marin will benefit from their largess for decades to come.

He loves Marin County and recognizes that he is in a position to improve the lives of nearly all its residents, especially the young ones whose education was foremost in the mind of Beryl Buck.

A San Rafael resident since the day he was hired (he lives in the Smith Ranch section), Peters is a Fourth Street aficionado—"I don't cook, so Fourth Street is my kitchen"—and one of those much-envied commuters whose trek to work is roughly three minutes each way. He loves Marin County and recognizes that he is in a position to improve the lives of nearly all its residents, especially the young ones whose education was foremost in the mind of Beryl Buck.

Dr. Tom Peters is truly a rare local gem whose ability to face challenges and make tough decisions based on solid conviction make him the perfect fit to lead an equally rare gem of a foundation into the first several years of a daunting new century.

Elaine Petrocelli

"Sense of community" may be one of the most overworked expressions in modern life. But when the term is witnessed in its most evident, proactive form, it is a refreshing sight to behold.

That's the feeling one gets in Elaine Petrocelli's slice of Marin—Book Passage in Corte Madera, a center of learning and citizen interaction that just may very well be the pulse beat of The County.

Petrocelli exudes a sense of vibrancy and vitality, twin qualities that stem from a lifelong passion for reading. She reads five books a week, alternating from mystery to nonfiction and fiction. In spite of her busy schedule, she reads in the morning before breakfast and every evening. She always has an aptly sized volume stashed in her purse in case she can steal a few minutes to read.

A Marin resident for 37 years, Petrocelli opened her first bookstore in Marin 28 years ago. A second Book Passage opened in San Francisco's Ferry Building in 2003. This addition to San Francisco's culture is situated at the doorstep of the Golden Gate Ferry Terminal. Petrocelli often takes the ferry between stores and, of course, spends the journey reading.

Book Passage, which she runs with husband Bill (a Marin attorney turned booksmith), is far more than a storehouse for books. It is an exciting intersection of writing conferences, plentifully attended classes, children's events, cafe scholar roundtable sessions, emerging and celebrity author presentations, and a gathering place for friends, families, book club members and blind dates. Overshadowed to the west under the austere gaze of Mt. Tamalpais—The County's ultimate muse—Book Passage does, indeed, take on the magical aura of an Olympian forum of people, ideas and civic discourse.

When Petrocelli had to take time off from her life's passion following a heart attack in Year 2000, she accepted her dear friend and San Rafael resident Isabel Allende's gracious offer to help at the store. Petrocelli gives frequent speeches to the community in which she tells the audience about the most interesting new books. While she was recuperating, Allende took over the lectures, introduced authors, and even made cappuccino in the Book Passage Cafe. What other book emporium anywhere can claim an internationally renowned author and activist as a member of its team? (See the profile of Isabel Allende on another page of this book.)

The store is sprinkled regularly with visits and readings by local authors such as Sheldon Seigel, Amy Tan, Judith Greber, Orville Schell, and Anne Lamott. Over 500 authors speak at Book Passage each year. Book Passage has hosted Julia Child, Alice Waters, both Hillary and Bill Clinton, Al and Tipper Gore, and Jimmy Carter.

For inveterate book reader Elaine Petrocelli, this is the zenith of dream jobs. "Every day I wake up," she proclaims from her modest, overcrowded office, "I simply can't wait to get here. Where else would I have met so many fantastic people—authors, customers and employees alike? When I was a young teenager growing up in Indiana, I would take a train to Chicago on Saturday mornings, hang out in art museums, and spend ages selecting one treasure in the nearby bookstores. Then I'd be in heaven reading my new book on the train home. I never told my Mom where I went, but I finally confessed to her when she was 85! But seeing where my adventures led me, she wasn't too upset with me."

Bill Petrocelli, who gave up law and billing time 13 years ago to book time at Book Passage, is the masterful creator of the company newsletter, *Book Passage News and Reviews*, which is chock full of the schedule of literary store events, scheduled classes, author snippets and hot books to watch. The energy and enthusiasm both Petrocellis bring to life literally jump off the pages of the newsletter.

Book Passage has helped put together Left Coast Writers, a literary salon led by author and teacher Linda Watanabe McFerrin. This provides a monthly evening of literary connections, support, counsel, provocative readings, writing tips, literary chat, unabashed networking, and great fun. Each meeting of Left Coast Writers spotlights a presentation by one of several Bay Area literary figures, like authors Tess Uriza Holthe, Gail Tsukiyama, editor Don George, publisher Malcolm Margolin, and literary agent Victoria Shoemaker.

Two popular Book Passage events are the annual Mystery Writers Conference and the Travel Writers & Photographers Conference. Both have been going on for over a decade. The Mystery Writers Conference each year features an outstanding panel of mystery authors, detectives, forensic experts, police and other crime-stopping professionals. The Travel Conference brings together some of the world's most famous writers and photographers for a truly unique four-day event.

In addition to the large conferences, Book Passage features a regular series of ongoing classes almost every day of the year. Many who have taken these classes have gone on to writing careers. In a typical week visiting Book Passage, one may have found a Mary Mackey class on writing family memoirs, an essay writing class with Adair Lara, a class by Marty Nemko on "How-To" writing, a Judy Brown comedy workshop, a class by Joyce McGreevy on gardening books, and a workshop by Dianne Jacon on cookbooks.

Book Passage is an exciting intersection of writing conferences, plentifully attended classes, children's events, cafe scholar roundtable sessions, emerging and celebrity author presentations, and a gathering place for friends, families, book club members and blind dates.

Book Passage is almost like a modern-day Grecian forum—the great gathering place of common folk who are compelled by love of knowledge, a thirst for dialogue, a hunger for interaction, and a raw passion for the written word.

Elaine Petrocelli laughs aloud at the similarity to an educational institution—"My kids refer to me as the President of Book Passage University, but the standing joke is that BPU is a short-version Latin phrase meaning 'We are not accredited.'"

Speaking of the children, Petrocelli is thrilled that they all turned out to be voracious readers and writers. Grant's interviews with visiting authors can be found on the store Web site, *bookpassage.com*; Nicole is a pharmacist for Genentech; Kathryn is the Book Passage Marketing Director; and Michael is a journalist.

Elaine and Bill Petrocelli make an invaluable, indelible and ongoing contribution to the literary, cultural and social life of Marin County, a legacy that simply (and, come to think of it, ironically) cannot be measured by mere words.

Michael Pritchard

On the day I interviewed Michael Pritchard, he came to my office high above the streets of San Francisco. It was noon, so we joined the lunchtime stampede of city workers fleeing the highrise. It was like a downward vertical standup comic routine, if you'll pardon the dizzying triple directional.

The elevator door opened about every third floor. Just watching the initial looks of awe and amazement as people boarded was entertainment enough. Michael has this presence. The man is as big as a house, so he doesn't ride elevators. He *wears* them.

It was like a 34-floor vertical-drop monologue, Michael spinning one-liners, quippy quotes and hushed intimacies to each and every passenger. Normally, business people in the Financial District are not a cheery bunch on their way to lunch. When the elevator door opened after what felt like an eternity of guffaws, chuckles, ripostes, puns, and major yuks, the passengers exited howling like banshees. The man knows how to stir a room, even if it's the size of a cracker box.

There are many things that are impressive about Marinite Michael Pritchard—his girth, his merriment, his eloquence, his astonishing memorization of perfectly timed quotations, his open-hearted spirituality, his loyalty for his wife and family, his compassion for people in pain, and his riotous sense of humor that acts as a great big balm salving souls who suffer from the mere act of being alive.

But *the* most impressive thing about Michael Pritchard has to be the fact that he has forsaken a sure-thing Hollywood career for a loftier calling of tending to the gashing-wound psyches of teens in trouble. Instead of wasting his deliciously profound sense of humor on a mind-numbing sitcom or jived-up reality show or a seat on "Hollywood Squares," Pritchard toils in the fields of the young, bringing hope to desperation, light to cynicism.

Drawing upon his years as a youth probation officer and reaching deep into the pools of his mansion-sized heart, Pritchard tirelessly attends and addresses school assemblies, youth conferences, drug/alcohol seminars, and PBS programs. His message is simple—you, a troubled teen, *matter*. You need to cull strength from chaos, you need to reach into your soul and trust who you are, you need to make choices that enhance individuality and shun depravity, and you need to let God work His wondrous ways in your life.

He disarmed occupants of the San Francisco elevator the day of the interview by looking around the stress-dripping box and saying out loud to everyone in particular: "No matter how rich you become, how famous or powerful—when you die, the size of your funeral will still pretty much depend on the weather."

There is some method to this exquisite madness—he is a very well organized professional whose umbrella "company" (for lack of a better term) is Heartland Media Foundation, an entity dedicated to the promotion of youth development, focusing on building character, resiliency, emotional intelligence and leadership skills. With Pritchard as its centerpiece star, Heartland Media Foundation works hard to prevent youth violence and to foster safe school environments.

Rarely has there been a personage who so fearlessly and openly and bravely just walks around spouting light and humor and excellence.

A strong family man, Michael has been married to Mary Jo Pritchard for 25 years. The couple's children are Connor, 22, a Loyola graduate; Brian, 19, a Psychology major at Chico State; and Katy, a Marin high schooler. Mary Jo is an author, playwright, and director. Her most recent production is "Trailer Town."

While encountering Michael Pritchard in the flesh packs a jolt for anyone wishing to make life changes, the comic/probation officer also offers an extensive packet of educational videos on conflict resolution, teen violence, inciting emotional awareness, and inspiring courageous leadership in the young. His comedic skills have earned him appearances with Robin Williams, Jerry Seinfeld, Whoopi Goldberg, and Dana Carvey; and he has been the opening act for performers like the Grateful Dead, Boz Scaggs and Diana Ross—but he has steadfastly resisted Hollywood's many advances to trade in a socially redeeming lifestyle for a financially more rewarding career as a star.

Perhaps because of the overloaded elevator, the lift lurches between two of the lower floors. There is an audible gasp among the passengers. Michael drones on undeterred—"Fear is that little darkroom where negatives are developed." The man is relentless. Only a guy of his depth and stature could make an elevator full of staid business types turn into a standing ovation.

Shelby Ratto

People who voice their worry and concern about the young generation being composed of slackers and cynics haven't met Shelby Ratto of Marin.

If an optimist gives energy to aspirations, then she will be a success at anything she chooses in life. To date, her goals have turned out swimmingly, and success has a way of multiplying itself.

Born at Marin General Hospital and a resident of San Rafael, Shelby (now 22) attended Marin Catholic High School in Kentfield, a place that warms her memory—"I absolutely loved Marin Catholic," she smiles. "It was a perfect microcosm of Marin, with students coming from all over The County. I was fortunate enough to be student body president and even more fortunate to have been able to work on youth projects with comic Michael Pritchard, who is such an amazing role model for young people.

"I went to school with Michael's son. He and his wife Mary Jo are like family to me. I used to call on him for help with school activities. He would speak at school functions and conferences. He was a mentor to me.

"People can do anything they want if they have the right tools and are given the right sort of leadership. And, to me, leadership is as simple as one person doing something and others following. I really like doing things that make other people's situations better. People, especially my age, are so eager for something new these days, and they are looking hungrily for true leaders."

After Marin Catholic, Ratto attended Gonzaga University in Spokane, another zenith educational experience in her quiver of academia—"Gonzaga is a wonderful school and Spokane is a great place," she raves. "I like the Jesuit ethics and their mantra, which is 'educate the whole person.' I also chose it because it has a first-rate business school, and I have always believed if you are truly going to make a difference in this life, it is essential to be grounded in a solid business background.

"I really admired the president, Father Spitzer, who is legally blind but has the vision to put Gonzaga in the vanguard of progressive education—there is a broad liberal arts program which has heavy emphasis on rhetoric and writing, and the student gets deeply immersed in critical thinking and learning how to form opinions and convictions for oneself. I was also super-involved with campus issues—bigtime."

She also liked the fact that Gonzaga was a visibly active entity in the community of Spokane. Made up of a hard-working populace, the mostly warehouse, blue-collar city was an ideal spawning ground for someone of Ratto's working-class organizing ethos. She says she came to care for the people in her school's community, she developed strong bonds with both the mayor and the city manager, and, once again, she sharpened her leadership skills on youth-oriented projects.

One week after college graduation, Ratto took a job working in advertising for a marketing company in Seattle—a high-tech business with mostly young people who sell advertising to clients all over the globe. Clients are in travel, television networks, and online retail.

"I am not getting rich," she laughs, "but I am learning a lot. It's a young firm with a young CEO, the kind of IT startup you hear a lot about. It's very exciting to be able to work with so many other young people, and there's no doubt in my mind this is going to lead me somewhere."

Ratto ascribes much of her rosy outlook on life to the influence of her parents: "My father was the oldest of 11 children, so you could say he was a naturally born leader, and my mother, the oldest of three, shares his strong feelings about being a positive role model for siblings. The most important feeling that came with me from their loving parenting was, very simply, that with hard work and a sense of purpose I could do anything."

Her attitude and spark give substance to that "sky's the limit" belief—she is both bubbly and realistic, dreamy and pragmatic, passionate yet fundamentally sound, gung-ho but thoughtfully precise about her words and expressions.

She is also empathetic about her peers—"There is a lot of pressure on kids in Marin schools because the bar has been set pretty high. Kids know they have to succeed in order to get a good career and own a home. I support my friends by seeing with them that the so-called 'pressures' of Marin can actually be motivation and fuel that serve as an active, posiitve force rather than an obstacle. It makes me feel better when I become an example more by my action than by my words."

"People, especially my age, are so eager for something new these days, and they are looking hungrily for true leaders."

The only downside of this sparkling young leader's boundless potential is that her current absenteeism is clearly Marin's loss.

"I absolutely miss Marin so much," she says of her current geographic status. "The pace in Marin and the Bay Area is so much faster than in the Pacific Northwest. The talent level in Marin is so broad and sophisticated, so inspiring and creative. I don't know what I will do when I come back, but I will probably be there soon. I'm dying to get involved in things, and I'd like to run for San Rafael City Council.

"To me, politics is about getting other people excited about what can be done. It's about pointing out the possibilities, bringing a few people to the political fold who are positive and hopeful.

"The best thing we can do as a nation is to be optimistic, not in a blind way, but in a way that welcomes diversity and critical thinking. Times are very tough right now, but who knows what the future brings? There's always room for change, and I am a firm believer that change begins at the local, grassroots level."

There is something so crystal-clear and energetically doable about her words that one can't help but wish Shelby Ratto anything but the very best Marin County—and the world—has to offer this essentially very giving person.

"My long-term goals," she concludes, "are to live in Marin, get involved in the community, and raise a family. There is really no place anywhere more beautiful than Marin County. I really feel now there is a plan for me, and it will all start as soon as I can get back to Marin."

Herb and Debbie Rowland

The next time you are driving north on Highway 101 toward Novato, just past the Hamilton exit, look west toward the sloping foothills, and you will espy a scene that is vintage California—the sight of a white farmland estate surrounded by acres of fine grapes, tall trees, and a dignified, gated entrance marking the place as something very special.

Special, indeed—this is the locale of one of Marin's best wineries, Pacheco, which also happens to be situated in the oldest Mexican land grant in the State of California, established in 1842, a good seven years before the fabled Gold Rush put California on the map forever.

According to Carla Ehat Kent, who interviewed Herb Rowland Sr. in 1975 for the Oral History Project of the Marin County Free Library, the Pacheco estate, situated on a 70-plus acre parcel of the original 6,659-acre Pacheco grant, was first titled "Rancho de San Jose." This grant was given to Ignacio Pacheco by a grateful Mexican governor, Juan Alvarado, in 1840 as a reward for Pacheco's military and civilian services to the Mexican government.

Herb Jr. and Debbie Rowland, current inhabitants of the mansion and co-owners of the winery that bears its name, met at U.C. Davis in 1970. The ranch has been owned by Herb's family since its inception—his grandmother is Abigail Telesfora Pacheco (known to family and friends as Gail).

"She ran off with a gringo," laughs Rowland, "and that's how the Rowlands got into the Pacheco picture. Ignacio Pacheco, for whom our little Novato town of Ignacio is named, lived at the ranch in 1878 when his son built the home, and he installed indoor plumbing, making it the first-ever Marin home with such a modern amenity."

The land-conscious family, according to Herb Sr.'s memoirs, "did a wonderful job hanging on to the estate through a lot of difficult times. One of the things we are proud of is that this is one of the very few land grants where an original grantee, or one of the grantee's descendants, is still in residence."

"We want to keep the ranch the way it has always been," says Herb, "well-groomed, productive, stately and homey. We want visitors to feel welcome, and we want to keep the grape-growing tradition productive and successful."

"We are one of the first wineries in Marin to be estate bottled," says Debbie Rowland. "We sell bottled wine on the premises, but by appointment only. Otherwise, you can find our product in local restaurants and wine shops.

"The winery is family operated, with a total of 10 people involved. We do virtually all the work ourselves. In the spring there is disbudding to do, which is labor-intensive, so we do hire some people for that. Spring and summer, we do vine maintenance and replacement. After about 30 years, some vines need replacement. Summer is the growing season and fall is harvest. After harvest in the fall is the fermentation and actual wine-making. It takes about 18 months to two years before the wine ends up in the store. Wine marking is an art. It's part chemistry and part vineyard management, but it all starts with the grapes.

"We want to keep the ranch the way it has always been—well-groomed, productive, stately and homey. We want visitors to feel welcome, and we want to keep the grape-growing tradition productive and successful."

"I do the day-to-day operations of the winery," says Deb Rowland. "Aside from that, I sit on the board of Novato Community Hospital. The day-to-day operations at the ranch include sales and bookkeeping. We produce about 500 to 800 cases of Cabernet Sauvignon annually, depending on weather and other factors.

"When Pacheco Vineyards started in 1970, my father-in-law did a lot of research. He went to the Hamilton Air Force Base and got all their records on weather. The first planting at the ranch was in 1970, then 1973 and 1983. But old photos show that there were some vines growing back at the ranch at the turn of the century.

"Our kids are quite involved in the winery. Both of our kids are at Cal Poly at San Luis Obispo. Our daughter is 22 and is majoring in Ag Business and Wine Marketing, and our son is 21 and studying viticulture. They are heavily involved in the ranch. It's nice to have the kids digging in and helping. We harvest all the grapes in one day in the late summer. I hope the kids end up taking the place over."

Richard Rubin

Richard Alan Rubin may very well be the most actively engaged and visibly omnipresent non-elected official in the history of Marin—*sort of*: he was recently elected to (with no opponent) and chairs the Strawberry Recreation District.

Back in the '70s and '80s, he wanted to be an elected member of the Board of Supervisors in the worst way (pun unintentional). But the man he took on twice was a looming legend of electoral politics in The County, one Gary Giacomini. Rubin was twice defeated.

Trained as a lawyer and known to be a fighter for causes he believes in rather than reflective, Rubin nonetheless withdrew a bit into himself, taking a sabbatical from the public forum of verbal blows.

"I got out of mainstream politics," he says, "and concentrated on building my business. I had taught a government affairs and management/consumer marketing course at Golden Gate University and Berkeley. I was a regular contributor to the *Chronicle* and *Examiner* Op-Ed pages, and these helped my government relations business come together nicely. Richard Rubin & Associates is nearing its second decade, and we have a steady stable of clients who, fortunately, have remained faithful.

"The way I describe my business is that I develop relationships in the public/private sectors, creating interaction between them. In other words, I assist private companies get public contracts.

"It's basically public policy management. I am a problem solver, and I help companies get what they want. It's very eclectic work, and I deal with everyone from architectural to environmental, from engineering professionals to non-profits and beyond."

Politics has always been a burning passion for Rubin although, he says, "I now refer to politics as the development of public policy—it's what I do best. In dealing with complex issues, I work very hard to point out the myriad ways of approaching problems and solving them. I was elected a couple of years ago, for example, to the state executive board of Local Agency Formation Commissions (LAFCO)"—(Rubin was the first-ever member from Marin)—"which is a powerful yet little known state agency governing municipal services, local boundary reorganizations, fiscal controls, the whole litany of governmental issues and programs.

"One of my toughest assignments was to organize and chair the annual statewide CALAFCO Conference of 700 people in Santa Barbara, a vast cross-section of governmental types brought together to discuss and resolve an entire cornucopia of complex issues.

"My service in government, through LAFCO and other state and county boards, has cultivated many wonderful friendships. To me, nothing—not victory for a client, not even the Niners winning a Super Bowl, *nothing*—replaces lasting friendships. It is a richly rewarding feeling to know that I can call someone in San Bernardino, Fresno, or Los Angeles, and know that person will take my call, and we can exchange stories about old struggles. It's what drives me."

The other, most important drive in Rubin's life are his five daughters—twins Lynsey and Alexis and their sister Pilar from one union, and twins Jennifer and Ashley from a second union.

"What makes me happiest in life is watching my girls grow up in a healthy fashion and pursuing their dreams. Watching their growth really pleases me; nothing is more satisfying than seeing your kids progressing.

"One of my older twins, a psychologist, has just married her high school sweetheart, a newly-minted Stanford-trained physician; twin number two has mastered Sanskrit and is studying Eastern cultures. My daughter Pilar, like me, is a graduate of Kenyon College in Ohio, which makes me especially proud. She's decided to go to medical school and will follow in her grandfather's footsteps. The younger twins, both bright and athletic, will be entering junior high. All five have blessed me enormously."

Rubin just retired as Chair of the Kenyon Fund which broke records during his tenure, and was given the "Gregg Cup" for his efforts—the college's highest award for Distinguished Service by an Alumnus. An earlier winner was Paul Newman. "Gregg now gets to sit on my office desk for one year," says Rubin, "and he seems quite content in the Bay Area.

"Some would call all this activity over-extension," says Rubin. "I call it being involved in the life of one's community. Politics is all about community participation, and in its most noble sense, politics is public service. I feel deeply that you have to give something back in this lifetime. If you don't, you're simply taking up space. You're here, but not really actively present.

"Gratification for me is to see a girl whom you've tutored and mentored and supported graduate from a girls' chorus after you've helped her with a scholarship; to see a classroom built which without your help would not have been constructed—all sorts of community-oriented accomplishments which I find enormously satisfying."

"In dealing with complex issues, I work very hard to point out the myriad ways of approaching problems and solving them."

Rubin's next ambition is to continue his "off-and-on" work on a book he is writing as to why representative democracy has failed America; why American voters feel so alienated; why the right kinds of candidates are not being drawn to run for elected office; and why our voter turnouts seldom register more than 40 percent when so many other democratic nations produce 95 percent voter turnout rates.

"As de Tocquevile once wrote," muses Rubin, "mediocrity rises to the top, and American politics has become a melting pot of mediocrity. My personal political hero is Harry Truman—and, by the way, he was not elected to anything until he was in his 50s!—and it troubles me that politics and government have not attracted such well-defined, no-nonsense citizens as Harry Truman."

At this writing, Rubin is a fully engaged candidate for the Marin Municipal Water District Board of Directors, and, if he wins, there will definitely be no drought or shortage of rhetoric and spirited debate.

Like many men who put their professional careers at stake with frequent forays into public service, Rubin has a strong woman behind him—his wife, Marcia Smolens, a widely respected Bay Area lobbyist with a powerhouse list of clients. Smolens has seen City Hall under five different Mayors. Her firm repeatedly makes the list as the number one in The City.

"She is a formidable person by anyone's measure," Rubin says of his wife, "and you can quote me on that."

Spoken like a career politician.

Tom Ryshke

The remarkable thing about Tom Ryshke (pronounced "Rish-ky," as in "whiskey") is not that he is probably Marin County's longest-tenured bartender at 38 consecutive years being a mixologist, but that he has spent nearly the past 20 years doing so stone cold sober.

If you were a quip-seeking barkeep, you might say this is Ryshke Business, but, then again, maybe you should leave the quips to the barman.

Tom is somewhat blasé about his sobriety.

"I have been sober for two decades. It doesn't bother me to serve alcohol or be around booze. I keep an eye on people when they are drinking to make sure they don't get too far ahead of the game. I use a civil, gentle approach with people who are getting inebriated. I will come around the bar and tap them on the shoulder and ask to speak to them. Then, I will put my arm around them and start talking in a friendly way while I walk them slowly to the door.

"I will tell them that they have reached a point in their drinking that is not good and that they probably realize it more than I do. It usually works. I speak to them quietly and privately so no one else hears."

It *does* work, and it is probably Tom's greatest skill as a bartender—because he has been on the other side of the slab himself and has some regrets about his own past behavior, he doesn't judge drinkers harshly or humiliate them in front of others. His track record at 86'ing people firmly yet kindly is astonishing.

While he can speak with virtually anyone on any subject under the sun—a huge asset for someone who pours drinks for a living—Tom is also a very introspective, somewhat shy, self-reflecting man who is a voracious reader of books and a *bona fide* movie buff. A native of

Milwaukee, Tom settled in Marin in 1966. He met his wife, June, in 1969, and in 1971 the couple was married at the romantic Highlands Inn in Carmel on Christmas Day.

June Ryshke is a native San Franciscan who graduated from George Washington High School in The City. Tom has no children, but June has two daughters from a previous marriage—Pam, who lives in Marin, and Lynda of Colorado Springs.

Tom spent the past 17 years tending bar at what was once Ristorante Dalecio in Ignacio and at its successor, Ristorante Orsi. Tom was a fixture at both places until Orsi shut down for good on July 18, 2004. His previous stints around Marin are literally too numerous to mention, but his most glittering stretch as a a barkeep was a 12-year run at the glorious Alta Mira Hotel in Sausalito, rendezvous-cozy haven for movie stars, nefarious authors like Hunter S. Thompson, and occasional venue for such culture-bending film shoots as "Behind the Green Door," starring Marilyn Chambers, once famous for selling Ivory Snow on TV.

He says that Hunter S. Thompson, who used to stay at the hotel while penning books like "Fear and Loathing in Las Vegas" and his wildly gripping political articles for *Rolling Stone* magazine, was a truly colossal drinker.

"People think that his alcohol tales are fanciful and exaggerated," says Tom. "I can tell you they are dead-on true. He used to drink entire bottles of Green Chartreuse at one sitting while gazing at San Francisco Bay from the hotel bar. *Nobody* drinks Green Chartreuse."

Tom loved the Alta Mira because he got to know a lot of celebrities who stayed there—Broderick Crawford, John Forsythe, Ed McMahon, Sterling Hayden, Vic Damone.

"One of the highlights of my career was chatting with Jack Lemmon," Tom recalls. "His wife had slipped into the restroom, so I thanked him for all the great movies he had been in, especially my favorite Lemmon role in 'Save the Tiger.' A year or so later, I was watching Lemmon in a TV interview, and the interviewer asked him about autograph hounds and others who bother celebrities when they are recognized in public.

"Much to my shock and glee, Lemmon recounted my meeting him and genuinely thanking him for the good he had brought to me and my wife. I was completely bowled over that someone like him would remember our conversation."

Another favorite Alta Mira story of Tom's ranks as Only in Sausalito. A couple from Los Angeles was having drinks at the bar prior to dinner. When they went to their room to dress for the evening, they discovered the suite had been ransacked, but the only item stolen was the formal outfit the woman was planning on wearing that night—pantyhose, shoes and evening dress.

The police were called in to investigate, and soon apprehended the male thief strolling saucily down Bridgeway, Sausalito's main drag. He was wearing the entire outfit while staring lasciviously at himself in store windows. Said the transvestite of his transgression—"I looked so good walking down Bridgeway."

While he can speak with virtually anyone on any subject under the sun, Tom is also a very introspective, somewhat shy, self-reflecting man who is a voracious reader of books and a bona fide movie buff.

Some of the keys to Tom's success as a man of the planks—and, more importantly, as a person—are that he has kept his mind razor sharp through years of avid reading and movie-going; he has maintained a kind of innocently boyish curiosity and wonder about people and life; and he has adamantly refused to take himself seriously.

Though he is constantly exposed to the perils of alcoholism and the wreckage wreaked by those who have abused the drug, Tom is not one to preach or condemn others.

"I am one of the lucky people," he confesses, "who reached a point in my drinking where I had no choice but to stop. But I know how insidious and vexing the problem can be. Unfortunately, when you tell a problem drinker he or she needs to stop, your words usually make them drink with even more vengeance. Change has to come from within, and sadly, many people don't get the message soon enough.

"I regularly read the works of Charles Bukowski, a notorious street drunk upon whose life the movie 'Barfly' was based. If I ever get a craving for booze, his debauchery-soaked words soon set me straight.

"Right now, my drug of choice is Haagen-Dazs," he laughs.

Margaret Sabin

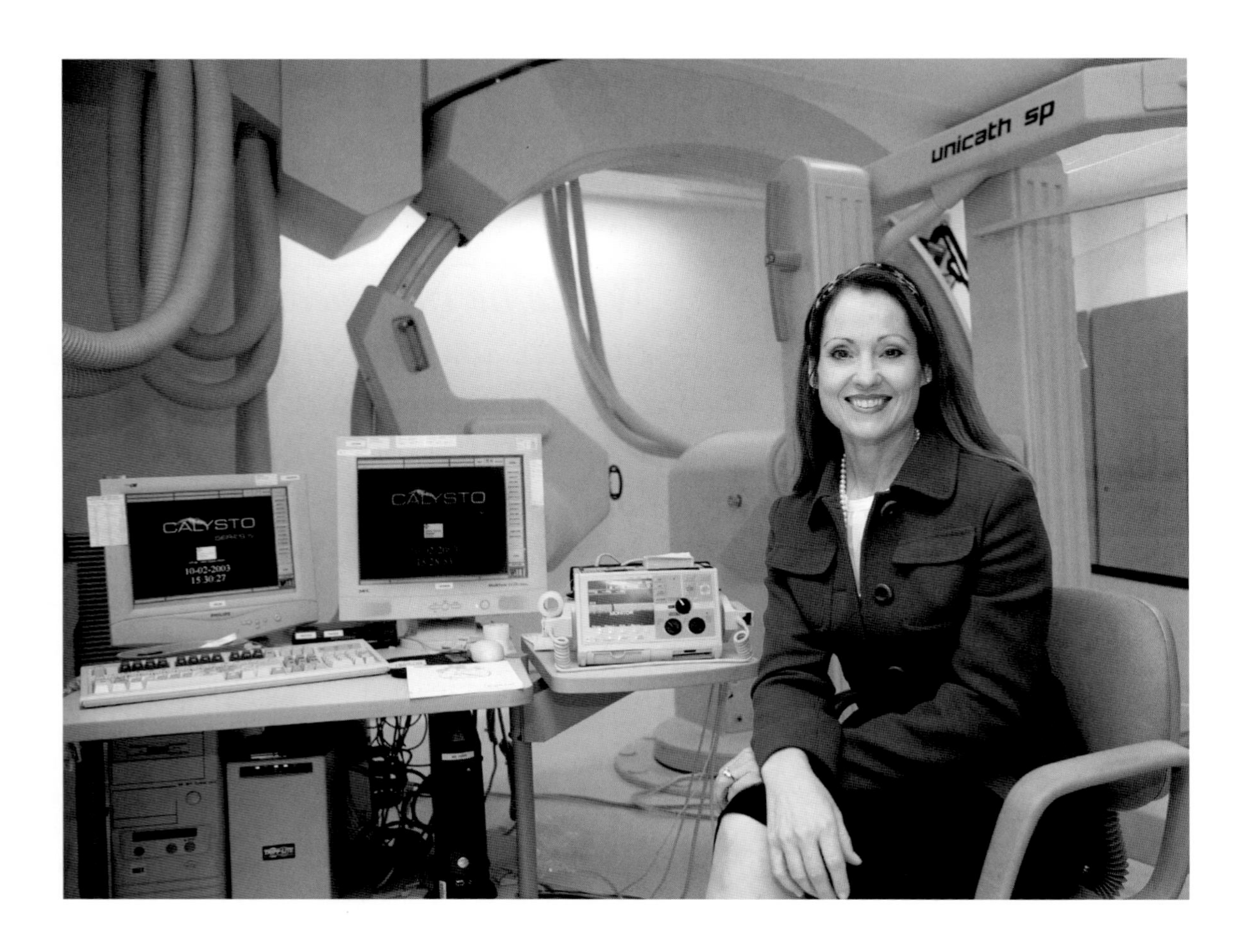

The first thing one notices about the CEO of Marin Community Health is that she is anything but a stereotype CEO.

Margaret Sabin is eminently approachable and open-minded—and very strong. Yet, she exudes a kind of tangibly free spirit that seems definitely at odds with your typical Chief Executive Officer.

She's passionate about what she does—and that's providing quality patient care to the Marin community. She can be tough when the occasion calls for it and can laugh during a silly moment in crisis.

But at the end of the day (and her days usually extend late into the evenings), she knows where she's going and has a plan on how to get there.

For the past three and a half years she has been CEO of Marin Community Health, which includes both Marin General Hospital and Novato Community Hospital, affiliates of the Sutter Health Network. Prior to her appointment in 2001, Sabin had been CEO of the Steamboat Springs, Colorado Health Care Association. Margaret, her geologist husband Andrew Sabin and their four children, ranging in age from 5 to 22, have lived in Marin for three years.

They had spent the previous 12 years in Colorado, not a bad place itself for scenic attributes, but Margaret Sabin still refers to Marin's beauty as "incomparable."

In a hospital district long beset by "medical politics," Sabin is a breath of fresh air.

"I have devoted my entire life to health care," she says, "and I am passionate about wellness. There will always be a small handful of people who would like to turn medicine into a political venue, but I just keep asking the question, 'Does this serve the ultimate best interests of the community?'

"The answer is usually no."

A graduate of Villanova University in Pennsylvania and George Washington University in D.C., Sabin has lectured extensively on the subject of managed care and has authored and co-authored several chapters on reimbursement in ambulatory and emergency settings in books published by the American Hospital Association and the American College of Emergency Physicians.

"I come from a big family in Accokeek, Maryland—four brothers and two sisters—and my father died at what I think is a relatively young age, 72, by today's standards. Because of that and because I am so motivated by my four children, I am ironclad committed to both wellness and exercise. I've been at it for 24 years, but there has never been a better climate than now to get individuals involved in taking responsibility for their own optimum health care."

As overseer of both Marin General and Novato Community, Sabin is responsible for a combined budget of over $270 million a year. It's a very tricky dance in today's super-complex medical world to keep budgetary matters balanced while first of all caring for patients and keeping doctors, nurses and staff happy, as well. Health care costs are skyrocketing, employers are justifiably concerned about their premiums, and quality doctors need to be drawn to the hospitals.

"Enhanced patient care," she says "has been my goal since Day One in 2001. We all work hard, we are extremely proud of what we do, and we are absolutely determined to show the community—from Northern Marin to Southern Marin—that we are an excellent health care system."

One of her first executive acts was to upgrade the Marin General Emergency Department, overseeing a $300,000 remodeling project that has modernized the unit. She also instituted a committee called Employees in Power, a group made up of non-managers who meet regularly to measure employee morale and to come up with ways to improve it.

"Marin General Hospital and Novato Community Hospital are significant assets to the community," adds Sabin, "and our employees are our army. Addressing employee needs is important to allow us to continue building the kind of hospital that really meets community needs. We want to raise the bar and make Marin Community Health a national leader."

A lot of buzz during the past few years has been swirling around the new-version Novato Community Hospital, a bright, sparkling, fully modern addition to the landscape alongside Highway 101 in Novato. Costing $38 million, the new facility is a glittering testament to health care in Marin.

It's loaded with high-tech state-of-the-art equipment and services, including a new scanner that can more accurately detect cancer, heart disease and neurological disorders in their earliest stages. One of the things that Sabin likes to point out that makes this spirit-enhancing architectural gem such a special place is its Healing Healthcare philosophy: "Novato Community Hospital is rated by patients in satisfaction surveys. They characterize our care as competent, compassionate, and delivered in a way that conveys dignity and respect for their values. Patients rate our staff particularly high on Healing Healthcare attributes: warmth and caring shown to patients and their families, sensitivity and responsiveness, the ability to listen, and the inclusion of patients and family in care decisions."

"I never forget that my profession is first and foremost about people. In that regard, it is truly a sacred profession."

As non-profits, both hospitals help the community in many ways. In 2003, Novato Community Hospital and Marin General provided more than $39 million in support of 150 community programs that directly benefited 118,000 local residents, primarily children and youth, the elderly, the homeless and disabled. The majority of this money represents the difference between the hospitals' costs of providing certain public programs, such as Medicare and Medi-Cal, and the amount the government reimburses them for these programs.

And, Novato Community in conjunction with Marin General has successfully raised over $2 million to improve breast health screening in Marin, a locale that has gained national notoriety for its uniquely alarming high incidence of breast cancer.

It is an ideal challenge for someone like Sabin, who says, "I never forget that my profession is first and foremost about people. In that regard, it is truly a sacred profession."

Toby Scammell

USC Head Football Coach and Greenbrae native Pete Carroll, whose 2003 Rose Bowl-winning Trojan squad is the number one team in America in 2004, may be the most famous Marinite associated with that college, but there is another, much younger Marin man who's causing academic heads to turn in his direction.

He is Toby Scammell, an infinitely confident and seemingly self-assured product of local schooling, whose ambitious business sense has already created controversy and raised collective eyebrows.

A sophomore who majors in International Relations (and whose stoic, unblinking eye on policy matters conjures instant images of Henry Kissinger), Scammell launched a Web site last summer called *TerrorPlaybook.com*, which has a much more ominous sound than Pete Carroll's playbook for Trojan team defense.

Controversy and eyebrow-raising stem from the fact, obviously, that his Internet service offers subscriptions to people seeking information on which companies would be alternately helped or hindered by impending acts of terrorism. So serious was his own concern for both appropriateness and safety that he decided to contact the local FBI office in San Rafael prior to the site's launch.

The Feds gave him clearance, but the fight for positive public relations is something he may never fully surmount. As he explained to the *Marin IJ* in a story detailing the young man's vision: "We're living in a new era, where terrorism is just another scenario that you have to account for. To ignore it is doing yourself a disservice," he concluded, citing figures indicating that, in the wake of the 9/11 terrorist attacks on America, the NASDAQ dropped more than 16 percent and the Dow dipped 14 percent.

The Australian-born 19-year-old came to Marin in 1991 at the age of six. He attended Neil Cummins School in Larkspur, Kent Middle School, then Redwood High. He and his two brothers have vivid recollections of lively dinner conversations around the family table—their father was in international business, so there were some intellectual challenges to be met before the gravy was dished.

"I got involved in community issues through school," he explains, "because I wanted to get some leadership experience. I was never into drugs or alcohol. I used my personal experiences to talk to many younger kids. Plus, I did a lot of public speaking. It was all a very positive experience."

So how did he get motivated to create the controversial Web site?

"I've always had an interest in investments," he says. "I've been investing for about four or five years, and my main interest has been security issues. I started another Web site a few years ago, and then I launched *TerrorPlaybook.com* because I did my research and found that nobody had come up with a list of companies that might be affected by terrorism in one way or another.

"There are 300 to 400 companies listed in my report. I sell subscriptions to the report online, where customers can securely access the files. It's mostly small money managers that have been signing on. I've had some negative response to the company since a story on me came out in the news. Some people said 'You are profiting from terror,' but other people who e-mailed me said 'Terror is not going away any time soon.'

"*TerrorPlaybook.com*," Scammell continues, "is a part of Scammell Enterprises, which is a sole proprietorship that I created. *TerrorPlaybook.com* has made some money for me since I launched it, but there are some costs involved, like $500 for press releases and costs like that. But it is a learning experience."

If and when an actual terror attack occurs, Scammell says his service will be capable of producing immediate and useful information for subscribers who have shelled out $180 for a full year's subscription.

"I don't think there is any other service that's available to the public like ours," he surmised to the newspaper. "Our whole goal is to allow people to prepare for and react to the next terrorist attack."

Scammell says he is urgently concerned about being misunderstood, explaining that we, especially in the Bay Area, are surrounded by companies and corporations whose bio-tech-oriented output could be used as weaponry upon the very people such technology is designed to serve.

Whether his work is providing a service or capitalizing blasphemously from a profoundly disturbing worldwide situation remains to be seen, but there is no doubting the kid has brass. All of us have done things in our youth that made perfect sense at the time, even though others may not have understood or accepted our actions. The surest test of a person's decisions are played out in the aging wine cellar of time. Scammell's decision is a bold one, it will be debated and processed, and someday only he will be able to say whether it was wise or foolhardy.

"We're living in a new era, where terrorism is just another scenario that you have to account for. To ignore it is doing yourself a disservice."

In the meantime, the student says of Marin: "I'm in my sophomore year at USC, so I'm not coming back to Marin in the near future, but I'm not closing any doors, either. Marin is a great place, very safe with a good educational system, and people have some respect for each other, compared to USC, where there is so much crime and so many gangs. Maybe the down side of Marin is that there are a lot of very privileged people there, and some older people who might have a chip on their shoulder who are a bit snobbish towards others. But that kind of thing is unavoidable.

"Right now," he concludes, "I am concentrating on my studies. I want to get top grades, and working so much on my business could have an impact on that. I may do an internship next year in the intelligence field. In the future, I may go to law school. Otherwise, I am just busy being a regular student."

There's no neat way to wrap up a profile like this with a cute ribbon. These are sober, troubling times. Regardless of what you may think of this young man's enterprise, one really sad reality to ponder is that our college kids now have much more on their minds than trying out for Pete Carroll's vaunted defense.

Bob Smoke

Seton Smoke Capital Management is an impressive enough firm located at Drake's Landing in Greenbrae, but what gives it special distinction is the avocation of its President & CEO, Bob Smoke.

He is a pilot who ferries needy children and adults from outlying areas of California and the Northwest to local medical facilities such as UCSF and Stanford Medical Center where they can receive the specialized medical treatment they so desperately need.

Smoke—who grew up on an island in the Great Lakes and came to Marin in 1976—says his life has been so blessed that serving others less fortunate is second nature to him.

"It's not terribly complicated," he says. "We are so blessed here in Marin with the climate, the beauty, the great people, and I have been so fortunate to have succeeded in both family and business matters, that doing something worthwhile for people who don't have the wherewithal is simply a joy.

"The essence of my business is to look out for my clients—I am not in it, obviously, just for myself. So the same philosophy applies to my personal life. The organization is called Angel Flight, and it is a band of 5,000 pilots across the country who give their time and resources to airlift patients suffering from all kinds of maladies.

"I fly indigent people from the East Bay to Seattle, for example, for chemotherapy, or, in other instances, I transport children who have suffered disfiguring burns to special summer camps where they can meet and have fun with other kids who suffer the same hardships."

Angel Flight volunteer pilots pay all the costs of the mercy missions, but the organization seeks funds to support coordination and outreach programs. Most of the pilots fly four-seaters—Smoke flies a Cirrus—and have only their private or instrument licenses. While Angel Flight members come from all walks of life, they are unified in their commitment to combine their love of aviation with a unique way of helping people.

Smoke is a Kentfield resident who with his late wife Suzanne fathered two children—Sabrina, 21, a student at Cal, and Jordan, 16, who is finishing high school. His current wife Ellen, a Wisconsin native, brings two children of her own to the blended family, Alex and Grant.

"I have a wonderful, warm, loving family," says Smoke, "and my good fortune simply gets magnified when I render assistance to people who are having difficulty in life."

Seton Smoke is a solid financial management firm that seeks to be responsive to the needs and concerns of its clients. Foremost in their services to clients is educating them about all aspects of the investment process.

"The key to serving our clients," says Smoke, "is our team of investment professionals. We are an independent investment management firm with no affiliation—and hence, no conflict of interest—whose sole products are sound investment management and financial advice. Our clients always come first."

Smoke pioneered Seton Smoke's investment strategy of making institutional quality investment management available to individuals. Before merging with Seton Capital Management in 1991, Bob had founded Robert D. Smoke & Associates in 1983. He had previously served as an officer at Bank of America's Private Banking Group, and prior to that was in the tax department of a "Big Eight" CPA firm.

Smoke has been a popular speaker for events sponsored by the National Association of Personal Financial Advisors and California CPA Society. His investment opinions have been vigorously solicited by the *Wall Street Journal, San Francisco Chronicle*, and many other investment periodicals.

In a more finely tuned definition of its services, Seton Smoke is a leading provider of comprehensive wealth management for affluent investors. The firm uses a disciplined, institutional level investment process with advanced information resources for each portfolio. The company offers personalized, comprehensive investment management service for individuals, pension and profit-sharing plans, trustees, executors and other fiduciaries, as well as corporations and non-profit organizations.

Seton Smoke, which moved its offices to the Greenbrae location at Drake's Landing at the turn of the century, has seven professionals on staff managing 185 clients with $325 million in assets. Clients are located across America, with largest concentration in California.

But of all his clients, it is clear from talking with Bob Smoke that the ones who are closest to his heart are the needy passengers on his flights of mercy.

"I can't stress enough how enormously gratifying this is," he says. "Just to see the relief and excitement in the eyes of those I transport is payment enough. We walk a fine line, because of course we are not medically trained, and therefore the passengers must be ambulatory and able to sit up in the aircraft for the duration of the flight. We are not an air ambulance service, but the only criterion is that the patient seeking help should have a very clear financial need to benefit from our assistance. Also, obviously, they live in a rural area or are susceptible to infection and cannot be exposed, for example, to crowds at airports."

"I have a wonderful, warm, loving family, and my good fortune simply gets magnified when I render assistance to people who are having difficulty in life."

When he's not flying like an angel through the skies of hope, Smoke is firmly ensconced in his Greenbrae offices, working hard to grow his firm with his able associates—Junior Vice President and Portfolio Manager Jack Scaff III, Junior Vice President Michael Gandy, and all around indispensable Girl Friday Nancy Powers.

Bob Smoke has strong feelings about the vagaries of the economy in shifting times—"The excesses of the 90's," he says, "created a mindset of entitlement. Limo commuting by 25-year-old Wall Street analysts. Five thousand dollar bottles of wine poured to celebrate an acquisition. Million dollar spousal birthday parties. Performance bonuses and unauthorized perks available for the taking.

"Unfortunately, the visible excesses were merely reflections of the vast unseen conflicts of interest that would adversely affect the American public.

"The names of some of the most flagrant abusers of the public trust will be on our lips for some time to come as the criminal prosecutions work their way through the legal systems. Seton Smoke regularly reviews investment alternatives through a variety of screens and always with the best interests of our clients in mind.

"If we learn that a manager or firm that we rely on in the management of our clients' assets has behaved unethically or illegally, rest assured that we will end the relationship promptly if that is in the best interests of our clients."

Lise Sonnen

There was a time in The County when BMW instantly conjured up in people's minds the not-so-flattering term "Basic Marin Wheels." Thanks to high-octane wags like Herb Caen and other purveyors of "Only in Marin" humor, this somewhat spoiled moniker stuck in our collective craw for years, lodging near other malign assignations like hot tubs, peacock feathers, insufferable foodies, and obnoxiously sweet gurus.

Lise Sonnen, owner of Sonnen BMW, laughs off what others might take too seriously. She exudes the manner of someone who doesn't let anything bother her, an inner serenity she ascribes to her essentially spiritual nature.

"My business philosophy and my personal philosophy and my community involvement are basically all one and the same," she states stoically. "My beliefs are purely spiritual. I don't get involved in community issues, for instance, just because community involvement is good for business. I get involved because it's just me, it's the right thing to do, and it makes me feel happy.

"I take great pride in my business and my 100 employees and the community in which I live."

She is a remarkable woman running a remarkably successful business, but the matter-of-fact tones with which she describes her life belie *anything* remarkable. Perhaps there's a success secret in that sort of resigned, serene, accepting attitude. Whatever it is, her life story falls from her lips in staccato-like snippets of fact:

"My parents were divorced, so I grew up with my Grandmother in Copenhagen, Denmark. I got married at 18; I had my first daughter at 19. I graduated from college at 19. I owned a fashion store in Copenhagen at 19, and imported clothes from all over Europe.

"I started a travel agency at 20. I was the first female travel agent chartering planes in all of Scandinavia. I had studied English in Denmark, also Business and a little bit of Law. Then I came to New York for a brief three-week stay, then came to San Francisco.

"I fell instantly in love with this country. You might say I just got stuck here. I stayed six months in San Francisco, then moved to Mill Valley, attended the College of Marin, studied all sorts of crazy things, including more Law and English."

It was during this period in her life that she met Elmer Fliegauf, who had started and owned Mill Valley Imports on Miller Avenue in Mill Valley. Sonnen worked for him until his death of a heart attack in 1981 when, faced now with a bankrupt business and a local population of people "who basically didn't know what a BMW was," she tried to figure out what to do next.

Her first step was to move the dealership to the Strawberry Shopping Center. (Now divorced, it was during this time that she was married to Peter Sonnen.)

"I was the only woman in that business in Marin for a long, long time," she recalls, "so I was extremely determined to make something happen. I worked very hard, expanding the business from six employees in Mill Valley to 45 in Strawberry. When I am faced with a challenge, it simply inspires me to win."

After nurturing the business along to respectable levels for 15 years in Strawberry, Sonnen moved to its current, highly visible site in San Rafael alongside East Francisco Boulevard, were she doubled her employment rolls and tripled her BMW inventory.

Sonnen BMW prides itself on being an Internet-certified dealership, which means that customers can experience the benefits of Internet correspondence—everything from having convenient doorstep delivery to requesting a service appointment when a phone call is not handy.

Quite a remarkable turnaround from the modest Mill Valley days when nobody knew what a BMW was to a time now when BMW actually, albeit jokingly, is the hood ornament logo for an entire county, no?

Sonnen continues to be blasé in both interview and outlook:

"I don't know where I got the will power to succeed," she admits, "but I was always very determined to make it in life, even from an early age. And America is perfect for someone like me—it is truly a country of opportunity. And I love the different combinations of people we have here in the United States, the rich diversity, the tolerance and understanding. Europe is perhaps not so tolerant of newcomers."

Like so many successful Marinites not driven entirely by monetary gain, Sonnen is an ardent believer in returning goodness to the community that supports her business.

"I love the way that people in Marin get so involved in their community," she enthuses. "Personally, I am heavily involved in the community—I am a member of the Mill Valley, San Rafael, Tiburon and Sonoma Chambers of Commerce (former board member of both Mill Valley and San Rafael); I have been a speaker at the Women's Conference twice in both Marin and in Sonoma; I have been the president of Rotary; and I have participated in and contributed to Marin Special Olympics and many other local charities.

"I was the only woman in that business in Marin for a long, long time, so I was extremely determined to make something happen."

"Getting involved in the community gives to me as much as I give to it. Making money is not what's important to me in my business. It's the people, getting involved with people. In Marin, we all pitch in here. There are some exceptionally interesting and talented people in Marin.

"In terms of my business and why they come to me, I can tell you that buyers are all ages and both genders, but you might be surprised to know that a good 40 percent of all my customers now are women. For all buyers, owning a BMW still says 'I have arrived and I knew how to get there fast.' People in Marin are very demanding, and they know what they want in a car, just like they know what they want in life.

"I save a little something special for myself," she adds with a twinkle in her voice. "I have a secret paradise in Sonoma, three acres where I grow wine and where I go on weekends. This is a sacred place for me. I give and give all I can when I am in Marin, but God help the person who bothers me with business when I am in Sonoma."

Sonnen has two daughters, Charlotte Vogt and Susanne Lamelza, and four granddaughters—Sophia, Lilly, Emily and Sarah.

As for changes in Marin, says Sonnen: "There have been so many changes since I moved here. Things are very congested now, of course, but I can honestly tell you Marin has never lost the charm that attracted me here in the first place."

Dick Spotswood

Throughout the information-voracious labyrinth of California government, there is a well-known, widely read daily political junkie journal called "The Capitol Morning Report." It is published Monday through Friday, usually runs about seven or eight pages, and has as its only illustration the mere shadow of a black coffee cup.

Distributed primarily through e-mail subscription, the daily fix—edited and published by a former *Los Angeles Times* Capitol reporter, Bob Fairbanks—"The Capitol Morning Report" is a no-nonsense, meat 'n potatoes sheet that is filled with political gossip, governmental appointments, updates on important legislation, inside dope about lobbyists and their clients and employers, background information about legislative staffers, an occasional profile of someone legendary (or just plain ordinary) in state government, and even a brief listing of condos for rent and homes for sale near the Capitol and in outlying areas.

It is a habit-forming bit of political caffeine, and political insiders, who may not admit it, would be lost without it.

This is a rather long-winded introduction to the profile of a Marin man, Dick Spotswood, who has created his very own version of "The Capitol Morning Report." His political newspaper column, published weekly, is called "North of the Bay," and it is gaining widespread acclaim as a very knowledgeable, politically astute, well-written two-pager that covers politics and politicians in Marin and Napa/Sonoma Counties.

Spiced with fetching dollops of inside lowdown and garnished with expanded profiles of some of the North Bay's more visible and vocal political luminaries, Spotswood provides a fair, objective, balanced and informative look at just what's happening north of the Golden Gate Bridge.

"When I was in college at Cal Poly in San Luis Obispo, I was involved with Young Democrat politics, and that continued when I attended University of San Francisco. I published a newsletter called *Yerba Buena Democratic Club News*. Much to my surprise, it was read by the players in San Francisco, although it didn't really have a big circulation.

"I was introduced to Bill Press (who once served as aide to Marin State Senator Peter Behr and who is now a nationally syndicated TV political commentator), and he was looking for a driver/advance man to work for San Francisco Supervisor and California Democratic State Chairman Roger Boas.

"My first real campaign was working for Pierre Salinger for California U.S. Senate in 1964. (Salinger served President John F. Kennedy as his Press Secretary from 1961-1963.) I was at St. Ignatius High School at the time, and everyone was encouraged to get involved in politics.

"In the early 70's, Joanne and I got married and it looked like my political fortunes were running out in San Francisco. I had run for office as BART Director in The City, but finished third or fourth, which was respectable, but I was a terrible political fund raiser. So I decided to practice law, settle down, raise a family, get out of politics.

"We bought a house in Mill Valley in 1976 and, quite by accident, I became president of the neighborhood association, the West Blithedale Canyon Neighborhood Association. So through that, I met a few people in Mill Valley, some who were City Council members. One of these folks was the legendary Mill Valley political activist Jean Barnard.

"She and the others suggested I run for City Council. I was 33 and got elected, coming in first. Nobody knew me so I didn't have any enemies! I served three terms and also three terms as Mayor of Mill Valley.

"One of the things I am interested in all my life is transportation, especially railroads and trains. I collect train books, I have a model train, and I've traveled everywhere by rail. I was elected to serve as a Director of the Golden Gate Bridge Board. In 1987, during planning for the 50th anniversary of the fabled span, there was a lot of opposition from Marin to having a big party. People were afraid of chaos, they were concerned about safety.

"I expressed a lot of those reservations, especially around rock impresario Bill Graham's plans for a mid-span party. It was an emotionally charged controversy. Of the 15 of the 19 board members present to vote on the celebration, I was the lone dissenting vote. I still get chills recalling how the bridge flattened from the

"Each of the communities in Marin has a distinct personality, which is why it is so much fun to write about The County."

weight of the estimated half million people partying on the day of the 50th bash.

"In 1989 when Loma Prieta struck The City, I was en route to Marin with my parents, so I stopped by the Bridge District offices. General Manager Carney Campion was out of state, the guy next in charge was at the World Series game, so I was left in charge of media queries. One of the issues was whether or not to waive bridge fares following the quake. I made the executive decision to waive those fares, which I still believe was a very good PR move."

Spotswood ran for Congress in 1991 but hated the fundraising aspects of the ambition, so he bailed to create his political journalist dream, hatching his column with the help of old friend Paul Anderson of *Marin Scope* newspapers. His column was featured in all of Anderson's papers, and soon the *Novato Advance* picked it up, as well. His political column now appears in the Sunday *Marin Independent Journal*.

"Each of the communities in Marin has a distinct personality, which is why it is so much fun to write about The County. One of the things I have long advocated is the construction of a light rail line between Sonoma and Marin. I have spent 20 years working on this, but have yet to convince the majority of Marin/Sonoma taxpayers that they should pay for it.

"In real life, I am a lawyer. Joanne, my wife, was a bank vice president but now has her own business, Paper Trail Press, which publishes greeting cards. Our daughter Beth works in theater, and our son Alex wants to be a sports journalist."

And, if "The Capitol Morning Report" ever needs a Marin correspondent, Dick Spotswood can take the train to Sacramento.

Diet Stroeh

Drastic times call for drastic measures; they also call for good people with strong commitment to action.

In 1976-1977, Marin was a parched landscape. The reservoirs were bone dry. The skies were barren. Gardens were dying. People had little water to drink. Bathing, doing the laundry, or washing dishes was on a days-on/days-off basis.

J. Dietrich Stroeh was General Manager of the Marin Municipal Water District. Luckily for Marin, this strong leader with a self-deprecating sense of humor and a hunger for action was at the helm of a district so brutally victimized by a drought of nature that his drastic action resulted in the installation of an enormous, snake-like pipeline on the top deck of the Richmond-San Rafael Bridge that brought water from the East Bay, thereby saving Marin.

"We entertained all sorts of options," recalls Stroeh, "like washing out and cleaning oil tankers to create ships with potable water. Congressman John Burton proposed a Sixth Naval Fleet plan, whereby the fleet would be floated into San Pablo Bay, using its desalination for a water supply. We considered an iceberg that would be towed up from Chile—we had visions of penguins frolicking in Tomales Bay! Burton also floated the notion of loading East Coast train cars with snow to be transported to Marin.

"Then in 1976, the first year of this drought ordeal, we really got serious about trying to figure out what to do.

"I have to admit, we started a very undemocratic approach to rationing in 1976—our mandate to people was don't wash your cars, don't wash down your sidewalks.

"But in 1977, we became more democratic—we figured out how to allocate 46 gallons of water per day per person in the district. But we did it in a way that put the choice with the people, not ordering them from above.

"We began a rationing program; we looked for alternative sources of water. Slowly, people began to realize that we were in deep trouble.

"Rationing became fun—it was like a rallying cry for The County, akin to World War II when people conserved on tin cans, using cigarette packs with aluminum foil, instead.

"In effect, we had 170,000 meter readers who would monitor their use on a daily basis. We held classes on how to read meters. There was a sense of fun and community about this—if you went to someone's house on Friday or Saturday night, you brought your own water out of courtesy. It became a way of life. And the district was working its ass off.

"The question was simple—how much water will we have with no rain? It takes 12,000 acre feet to live the whole year; at this pace, we would run out by September, 1977.

"So—we divided 170,000 district water users, and figured out an even distribution program of 46 gallons per person per day.

"Then we asked—what if everyone uses more than their allotment? The answer was simple—they can't. We would have a strict and enforceable penalty program. And we would also have different levels of use—our customers included scores of restaurants, San Quentin, hospitals, and schools. If customers went over their quota, they would have to pay dearly.

"Penalties were stiff. The worst offenders would eventually go to double rates. We brought it to the board, and the board appointed a top billing officer to work for me—a hearing would be set up to hear each offender's circumstances.

"We had people who came with various complaints and concerns—one guy's neighbor was stealing water by hooking up a hose to the guy's nozzle if he went on vacation. But the overall public relations was more impactful than the few people who may have cheated.

"One guy in Ross had put a check valve in backwards, thereby feeding public water into his well; he received a $20,000 bill.

"Other examples abounded—many people would go to San Francisco to take longer showers or to do their laundry at friends' houses. There was almost a 'Marin Goes Third World' atmosphere all over. There really was a lot of fear about typhoid fever and epidemics. In the end, there was not one known case of anyone getting sick from the drought.

"There were certain patients—people in water therapy with skin disease, for instance—who would get better allotments. People always had the option to appeal their case—this is why it was such a democratic program.

"I remember we got a program going with Chevron, in which we received 4,000 clean barrels from the oil company. We would give them to people who wanted to save water. They were vehicles to collect water.

"We seriously considered desalination, but it was costly and time-consuming—it would take three to five years to build a plant, because bay water from the Delta is the worst kind of water. It simply wasn't feasible, and terribly expensive.

"We began a rationing program; we looked for alternative sources of water. Slowly, people began to realize that we were in deep trouble."

"The thing that got us into all this trouble is that Marin is unique—we rely on lakes and reservoirs; the Russian River as a source was simply too untried. As PR guy and general manager, I discovered that every day was a new press conference.

"Then the memo of understanding I negotiated to get water to Marin via the pipeline was actually done without authorization. Authorizing the materials and the pipeline itself, yes, this was ratified by the board. We built the pipeline in about three months, and pretty soon there was water for everyone. Months later, Marin was almost submerged in record rainfall!

"So that was it—forging a deal with CalTrans for one dollar to use the bridge to place a pipeline for Marin's water; CalTrans wanted the pipeline in a permanent position.

"My opinion about taking the pipeline off the bridge? Totally stupid. Now we are back to Square One. With the pipeline in place, we would have had a permanent lease and a possible water source.

"When I left in 1980, everything had returned to normal and was going just fine. I needed a change, so I resigned from the District to start Stuber-Stroeh (an engineering firm) in Novato."

Stroeh, a longtime member of the Golden Gate Bridge Board and a very effective and highly respected "Marin insider" who says he works best and can accomplish more behind the scenes than in elected office, boasts proudly:

"I have three daughters—Erica (who runs her own day care center), Christina (teaches music and drama at San Rafael and Terra Linda High Schools), and Jody (a singer/entertainer)."

George and Donnalei Sumner

It's a good thing to be George Sumner. This is one cool dude. It's an even better thing to be George and Donnalei Sumner. This is one cool couple.

Talk about a fun life—actively engaged in community-minded, globally-inspired art, fully involved in activities and aspirations of the human spirit, omnipresent and super-available in the county they call home, and, most importantly, dynamically intertwined with each other and their children (George has a son, Sean, 34, and Donnalei has a daughter, Megan, 20). Sweet, fulfilling way to live, is it not?

Trying to describe who they are and what they do is as daunting as trying to describe a kaleidoscope—they are bright, shiny, fascinating, ever-changing, and full of play and light.

Breathlessly, here's a short list. George is a renowned painter. You've seen his famously chartered posters of the Statue of Liberty on the nation's 200th birthday, the Golden Gate Bridge on its 50th jubilee, dolphins kissing in space to bestow honor upon detente and the warming of the Cold War. You've taken rides in his joyously painted Golden Gate Transit buses, the ones with whales surrounding the windows. You may have sipped wine from bottles whose labels are splashed with his signature handiwork. Or you may have greeted him at the annual Sausalito Art Festival where he has held court for nearly 40 years beneath the shade of his booth while he teaches kids about loving the environment and caring for the future.

Years ago, you may have also spotted him gardening in Golden Gate Park, where he toiled as a city worker during the Summer of Love, chasing Janis Joplin with a pitchfork as she cackled her way through the shrubbery like a '60s version of Johnny Appleseed—only the seeds she was spraying around weren't apples.

George's parting tribute to his gardening career was planting the florid 100th anniversary arrangement in front of the Conservatory of Flowers, commissioned as he was to do so by then-Mayor Joseph Alioto, himself a larger-than-life painting.

The engine purring softly and strongly inside the art and heart of George is Donnalei. Easily the more sensible of the two and the one who keeps the divine madness of their chemistry somewhat rooted to Planet Earth, Donnalei grew up in Hawaii where her military Dad had married her Islander native Mom. The couple had Donnalei and her older sister Judi, "a very religious, kind, loving, honest person," says Donnalei, "who, as a lactation consultant, teaches young mothers how to nurse."

Still planted in the backyard of their quietly suburban Marin home is the gazebo where the couple exchanged their wedding vows, and still planted in George's eyes as he sings his wife's praises is that look of love that has never diminished—"She is a tremendous partner as a wife and business manager," he raves, "but she also has so many individual talents unrelated to my work. She's wonderful, absolutely wonderful with children. She does a lot of voiceover work. She used to read for the blind in Hawaii, and is planning to do the same, soon, in California. And now she reads for the Cancer Research Center and for children.

"She still harbors an ambition for us to collaborate on a children's book, with me as illustrator. Of her many roles—chef, bottle washer. sales rep, promoter—it's really her love of kids that is the unifying factor between us, because the bottom line in my art has always been my hope that it inspires children to reach for the stars."

It really is hard to imagine a life that has been more cutting-edge and exciting. George recalls almost offhandedly that he was one of 12 earnest, young, relentlessly progressive-minded idealists who sat at a table one day and came up with the dream of saving whales from ocean pillagers. This group became Greenpeace. One of George's most striking art posters is his tribute to the worldwide organization, a sea-blue rendition of a young whale titled "First Breath."

"If you keep your heart open and your mind young," he says, "good things come your way. Following a simple little lecture we did at a Marin grade school, where Donnalei and I talked about the living organism of the world's oceans, the students not only wrote us thank you notes but also followed through on their own with pitches to Autodesk, which eventually bestowed a grant to create shrimp restoration in the bay. Talk about grass-roots at its finest, eh?"

Chimes in Donnalei with profound simplicity: "George has made a difference with his art just as the children do so through singing, dancing and being good to each other."

Active lobbyists for the environment in both Sacramento and Washington, D.C.—taking vigorous stands against offshore drilling and illegal fishing—the Sumners still find time to retreat to the quietude and ineffable beauty of their beloved Hawaiian tropics, which has served as the inspiration for some of George's most breathtaking pieces of art.

"George has made a difference with his art just as the children do so through singing, dancing and being good to each other."

The couple has befriended countless celebrity and politically powerful personalities. An occasional painting partner is crooner Tony Bennett, and a close friend is former Soviet President Mikhail Gorbachev, whose peace-seeking think-tank in San Francisco's Presidio which bears his name is a close parallel in theory and vision to all that the Sumners hold dear to their hearts.

No life is perfect, of course, and one cross that George has carried for years is the somewhat tediously envious assertions about the commercial success of his art. He has always taken the high road, refusing to engage in any kind of heated debate about artistic purity. He merely shrugs and grins and reminds the listener that if a child's life is moved to heights of inspiration by his work, then that is the only success that means anything to him. Set in that context, artistic argument suddenly and swiftly seems somewhat trivial and downright pathetic.

What George and Donnalei Sumner are all about is celebration of life, painted in bold strokes of jungle parrot hues and splashes, dipped in the rich tones of lifelong friendship with throngs of admirers, and framed in the enduring portraiture of community activism, global awareness and the never-ending, always enchanting search for beauty and truth.

Nadia Tarzi

When speaking with Nadia Tarzi, one can't help but think of Edith Piaf, the "Little Sparrow" of France, who was petite, whose voice was soft, but who sang with boldness, power and passion. Her incredibly vulnerable yet distinctly eloquent phrasing brought identity and understanding of all things French to the rest of the world.

Nadia Tarzi, born in Strasbourg, France (but who has been living in America since 1989), speaks softly but with a powerful message, bringing boldness, power, passion, identity and understanding about her father's country, Afghanistan, to the rest of the world.

Her father, renowned and world-recognized professor of Afghan Archaeology, Zemaryalai Tarzi, taught Nadia how to be truly patriotic and genuinely caring for one's fellow human beings, a trait Nadia continues to practice in today's world that needs much nourishment and nurturing. Not surprisingly, Nadia is a member of the service-oriented San Francisco Rotary Club #2. She also works professionally in Marin as a certified massage therapist (CMT), health educator, and as a professional actress seen last as the lead "Lady" in "Orpheus Descending" at the Actor's Theater of San Francisco.

Her acting reviews were excellent, and, after a five-year break, she is resuming her 13-year career with renewed enthusiasm.

"My father taught me so many things," says Nadia, sparrow-like. "Life is very precious, and I am so grateful for every day I breathe and for every single person I meet. I try very hard to improve other people's lives. There is no doubt in my mind that it is the little things in life that make a difference in the world.

"Giving people—opposed to people who take—get very weary, extremely tired, but we are never going to give up. We have to contend with the cynics of the world, who are afraid of change. But we who give are carriers of light. It is a constant struggle—every time you make life brighter, the cynics rise up to make things dark. But I learned from my father never to give up."

Her father, who still teaches archaeology at Marc Bloch University in Afghanistan, instilled in his daughter such a love of all things Afghan that she took it upon herself, shortly after the catastrophic events of 9/11/01, to stage an "Awareness Event" in Berkeley. Working with associate Arlene Blum, the pair put together an outstanding exhibit that shattered people's myths about the little-known country and showcased its culture, history, and, of course, its archaeology.

One of her father's most pressing concerns is that Afghanistan, at the hands of the brutal Taliban who wreaked such enormous destruction during its occupation, is in grave danger of losing its profoundly important archaeological heritage. The savagery of the Taliban—laying waste to the famous Buddha statues in Bamiyan—left such a swath of destruction in her father's native land that Nadia has joined forces with her father to create the Association for Protection of Afghan Archaeology, a non-profit located in San Rafael.

"Our efforts are intensely devoted to raising funds to provide professional archaeological training, help restore the Museum and the Archaeological Institute of Kabul," says Nadia. "One way we strive to inform the public about Afghanistan's imperiled heritage is to publish children's books and organize lectures and exhibits at schools, vividly explaining the country's little-known cultural contributions to the world."

One outgrowth of her work is the creation of "Afghankite," an online research link covering Afghan issues. Nadia uses this and her slide shows to clearly demonstrate luscious Afghan landscapes, archaeology, Afghan people, their traditions, and the somewhat dire predicaments that have befallen them.

"It's wonderful to see the looks on children's faces," says Nadia, "when the realization clicks in that Afghanistan is not a beehive of terrorists that should be feared. It is very satisfying for me to influence people's preconceptions and misconceptions, especially when I am doing so in honor of my father's country. Children especially are the ones who truly appreciate the difference between truth and falsehood.

"Like many misinformed Americans, these young people had mistakenly thought the country was ugly, barren, dry and bereft of either culture or art. To be able to show the richness of the culture and the levels of civilization, however damaged, is very rewarding to me."

One specifically daunting project Nadia and her father are busily trying to finance is the reconstruction of four tons of pottery shards found in the rubble of the Archaeology Institute of Kabul. Once restored, these objects will be on exhibit at the newly remodeled Kabul Museum. She has been tirelessly seeking ways to attract restoration experts to the cause, including consultations with the Asian Art Museum in San Francisco to see if a room could be set aside to use as a partnering venue for fund raising.

"It's wonderful to see the looks on children's faces when the realization clicks in that Afghanistan is not a beehive of terrorists that should be feared."

As if her life's mission and her family life weren't busy enough—she is married to Tony Saccardi and they have two young daughters, Julietta and Natasha—Nadia is also wholeheartedly dedicated to the work of her friend and close associate Heidi Kuhn of San Rafael, founder of Roots of Peace.

The Afghanistan leg of the mission is called Harvest of Hope, which was inaugurated on September 11, 2002 to raise funds to clear mines from Shomali Valley, where Afghan grapevines have been grown for thousands of years.

Nadia's friend Heidi Kuhn, characterizing the pair's relentless mission to rid the world of horrifying land mines: "We feel very strongly that the modern rendition of turning swords into plowshares—evocative of the birth of the United Nations following World War II atrocities—is converting mines to vines and replacing the seeds of destruction with the seeds of hope."

Echoed Nadia Tarzi: "We are so fortunate that Heidi Kuhn and Roots of Peace have never shifted their focus from the urgent needs of Afghanistan. The extent of the devastation from both mines and archaeological plunderers is overwhelming, but our hearts remain filled with high hopes and love for humanity."

Sung with courage from the Little Sparrow of Afghanistan.

Mimi Tellis

It is impossible to mention Mimi Tellis, longtime Sausalito waterfront community leader and free spirit, without remembering back in time to the days when Sausalito was a truly exciting Bohemian arts colony and not a slick tourist attraction. As a teenager growing up in Marin and as a young man in his 20s searching and brooding for self, I always went to Sausalito to find soul. Sometimes I found it in the charming community theater that sat on the water a stone's throw from where Scoma's sits today. This theater was the domain of famed Shakespearean actor Jack Aranson and his family, and they brought great drama to life. I vividly recall seeing his one-man tribute to Dylan Thomas one night. It was chilling.

The Tides bookstore was the central nerve zone of downtown Sausalito—this is where intellectuals gathered to discuss books and look like Richard Brautigan, garbed in pea coat, long scarves, scholarly frowns. It was also a great place to meet girls. Later, not so Bohemian but an even better mating zoo was The Trident (now Horizons), which in the Sixties was like the Playboy Club of northern California. Instead of bunnies, waitresses floated around in braless outfits that were fetching and wildly imaginative. There was a cult following around these women—they were always coming and going to Europe or South America, and they were drop-dead gorgeous. On one Sunday morning at The Trident, I watched in awe as the following brunch diners came in to find great tables by the bay—Jane Fonda with Donald Sutherland, Bill Cosby by himself, David Crosby with his moustache, and Stevie Nicks of Fleetwood Mac.

I went outside to sit on a rock and write in my journal, and Nicks came out in all her feathers, sat down next to me, and said, "A penny for your thoughts?" I was so dumbstruck by her that all thoughts flew out of my head. She smiled beautifully and moved on down Bridgeway. Story of my life.

Sausalito is Marin's bit of magic and deserves many more books of its own—Sterling Hayden holding court and leaning on his cane inside the no name bar, fawning disciples genuflecting at his feet and absorbing every word. Julie Christie arriving at The Tides for a film shoot of "Petulia," wrinkling her brow as a fan handed her a handwritten note of adulation. That would be me, and yes, she read it and blew me a kiss. Like I said, Sausalito was an inspiring fantasy day after day.

Mimi Tellis and her family moved to Sausalito in 1955—this would've been in the thick of the Bohemian/Beatnik period, pre-Hippie, when freedom of expression and truth-seeking poets were challenging the establishment patterns of the soporific 1950s.

The Tellis family lived on three different Bay Area ferryboats—the *Vallejo*, the *Issaquah*, and the *City of Seattle*. In 1960, the *Seattle* became their home.

Mimi was always the creative, artistic type—she majored in theater at Northwestern University, where she was the college roommate of the famous movie star, Patricia Neal, and a fine actress herself.

When Mimi was married, she went with her husband to Europe and lived the Bohemian life for a while, perfect training ground for the Sausalito years still to come.

Says Mimi's son Chris: "She was a great comedienne, and still is. She was a wonderful singer, as well, performing at USO events, night clubs, state fairs, any place where she could bring a little warmth into people's lives.

"When we moved to Sausalito," Chris continues, "the whole community was thriving in the '50s. As kids, we would row around the waterfront, visiting artists, sticking our noses into people's boats and studios, getting paint on our faces. We were waterfront urchins."

And what an ideal paradise home it was for water bound kids—a large number of abandoned vessels retired to the Sausalito waterfront in those days, which set the stage for the then-burgeoning Sausalito houseboat community.

Sausalito had been a major ship building locale for World War II Navy vessels. Workers flocked here by the thousands from all over the country to help build the famous Liberty ships on the north end of the waterfront.

In the early '50s, when the Tellis family settled in Sausalito, it was the post-war epoch. The now-idle waterfront stared to attract writers, dreamers, artists, poets, moviemakers and colorful raconteurs of all stripes. This would soon become the most colorful city in the West, rivaling San Francisco's Barbary Coast heyday as the new capital of hedonism, freewheeling philosophy, and artistic license.

The aforementioned Sterling Hayden owned a houseboat at the harbor. Jack Kerouac and Allen Ginsberg were frequent visitors. Beatniks and painters from North Beach flocked to Sausalito for the available studio space, the cheap rent, and because they preferred the light in Marin over the foggier confines of Upper Grant Avenue. Jean Varda and Allan Watts shared a boat on the waterfront (hosting their famous gourmet lunches) from 1961 until Varda's death in 1970. Watts wrote books and held seances on board the vessel.

"Our family used to sail on Jean Varda's boat, the *Sakari*," recalls Chris. "On one voyage up the Delta, we passed an abandoned ferryboat. My father convinced the owners to sell it for $1,800. It was just a great big open space about 135 feet by 48 feet. We spent years turning it into a home."

"There's just too much to see, and frankly, I've just started."

Later in Sausalito, approaching the Hippie years, Otis Redding wrote his masterful ballad, "(Sitting On) The Dock of the Bay" while he stayed on a houseboat. Timothy Leary and his cronies from San Francisco's *Oracle* magazine held be-ins and group gropes during the Summer of Love.

In conversation and in memory, Mimi Tellis is as sharp as though it were still 1955—"It just doesn't seem that long ago," she recalls. "The memories, the colors, the characters are still present with me. People then seemed larger than life, and we lived and celebrated large. Every action felt very important to us, almost as though we were making history. But we were so busy having fun, we didn't really notice."

Mimi was a thoroughly modern woman of her day—she worked as a publicist for organizations like Guide Dogs for the Blind and many progressive causes. She was and is a fearless advocate for peace. Arrested several times as a pacifist protester for an array of causes, she is ardently in favor of nuclear disarmament; she has accumulated years of experience working on behalf of the disenfranchised and marginalized citizens of the Bay Area; and she has worked diligently and selflessly for such groups as the Interfaith Task Force of Marin. She often used her family's houseboat for meetings, benefits and fund raisers of all kinds.

Hooked on travel, her globetrotting has never stopped—this past year alone, she has been to India, Fiji, Russia, France, the Great Barrier Reef, Florida and Cuba.

In true Mimi Tellis fashion, she says: "There's just too much to see, and frankly, I've just started."

Phyllis Thelen

"My kids are my best friends," says Phyllis Thelen. What a great compliment from this well-known community activist and patron to the arts who has befriended hundreds of fellow Marinites since arriving here in 1958. "At the end of the day," she adds, "no matter how many people you've met or how many lives you've influenced, there is nothing like the bonds between yourself and your own children."

Phyllis and her retired-attorney husband Max Thelen have wonderful sons and daughters—Nancy Thelen Rehkopf, a marketing consultant who is president of Youth in Arts, one of Phyllis' other "offspring;" Jane Greene, retired as executive director of the Marin Ballet; Max III, who is Chief Operations Officer of PreCare; and William Thelen, a local builder. There are 12 Thelen grandchildren, as well.

The Thelens came to Marin in 1958 at a time when The County was a virginal landscape just waiting for creative types like Phyllis and Max to leave their imprint. Their daughters Nancy and Jane were eager to study ballet, so Phyllis signed them on to the Marin Ballet program, run by famed Marin dance instructor Leona Norman.

It was a pivotal time for this cultural slice of Marin, because, while the dancers were given excellent instruction, there was no place for them to perform. Phyllis, ever the doer, organized a small group of other dynamic parents to embark on a fundraising campaign to construct a home for the ballet, eventually settling at 100 Elm Street, the former Marist Fathers Seminary in San Rafael.

The group banded together. When the budget-conscious Marin County Supervisors balked at the initial bids to construct the Veterans' Memorial Auditorium, the project appeared dead in the water, but Phyllis and members of an ad hoc committee refused to take no for an answer. Demonstrating as much political savvy as they had tiptoe moxie, the committee lobbied the Board successfully to consider more affordable bids.

The result of their efforts was a multi-cultural center for the arts that continues to thrive today.

Once again taking a cue from her children who were now enrolled in elementary schools in Marin, she realized from her PTA involvement that school kids were not receiving much exposure to the arts through school programs only. Her own kids were itching to attain more culture, so Phyllis and representatives of other arts programs put together an innovative program they called Youth in Arts, which basically provided Marin students a chance to see top-notch performances by the Marin Ballet and the Marin Youth Symphony Orchestra.

"One offshoot of Youth in Arts of which I am extremely proud," says Phyllis, "is the Italian Street Painting Festival in San Rafael, which has gained international attention in recent years—the colored-chalk paintings on the street's concrete are mind-blowing for their creativity and brilliance, if even for a short time. The paintings aren't permanent, but the joy comes in watching the painters' passion mixed in with the astonished looks on spectators' faces."

Phyllis attributes her twin skills as a community organizer and artist—two talents that unfortunately don't always co-exist in the mind set of brilliant creative types—to, first of all, her childhood in Southern California, where she grew up on an orange ranch and fell in love with the surrounding landscape; and secondly, to the faith in self which she received from her father who gave her the confidence and belief that she could accomplish anything in life if she wanted it badly enough and if she worked hard enough to achieve it.

She was not only into painting and drawing as a child, but she was also an avid tinkerer of tools, building and repairing handmade toys and figuring out how to take things apart and put them back together again.

After graduating from the Connecticut College for Women in New London in 1948, Phyllis traveled widely and at length throughout Europe, expanding her horizons and keeping an ever watchful eye on all things artistic. On her return to California after three months abroad, she was hired by United World Federalists, where she worked as the student organizer hired to bolster United Nations visibility on campuses and make the mission of the peacekeeping organization a more viable part of people's lives.

It was during this stint that she met her future husband Max, who also worked for UWF as a member of the Speakers Bureau. After they got married, Phyllis took classes at the San Francisco Art Institute, studying oils, pastels and sculpting.

"Max and I have been a great team," she says. "As President of Art Works Downtown, I have to be the chief fund raiser. Raising money can be a little tiresome, but Max has shown me how if you tie together the artistic enterprise with some solid financial planning concerning property ownership, it can be a very streamlined, sustainable and ultimately successful venture.

> ***"It's how I've lived my whole life—turning small ideas into great dreams. All things are possible, especially in Marin."***

"When I first saw Gordon's Opera House on Fourth Street," she explains, "I had this vision how it would look as an all-encompassing place where artists could rent space for living and working and teaching. The financial guys tried to discourage me, saying the nearly $3 million price tag was prohibitive, but Max and I put our heads together and we raised a good chunk of the capital ourselves.

"I love developing concepts like this. Now we have this 40,000 square foot complex of 30 artists' studios, nearly 17 affordable work-live units, multi-purpose rooms, exhibition space, restaurants and retail stores. It's quite an enterprise and I view it as a happy marriage between arts and business.

"Marin is not only a county of great wealth but, more importantly, boundless artistic and creative energy. We've already shown through the years what a little bit of dreaming and community action can achieve. Now imagine stepping it up a bit—just think what those 80 acres of land out at the Civic Center could look like if we applied the same kind of business and artistic teamwork to build an even greater cultural complex than we already have. It's how I've lived my whole life—turning small ideas into great dreams. All things are possible, especially in Marin."

A member of the Marin Women's Hall of Fame, Phyllis Thelen has assured herself a place in the modern legacy of Marin County as someone who has demonstrated personal perseverance, artistic grace and business acumen in a county that has become very much her own personal canvas.

Ruby Unger

The title of the Woody Allen movie, or even the exact context, escapes memory, but in the film there is a Woodyesque line when the ever-exasperated comic, failing in his attempt to offer an adequate description of himself to yet another unattainable flame, blurts out—"But I'm not a person. I'm an *experience*."

The same line came to mind while interviewing Ruby Unger, who is equally impossible to describe adequately. Free spirits are like that. And that's a good thing.

Ruby Unger, a resident of Marin since 1980, is a member of the Screen Actors Guild, the American Federation of TV & Radio Artists, and Actors Equity Association. She has performed in films, on radio and in TV for the past quarter of a century. Her company, Unger Productions, writes and produces best-selling videotape programs and workbooks which are distributed to educators—subjects include disease prevention, witness preparation, bullying, self-esteem development, tolerance and the Bill of Rights.

"I'm kind of all over the place," she laughs from her Mill Valley home where she lives with her husband, Alan Unger, a widely respected international public affairs consultant. "But I wouldn't know how to do things any other way. I did stand-up comedy in the '70s at places like the Boarding House with Robin Williams—Robin actually started my career in comedy. He was crawling through the audience one night, and I crawled right towards him on the floor.

"He brought me up on the stage and we did a few completely improvisational minutes together. People get their breaks in life in strange ways. This was mine. The audience members were howling at us. I remember Robin sweating profusely, on 'Full Robin.' Needless to say, I got the comedy bug that night.

"What else have I been? I've helped the CHP organize their Walk-a-Thons. I've been a Community Service Director for the March of Dimes in four counties—Marin, Sonoma, Napa and Solano. Ironically, Robin was the MOD's guest celebrity, and he agreed to be helicoptered around to 13 different Bay Area locations, slaying everyone with his manic act.

"At the University of Wisconsin, I got my B.A. degree in TV, films and radio. To put my way through college, I worked in a factory for awhile. Then I went to Marquette University and got another degree in speech pathology. I'm somewhat eclectic," she laughs again, somewhat eclectically.

"I bounce from serious to comedic and sometimes manage to weave both together. One of my favorite projects was a video program designed to promote understanding and foster tolerance of the pivotal religions of the world. It's called, 'Respecting Beliefs: Muslims, Christians, Jews and Others.'

"Our target audience is Grade 5 through college-age kids, and we present serious religious questions to these students and their parents and teachers in non-threatening, compelling ways in our effort to dispel myths and to advance tolerance. I asked the kids, 'How would you explain your belief, your religion, to an Alien landing from Mars?' Basically, it's education and enlightenment presented in a fun fashion.

"My first television 'gig' came from answering an ad I saw in the paper," she muses, suddenly thoughtful, "to be a contestant on 'Name That Tune.' I won $18,163. You bet I remember the exact amount! I thought it was all the money in the world. I bought a home in Forestville. I had, like, ten grand in my pocket but could only declare an income of $15,000. The real estate agent took me to the only house I could afford."

If the story of her life is sharpening into a finer focus, you might also recognize her as "Ms. Nancy" on the KTVU/Channel 2 production of "Romper Room," where she starred on the kids' show from 1981-1987. Following this stint, she was hired by KCBS radio to be an overnight talk show host, but soon quit because the hours were "insane."

Among her many awards for public service-oriented entertainment, she is proudest of winning the prestigious Action for Children's Television Award for her child abuse prevention series of public service announcements. During the Persian Gulf War under President George Bush Sr., Ruby created for Channel 7/KGO-ABC TV more PSAs designed exclusively to inform and comfort the children of the Bay Area.

"This was really gratifying work," she recalls. "If you remember, there was such a surreal, hushed sense of impending doom about this war, different even from the conflict we are waging now. The economy was horrible, children were having nightmares, and I found a special niche to ease some of the anxiety."

If life is timing, she always seems to be in the right place at the right time. From 1994 through 1997, Ruby lived and worked with her husband Alan in the former Soviet countries of Ukraine and Moldova. As the Media Director for public education projects funded by USAID (United States Agency for International Development), she supervised radio and television programs on the subjects of economic reform and privatization.

Her production team won the first-ever Crystal Truth Award at the Yalta International Journalists Conference of newly independent Eastern European countries. She was also awarded the Public Relations Society of America international public affairs award for the same production work.

Ruby Unger is a somewhat breathless advocate of mixing dynamic social engagement with an oft-frivolous sense of self whereby she takes her work extremely seriously and herself not at all.

"But most notably," she howls, "don't forget that I am the Dalai LaMarr (like the Dalai Lama, only more Hedy) of W.U.F.F. (Women United for Fun and Men Who Dare), an international social organization dedicated to stress reduction through intense partying. There are 300 active members worldwide. We have a wonderful wiggly rubber Power Trout which is our amulet. Once you feel it and fondle it, you'll see exactly why it produces so many smiles and reduces so much stress."

As you have witnessed, Ruby Unger is a somewhat breathless advocate of mixing dynamic social engagement with an oft-frivolous sense of self whereby she takes her work extremely seriously and herself not at all.

"It's how I maintain my sanity," she declares, stroking her green Power Trout fondly. "That and Alan— he is such a gentleman and such a wonderful calming influence on my life. I am one very blessed and fortunate woman who simply wants to share the wealth of that blessing. It sounds too simple to even say, but the good you do comes back to you."

Once again, Ruby Unger is not a person. She's an experience.

Sim Van der Ryn

Sim Van der Ryn, former State Architect appointed by Governor Jerry Brown, is a renowned leader in sustainable architecture. For over 35 years, his design, planning, teaching and public leadership has advanced the viability, acceptance and knowledge base of ecological principles and practices in architecture and planning.

"I've been a Marin resident since 1958," says Sim. "When I first came to Mill Valley, I was told the last Greyhound from The City leaves at 6 p.m. It was true. You could pick up a bottle of wine at the store after work and go home. La Ginestra was the only restaurant I can still remember that was here then.

"The biggest change in The County," he says, "has been the density. So much of the office developments along 101 are terrible, cheaply built, and now are expensive to maintain. I used to go for walks up Blithedale Canyon. I was new to California in those days, and I did a lot of exploring. For fun and enjoyment, I went hiking—that's what I still do.

"The best thing about Marin over the years is that a lot of it hasn't changed. It was a lot of hard work by a lot of people conserving Open Space. You remember that there were plans to build a development called Marincello on the Marin Headlands? And all throughout the San Geronimo Valley? And in Bolinas and West Marin? Thank goodness all of that was stopped.

"The worst thing about the changes in Marin has been the breakdown in community. There's so much traffic and all the pressure that comes from growth—the stress and tension and all the worst aspects of suburban living.

"People are no longer laid back, and many poor people are being pushed out, especially in the service sector, and that's a real loss. But I am not going to whine about it. Change and growth happen everywhere. I've lived in Marin for 45 years—with a home in Inverness and a houseboat in Sausalito for 23 years. There's lots of prosperity here and nothing ever stays the same. In Marin I think we are just suffering from all the things any materialist society would experience."

Trained as an architect with a degree from the University of Michigan, the theme of Sim's career has been applying principles of physical and social ecology to architecture and environmental design—such as the visionary yet unbuilt plan to convert Hamilton Air Force Base into a sustainable community which resulted in a countywide referendum.

He has pioneered sustainable design at the community scale and the building specific scale. He has designed single family and multi-family housing; community facilities; retreat, resort and health centers; schools and learning facilities; office buildings; commercial buildings; and planned communities. Recently he has planned the nation's first ecological cemetery—Marin Forever on Tennessee Valley Road.

As Jerry Brown's State Architect, he developed the nation's first government-initiated energy efficient office building program.

As Professor of Architecture at UC Berkeley, a position he held for over thirty years, Sim was a key force in establishing Berkeley's international reputation as a leading school focusing on issues of socially and environmentally responsible design.

Sim also founded the Farallones Institute that helped to create national awareness of "ecologically integrated living design." The work continues today at the Ecological Design Institute (EDI), Van der Ryn Architects' non-profit partner.

"I began teaching at Berkeley in 1969, and there were a lot of crazy things happening then," he recalls. "I started feeling a little apocalyptic about cities, so I bought a cabin out in West Marin near Inverness. I paid $5,000 for a lot, but I didn't build on it right away. There was pressure by developers to build subdivisions in the area, and I didn't want to end up living in a suburb that looked like Daly City. I have two houses now. Mostly I live in Sausalito—on a houseboat once owned by Phil Frank the cartoonist—and I go out to Inverness. There's a real feeling of community here on the waterfront."

One advantage in having a former State Architect, writer of six books, and ecologically renowned thinker living in the community is that we might listen to some of his fresh ideas:

On density—"Americans hate two things. One is density and the other is sprawl. We refused to allow any density in Marin, so we got sprawl by default. The last piece of land in Marin is St. Vincent's. I had a competition for my students at Berkeley to design a plan for that land, and they came up with an interesting mix that included residential and agriculture. What we really need in Marin is diversification."

On workforce housing—"To get any sort of workforce housing, for our teachers and nurses, fire and police to live in Marin, we need political leadership. That's what it takes to get anything done. It takes people with vision. I used to be part of the County Planning Commission at the beginning, and I used to be excited that we could get some good things done. We tried to get the Solar Village project going in Hamilton. We could have had the land for one dollar, and that would have made the whole project doable, but we were double-crossed by a Novato politician. Then Reagan came along and that was the end of that."

"Americans hate two things. One is density and the other is sprawl. We refused to allow any density in Marin, so we got sprawl by default."

On developing San Quentin—"I was on the task force looking into the future of that land. Supervisor Steve Kinsey had a plan for it, but I was never able to figure out what he was doing. The warden always said the prison would never be torn down, and now she is in charge of the entire state prison system, so I don't think we are going to see San Quentin disappear. There are 4,000 people in Marin who volunteer their time and efforts at San Quentin. My feeling is that you must first find another site for the prison if you are talking about tearing it down. Maybe Vacaville would want it. Anyway, the state would obviously want a fortune for the land, not one dollar."

Sim Van der Ryn is married to his second wife, Ruth Friend, a highly regarded fabric designer, manufacturer and founder of a Marin political action organization called The Ruth Group. They met during the Jerry Brown years in Sacramento. His three adult children are Julia, a writer and teacher living in Napa; Micah, a film and anthropology teacher who has documentaries on PBS and who lives with his family in Samoa; and Ethan, currently living in New Zealand, who won an Oscar as sound designer and sound editor for his work on "Lord of the Rings."

Jan Wahl

Jan Wahl—a shining diamond in the shimmering diadem of Marin personalities—is irrepressible, passionate, outspoken, fearless, breathless, irreverent, funny and exhilarating. She is everything we seek in our search for the perfect movie. After a conversation with her, we want to go somewhere and reflect, let her words sink in, then leap into some kind of action. She is what might be called inspiration.

It is very refreshing to be in the company of someone who really likes what they do. Exudes the Bay Area's best known film critic: "I totally love my life."

The hat-wearing maven of movies grew up in West Los Angeles near Beverly Hills and Westwood at a time when there really was a glamorous Hollywood—"Buddy Ebsen lived on my street," she recalls. "We'd see Barbara Stanwyck at the store. Edward G. Robinson was always around.

"My parents were crazy about old movies. They'd sit us down in front of the old black 'n white TV, and we'd watch the classic films. My mother loved anything with Rosalind Russell and Katharine Hepburn. My father loved Errol Flynn, who had this great love of life. I loved Ginger Rogers, Irene Dunne, Barbara Stanwyck.

"My mother would drop me off at the Cherokee Bookstore when she went shopping or to the farmers' market. I would hang out with the old character actors and listen to their stories in awe. It was a great way to be raised, seeing these larger-than-life screen characters up close and personal. Through his films, I fell desperately in love with the young Clark Gable, and I also fell in love with the social-issue movies, the ones that have a lot to do with who I am and what I am all about today.

"These were the movies that actually changed the world, films like 'Gentleman's Agreement,' 'On the Waterfront,' 'To Kill A Mockingbird.' I'm a huge Sidney Poitier and Gregory Peck fan. 'Valley of Decision' with Greer Garson and Gregory Peck was incredible—all about unions, organizing struggles, factories in Pittsburgh, poor people raging against rich people. It was just so smart and wonderful.

"I love that kind of thing, so it makes me very happy when I see something magical like 'Don Juan De Marco' with Johnny Depp or 'Rain Man,' for example, movies which honor the tradition of storytelling and great writing. And I get very sad when I see camera trickery and demographic servitude replacing story."

While most TV viewers know Wahl for her flamboyant hats (she started stylin' them15 years ago "to put the *show* in showbiz" and they have stuck as her personal signature), they might not know she is also a very impassioned educator. She has taught high school at The Branson School in Ross and St. Mark's elementary in Terra Linda. The Branson course she has titled "Critical Thinking of the Mass Media," and her mission is to elicit from the already media savvy students lists of things that offend them—unjust stereotypes, humor that's cruel, music that crosses the boundaries of taste and morality.

"I come from a generation that used to say if you aren't part of the solution, you are a part of the problem, so it's my deepest conviction to help lead these beautiful young people through some of life's toughest experiences and choices," she explains.

After graduating from high school in Los Angeles, Wahl couldn't wait to move to the Bay Area—"I loved how radical it was here, and I was crazy about Janis Joplin's music. I also wanted to attend the Communications School at San Francisco State University, which I did, and that led me to my various careers at KCBS, KRON and KGO. I had a radio show on KNBR in the mid-'80s titled 'Hollywood Calling,' and I also had a store in Sausalito called Bridgeway to Hollywood which sold memorabilia and old movies. It was during this time I met and fell in love with my husband of 23 years. He is the polar opposite of me—quiet and thoughtful, he manages buildings. He is not at all an entertainment type of guy. I love him even more now than ever."

Wahl's outspokenness has been a key to her success as a Bay Area luminary, but it has ostracized her from Hollywood industry publicity machines that seek softball critics who pander, fawn and pay unblinking homage to their profit-minded shenanigans.

"I'm not at all happy with the industry today," she says. "I see too many movies with people I wouldn't want to know in real life. I just don't care about them. And there is a total lack of rich dialogue—give me dialogue and action, yes, but not one in place of the other. And I'm very troubled by the lack of good, strong roles for women. As Meryl Streep told me, they just aren't there.

"The magic of this place is that when you cross that bridge and head home after work, you are literally leaving the workplace behind and entering paradise."

"But they should be there. The term 'chick flick' is horrible and horribly demeaning to women. Young actresses are spending all their power into what they can't eat to stay what they think is thin and sexy at the expense of delving into powerful roles. Again, choices are made to make profit or to stay on the A List. As a result, good stories suffer, and the entire industry, and eventually the viewing public suffer, as well. It's just a bad time for women in movies—you have leading girls, not leading women. And they are so skinny, you want to say, please, eat a hamburger!"

Wahl saves her positive notes for living in Marin—"The magic of this place is that when you cross that bridge and head home after work, you are literally leaving the workplace behind and entering paradise." And she has rave reviews for Northern California's burgeoning talent pool, movie-wise—"Good God, John Korty of Stinson Beach ('The Autobiography of Miss Jane Pittman') is a treasure, then we also have Philip Kaufman ('The Right Stuff' and 'The Unbearable Lightness of Being')."

Marin, she adds, is also full of wonderful dogs, and her favorite movie dog is Asta from "The Thin Man" series.

As far as favorite couples in film are concerned, she hesitates not a bit to cite Spencer Tracy and Katharine Hepburn—"Their relationship was absolutely perfect for classic movie making. He was the baked potato and she was the souffle."

It was Tracy who said, "Just plant your feet and tell the truth."

What a superb line to put the wrap on Wahl.

Kathryn Werdegar

If you were a betting person, you might bet against the fact that there is a California Supreme Court Justice living in our midst. And if you did, the scales of justice would weigh heavily against your wager.

There *is* a California Supreme Court Justice living in our midst, and her name is Kathryn Mickle Werdegar.

What probably makes it seem unusual is the high degree of anonymity that goes with what is, ironically, a supremely high-profile post in state government.

But you never know with whom you might be brushing elbows—or, in this case, judicial gowns—in the produce section of Whole Foods. Or, say you are a mini-celebrity yourself, like a judge in one of The County's court systems, and you say to a potential woman juror, somewhat laconically and almost as an aside (or sidebar): "So, what do you do for a living?"

According to California Supreme Court Justice and Ross resident Kathryn Werdegar, that is exactly what happened one morning recently in a Marin courtroom when she, jury summons in hand, showed up to fulfill her civic duty as a common citizen. The judge glanced her way and asked the perfunctory question.

A bit thrown, Werdegar replied that while her husband David worked as a doctor, she herself was also employed. As it happens, she was a judge.

Yes, replied Hizzonner hurriedly, and just exactly what kind of judge are you?

"I am on the California Supreme Court, Your Honor," came her soft reply, fulfilling her duty to tell the truth, the whole truth, and nothing but the truth, so help her God.

And God help the judge, who, according to Werdegar, looked quite chagrined.

The story is refreshing because it speaks to the kind of person San Francisco native Kathryn Werdegar is—spontaneous, unassuming, low-key, certainly humble and gracious, but also free-spirited and joyous. She exudes the light-hearted air and personal humility of someone who certainly would fail the Screen Actors' Guild version of what a Supreme would look like.

She is a happy person who loves living and hiking in Marin, who enjoys the company of her many friends who don't tremble in her presence, and who had the good fortune of raising her two sons (Matthew and Maurice) in The County, instilling in them a love of the Great Outdoors through their enrollment in such Marin-oriented activities as the Elizabeth Terwilliger Nature Walks program.

Just another well-adjusted Marin housewife, correct?

Well, yes—that plus a rather formidable background that includes degrees in law studies from both George Washington University and U.C.'s Boalt School of Law; years of service with the United States Department of Justice in Washington, D.C., including a stretch with the Civil Rights Division of Justice during the John Kennedy administration; a stint as director of the criminal law division of California Continuing Education of the Bar; senior staff attorney with the California Court of Appeal and the California Supreme Court; and professor and Associate Dean for Academic and Student Affairs at the University of San Francisco School of Law.

Her husband, Dr. David Werdegar, is a widely esteemed family physician and professor at UCSF Medical Center who had also served a term in the '80s as Health Director in San Francisco, appointed to that post by then-Mayor Dianne Feinstein, and another term as head of the Marin Community Foundation.

Says Werdegar: "The best changes that have occurred in Marin are the ones that haven't happened. I think that we are blessed that we have resisted so many plans for development. And the schooling system continues to be excellent. There is still a great small town feel to The County, and a lot of people continue to be community-involved.

"If I won the lottery, I would put my money into environmental protection, perhaps Audubon Canyon. My second priority would be children. There is a lot of hidden poverty in Marin. Many people aren't aware that there are so many others in need. The Marin Community Foundation has done great work, and I support what they do.

"I'm concerned about the general direction of the economy," she continues, "not just in Marin, but nationally. The worsening of the economy leads to such things as closures of local libraries and erosion of our school system. In Marin, we have to continue to withstand pressure to develop property, but the rising cost of real estate has also led to many people being forced out of The County. I am worried where that will go."

Rulings by Supreme Court Justices are not riveting bedtime reading. If you watched any of the Al Gore/hanging chad/George W./Florida popular vote/*United States* Supreme Court sessions, you would no longer be fighting insomnia.

Werdegar, in fact, laughs at the generally low profile, lack-of-panache nature of her job. She recalls one evening when she volunteered, along with The County's trial court judges, to participate in a "Meet the Judges" night at the Civic Center. Did the citizens of The County eagerly avail themselves of this rare opportunity to engage in a dialogue with a Justice of the State Supreme Court?

"All I can say," reports Werdegar, "is that every one of the questions was directed to the trial court judges and related to traffic tickets, divorce wars, and other matters of immediate concern to individuals."

"I am on the California Supreme Court, Your Honor," came her soft reply, fulfilling her duty to tell the truth, the whole truth, and nothing but the truth, so help her God.

The only attendee who acknowledged her presence wanted only to deliver a tirade against one of the Court's rulings—"I might as well have stayed home," Werdegar remarks. "Yes, I probably should have."

Identifying political strains of Supreme Court Justices is really not much of a practicing art in California. We the People like to think that these scholarly leaders ascended to the high bench because of their lofty-minded spirits, their uncompromised sense of patriotism, and their extensively studied and supremely earned academic laurels. And The People would be fairly correct—having political hacks on the High Court is simply unseemly.

Once in a great while, someone really controversial like Rose Bird comes along, but she was a Jerry Brown appointee, and Jerry Brown couldn't make a doctor's appointment without offending half the voters in California. So—characterizing a Justice like Werdegar is a complex task, but let it be said that she has impressed legal eagles with her moderate-to-progressive opinions, from supporting second-parent adoptions by gay couples, to her fiercely voiced defense of First Amendment issues, and to her impassioned advocacy of civil rights in complex racial conflicts.

Justice may be blind, but while people-watching in Marin, you should always keep your eyes open.

Cecilia Zamora

The quietly passionate and wholeheartedly committed Executive Director of the Latino Council of Marin, Cecilia Zamora, has been a Marin resident since 1988. Prior to that, she had lived in San Francisco's ethnically mixed Noe Valley since 1976, the year she came to the Bay Area from San Luis Obispo where she had attended Cal Poly State University. Originally from Hacienda Heights, she grew up in that L.A. diversity ambience that's here as a microcosm in Marin, so she's fully capable and aware of all that goes into the stew of her always exciting job.

Zamora, current President of the Hispanic Chamber of Commerce and Chair of the Marin Women's Commission, presides over a dynamically active community organization that serves as a conduit between the ever-growing Latino population in Marin and other organizations around The County. Her sensitive position calls for someone astute in communications and counseling skills, an expert "networker," a tireless advocate for people struggling with language barriers and racial impasses, and, at times, a gifted charmer who knows how to work a room.

From reports heard in hushed circles of admiration from all corners of Marin, Cecilia Zamora fits the bill—on all counts.

Formerly a marketing/communications person who knew there was always something beckoning her beyond mere business niche and financial security, she took the position with the Latino Council of Marin with eyes wide open not only to the burgeoning problems that were coming about with the rising Latino populace in Marin, but also, on the flip side, to the abundance of opportunities that were waiting to be triggered.

"Basically, I view my job as a facilitator," she explains, "as someone who can convince and cajole people, sensibly providing them with the confidence and know-how to seize opportunities that will carry them into this promising new century. Marin brings a very interesting—make that *fascinating*—perspective to this challenge because it's changing so rapidly. Adapting to those changes, staying on top of them, and guiding people through the channels is what gives definition and satisfaction to my job."

The Canal Area is, of course, one of the most watched and compelling social melting pots in all of Marin. When you consider that 25 years ago, the Canal was 78% Caucasian, you get a handle on just how fast this area has turned almost completely inside out. Today's Canal boasts a majority of Hispanic/Latino (with a significantly growing El Salvadorian population), Asian, and Afro-American makeup, with Caucasians now a distant minority.

In the myriad of issues Zamora can select like choosing food from a Lazy Susan—housing, health, employment, education, family stability, children's rights, immigration concerns, teen pregnancy and drugs and youthful violence—she is a passionate believer in the concept of teaching leadership.

Herself a graduate from the Leadership Institute of the San Rafael Chamber of Commerce, she steadfastly urges others to enlist in the program. Successful citizenship, she believes, is rooted in the tenets and principles espoused by the Leadership Institute, which exposes participants to the full panoply of civic issues like health and human services, transportation, the environment, the arts, local government, law enforcement, education, and community diversity.

Zamora, formerly a headhunter in high-tech recruiting for 10 years prior to her non-profit career, is an avid believer in this program—"What better way," she asks, "than to witness firsthand who is asking the tough questions, who is absorbing how business intersects with politics, and who aggressively asserts their rights as citizens who care for their community? The Leadership Institute swiftly and accurately identifies talent that might not otherwise rise to the surface."

Zamora, who has served on the community editorial board of the *Marin IJ,* voiced her enthusiasm in an Op-Ed piece she wrote for the newspaper:

"Team-building is a critical component of the Institute's leadership development philosophy. At the heart of the program is the opportunity to experience a group of dynamic, diverse individuals from many industries and disciplines. The skills achieved in this group setting, which include leadership vision, facilitated debate and conflict resolution, are geared to assist future leaders in mastering collaboration and collective problem-solving."

The Latino community of Marin is rich in leadership potential, and it is to this goal—seeing that it be properly identified—that Zamora has devoted the scope of work of her direction of the Latino Council of Marin. The ethnic diversity of Marin County is fast transforming the region's profile, and through the efforts of people like Zamora, the richness and human potential of that diversity has been given eloquent voice.

Zamora is a passionate believer in the concept of teaching leadership.

Zamora—who lives in San Anselmo with her life partner Alan Voigt, a Merchant Marine—was recently elected to serve on the board of the National Association of Commissions for Women. Her election is for two terms, and she will represent Region 9, which embraces Hawaii, Nevada, Arizona and California. As such, she is the only Californian on the national board.

Her rising star as a hard working, vociferous community activist has also caught the attention of the California Hispanic Chamber of Commerce. In 2004, that organization honored her with a group of Latinas throughout California. She was also featured with another assembly of about 20 women at the 25th Annual Convention of the California Hispanic Chambers of Commerce in Anaheim, that organization's Latina Businesswoman's Luncheon spotlighting her work as an effective liaison between the Latino community and the business world at large.

Other designations she has received include the 1998 Spirit of Marin Award and the 1998 Community Leader Award from Congresswoman Lynn Woolsey. Her involvement on other boards includes United Way of the Bay Area, Workforce Investment Board (a supervisorial appointment), and Chair of the Marin Community Health Foundation (both Marin General and Novato Community Hospitals).

Cecilia Zamora is a Class of 2000 graduate of the HOPE (Hispanas Organized for Political Equality) Leadership Institute, and she has recently been accepted to the 2004/05 Women's Policy Institute of the California Women's Foundation.

Roots of Peace

I am very proud that the creative team which has produced *100 Faces of Marin* has agreed to contribute 5 percent of book proceeds to Roots of Peace. This is a truly remarkable and worthwhile Marin-based charitable organization dedicated to eradicating 70 million land mines planted in 70 countries around the globe.

The fact that this book may help make a difference toward that endeavor pleases me to no end. One thread that runs seamlessly through the lives of our 100 Marin faces is how generously they take their successful careers one step further—into the realm of community giving. It is only appropriate, then, that this book, which celebrates their generosity, is itself a vehicle for giving. It is, in fact, the easiest decision our team had to make.

We live in a fearful, dangerous world. To do something positive is to defeat the fear and lessen the danger. Our belief is that it is always much better to light a candle than to curse the darkness. Thank you, Roots of Peace, for keeping the candle lit.

Peter Anderson
October 24, 2004

Roots of Peace was founded in 1997 with a clear mission—to rid the world of landmines by transforming toxic minefields into thriving farmland. Our vision of turning "Mines into Vines" seeks to restore the promise of hope and prosperity to afflicted communities throughout the world. We invite you to join us.

www.rootsofpeace.org

100 FACES OF MARIN

would like to thank the following sponsors

Alexander's Decorative Rugs in Mill Valley provides world-class, trustworthy customer service and undying dedication to seek out the most intriguing and exceptional antique and specialty natural dyed, handspun wool rugs for their esteemed and discerning clientele.

Established in 1991 in San Francisco and in 1996 in Mill Valley, Alexander's founder and president Richard Habib strives to offer a lifestyle, rather than just a commodity. Habib proudly refers to his ever-evolving collection of both museum-level antique Oriental, Persian and European rugs and new productions from Nepal, Tibet, Pakistan and locations across the globe, as "art to go under your feet." Alexander's deep commitment to enhance both the sensory and physical level of their customers' surroundings has resulted in national and regional recognition. Rug Retailer of the Year by the Oriental Rug Importer's Association, the Mill Valley Businessman of the Year in 2000, and winner in the Pacific Sun's "Best of Marin" for the last four years are just a few of the awards bestowed upon Alexander's.

Alexander's seeks to educate their clients so they can fully understand how to determine a rug's true value, offering lectures by noted designers and world-renowned experts. Appraisals, cleaning, consignments, purchasing, repairs, and restoration are all part of the extraordinary customer service that Alexander's places above all else.

Alexander's Decorative Rugs is an integral part of the community, serving on various non-profit boards and sponsoring many charity causes and artistic events, such as the American Heart Association, the Marin Breast Cancer Watch, and the Mill Valley Film Festival.

Bank of Marin provides the same products as the big banks, including multi-million dollar commercials loans, internet banking, and cash management, but with the legendary service and community commitment that is our trademark.

Bank of Marin enjoys a reputation for providing personal service and successful partnerships. Service that is individualized, flexible, and responsive has set us apart and contributed greatly to our success. Bank of Marin believes that banking is about meaningful, long-term partnerships. We strive to add value to those relationships by taking time to listen, to understand, and to care; time that our dedicated staff gives willingly.

Our goal as a community bank is to provide extraordinary personal service to our customers and demonstrate a serious commitment to the communities we serve. We are passionate about supporting community non-profit groups including chambers of commerce, youth and art programs, and our local schools through financial contributions and employee volunteerism.

Bank of Marin offers a welcoming, friendly work environment and promotes a balance between work and life issues. Our team of officers and staff is both our most valuable asset and our most differentiating characteristic. Our success as a community bank over the past fourteen years is largely due to our extraordinary staff.

BIRKENSTOCK®

Birkenstock Footprint Sandals, Inc., based in Novato, CA, is a 100 percent employee-owned company and is the original U.S. importer and distributor of Birkenstock footwear made in Germany. Birkenstock is a mindset of free spirit and individual expression that starts from the ground up. We believe that comfortable footwear leads to happiness and well-being, which is why our products are designed around the concept that the shape of the shoe should follow the shape of the foot.

Birkenstock has proudly operated in Marin for over 30 years. We sponsor several programs that contribute to the community by giving paid time off (48 hours per year per employee) for employees to volunteer. Our Giving Back program focuses on four main areas that represent some of our deepest concerns: human needs, health and wellness, learning, and the environment. Each area has a committee of employees devoted to it, which make donation decisions, organize volunteer events, and educate employees about related issues. These committees provide grants and product donations to nonprofit agencies within Marin County.

Birkenstock has more than 400 styles, colors, and textures of sandals, clogs and shoes, and a line of insoles and arch supports, all designed around our original footbed concept.

California Land Title of Marin has been serving Marin County for more than 50 years, providing title and escrow services that are vital to home ownership, commerce and the building of a community. The locally owned Marin-based company has grown to maintain offices in Greenbrae, Mill Valley and Novato with its headquarters at 700 Irwin Street in San Rafael. In a 2003 national industry survey on the performance of Title Companies, CAL LAND was rated #1 in the Bay Area for customer satisfaction in Transaction Turnaround Time, Error-Free Work, Problem Solving, Responsiveness to Requests, Personalized Service and Sales Representatives. CAL LAND is underwritten by four of the nation's leading insurers; Chicago Title, Commonwealth/LandAmerica, Stewart Title and North American Title. They are the "Title & Escrow Company of Choice" for major developers and homeowners alike.

Respected throughout Marin County for the quality, service and commitment of their work, "giving back" is one of the cornerstones of their business philosophy. As part of this commitment to the industry and community, the Company's principals and several employees serve on Boards and Commissions throughout Marin, including the Marin County Escrow Association, Northbay Family Homes, Marin Builder's Exchange, Marin County Board of Realtors, Chambers of Commerce and other non-profits. In addition, the Company is an avid supporter of numerous charities and organizations as well as playing a strong role in the dynamics of local business, schools, politics, affordable housing and regional development.

The Dutra Group has a heritage of over four generations providing services to its ever-expanding client base in Marin County, the Sacramento Delta, the San Francisco Bay Area and beyond. Dutra Dredging and Dutra Materials provides a solid organization of experienced professionals as well as the latest technology and equipment to ensure that client demands are met in dredging, marine construction and aggregate manufacturing and transportation.

Dutra Dredging supports a wide range of customers from governmental agencies to private industry members. From new projects to maintenance dredging with an emphasis on environmental protection, our company utilizes the best people, equipment and facilities to meet the needs of our diverse client base.

Dutra Materials' primary source of long-term aggregate reserves, the San Rafael Rock Quarry, is strategically located on the San Pedro Peninsula in Marin County. This century-old quarry has in excess of 30 million tons of aggregate reserves with the only waterside distribution center in the Bay Area. Dutra Materials' uniqueness is in its commitment to be the most cost-effective transporter of high quality aggregates by water distribution methods in this region.

With our combined Dredging and Materials resources, The Dutra Group brings a strong commitment and competitiveness to produce high quality work and products for our valued client base.

HANSON BRIDGETT

MARCUS VLAHOS RUDY·LLP

Hanson Bridgett North Bay opened in 1997 under the auspices of Gary Giacomini, native Marinite and a former and long-time Marin County Supervisor. The marriage of Gary and Hanson Bridgett was a natural, given what they already shared: Gary served as a California Coastal Commissioner for 10 years, while Hanson Bridgett Partner Ray McDevitt was instrumental in writing the Coastal Act that created the Commission; Gary's son Andrew was an associate with the firm when the Marin Office opened and is now Managing Partner; Gary served for 20 years as President of the board of directors of the Golden Gate Bridge, Highway and Transportation District, where Hanson Bridgett partner David Miller has served as General Counsel since 1976.

Six years later, the partnership between "Mr. Marin" and the 120-attorney law firm has repeatedly proven itself. "We appreciate the warm welcome we have received here," Giacomini said. "Of course, our areas of focus—land use and real estate, estate planning, labor and employment, litigation, general business law, and tax-exempt financing—are well-tailored to the needs of Marin clients."

However, it is Hanson Bridgett's understanding and commitment to the region that has allowed the firm to find its niche. "We are uniquely situated in that we have the full resources of one of California's largest firms." he said, "But, like myself, the attorneys who work out of our North Bay office live here and play an active role within their local communities. We don't just work here. The North Bay is home."

JACKSON'S

HARDWARE • TOOLS • DECORATIVE PLUMBING • RENTALS • PAINT

HC Jackson founded Jackson's Hardware in San Rafael in 1964. The store was 5,000 square feet and had 5 employees. At a previous employer, HC had experienced first-hand what happens when employees are not treated well, and he was determined for things to be different when he started his own business. His philosophy for success has been "the more you share, the more you make."

HC's goal in starting his retail business was to have the best hardware store in Marin. He initiated a profit-sharing plan for Jackson's associates (as the employees are called) in 1968, long before it was common to do so. Full medical, vision and dental coverage for associates and their dependents is part of a solid and progressive benefits package at Jackson's.

HC's belief in everyone sharing in the success of the company led him to form an ESOP (Employee Stock Ownership Plan) in 1989, and by September of 1998 the associates of Jackson's had purchased 100% of the company. Jackson's President and General Manager Bill Loskutoff attributes their continued success in an extremely competitive market to Jackson's focus on personal service to all their customers, and carrying a complete selection of high quality products.

Today, Jackson's Hardware is an award winning, 100 percent employee-owned company over 50,000 square feet in size, with 62 employee-owners.

Marin General Hospital opened its doors in May 1952 and is the largest acute care hospital in Marin County and accredited by the Joint Commission on Accreditation of Healthcare Organizations. MGH provides primary and secondary levels of care in addition to the Marin Cancer Institute, the Marin Heart Institute and a Level III Trauma Center with 24-hour neurosurgery coverage.

Novato Community Hospital, established in 1961, opened its new $40 million facility in the spring of 2000 and offers state of the art patient services to Northern Marin residents. Accredited by the Joint Commission on Accreditation of Healthcare Organizations, the hospital has a knowledgeable and caring professional staff that provides patients with highly personalized healthcare in a tranquil environment.

Marin General Hospital and Novato Community Hospital are affiliated with Sutter Health, one of the nation's leading not-for-profit networks of community based healthcare providers, delivering high quality healthcare in more than 100 Northern California communities. Sutter Health affiliates share a fundamental belief that local communities are in the best position to identify and meet local healthcare needs.

Marin Independent Journal

Nearly 100,000 Marin residents look to the *Marin Independent Journal* each day for complete local daily news and information. Expanding its reach to Web users, *www.marinij.com* provides daily news highlights as well as other useful information for residents and Marin visitors.

Other products produced by the *Marin IJ* include *From House to Home*, *Marin Homes*, *Classified Gazette, Marin People*, IJ Weekend and Wheels in Motion sections. From *House to Home* magazine, a glossy bimonthly publication provides home furnishing & design tips targeted to the sophisticated Marin homeowner. While *Marin Homes* is a monthly real estate magazine distributed free throughout Marin with more than 300 rack locations. The *Classified Gazette*, and weekly sections such as IJ Weekend and Wheels in Motion offer shopping, dining and entertainment information to Marin's active audience. *Marin People*, the IJ's Total Market Coverage product is delivered weekly to non-subscribers. And, *Marin 101*, a complete user's guide to The County and Northbay, is published each year in September.

As the newspaper of record in Marin County, the *Marin Independent Journal* is a strong supporter of local nonprofit organizations. The *IJ*'s Sharing & Caring grant program partners with four nonprofit organizations each year, establishing a matching grant that assists them with fund-raising endeavors.

The *IJ* also demonstrates its commitment to the community by sponsoring many events and programs established by local nonprofits. Over the course of a year, the *IJ* sponsors more than 100 fund-raising events and public awareness programs across the county.

Marin Joe's is the basilica of Marin restaurants. Since 1954, when the county was a sleepy suburb with a handful of coffee shops and few top-flight dining houses, the Della Santina family has carved a niche as the preeminent place to eat.

Fad foods have come and gone. Stylized temples of dining have made a flash impact on the terrain and vanished. But one thing is constant on the Corte Madera/Mill Valley border that is home to Marin Joe's—the telltale sizzle of the grill sparking forth scallops and prawns, Piccata and Scallopini, sirloins and filets, burgers and pot roasts, Joe's Specials and Zuppa Maritata, Chicken Caccciatore and Liver Venetian.

Marin Joe's is the cathedral of garlic, fine wines, convivial dining, and enduring dependability. In an age when the worship of fine food has reached an almost absurd level of reverence, the Della Santinas have never forgotten that families eating together, friends gathering to celebrate comprise the first order of restaurant business. Fine food and drink are essential, but the never-ending buzz of folks clinking glasses and sharing hearty laughter give definition to Marin Joe's soul.

Proprietor Romano Della Santina—a wise, kind, jovial man who presides over his tables not unlike a merry Pope—measures his success not by numbers of dinners sold or cases of wine consumed, but rather by the progressive march of generations who file through his doors displaying decades of loyalty. Romano and his co-prorpietors, sons Ralph and Paul Della Santina, never forget a face.

(*Text from* 100 Faces of Marin)

Marin Santary Service
Marin Resources Recovery Center

Marin Sanitary Service has been locally owned and operated since 1948. We provide solid waste, recyclable and yard waste collection in Marin County, debris boxes, provide safe and secure document shredding services, and operate Marin County's only indoor dump (Marin Resource Recovery Center), the first such facility in the entire nation. We are able to recycle 74 percent of everything that is brought to the Recovery Center. We also contract with the San Rafael Fire Department to provide household hazardous materials reception services.

Marin Sanitary Service also operates the Marin Recycling Center for drop-off and buyback of recyclable materials such as aluminum, glass, cardboard and paper. We opened our Environmental Classroom in 1991 and have given recycling programs and tours to many thousands of Marin's schoolchildren, teaching them how they can help save our natural resources through recycling. In addition, Marin Recycling initiated curbside recycling in the United States.

Patty Garbarino has been president of Marin Sanitary Service since 2000. She is responsible for policy development and implementation, as well as the overall management and oversight of the operations of the company. In addition to her administrative and management responsibilities, Patty remains directly involved in all aspects of the company's governmental relations, the Public Education Department and community relations.

Randy Block has lived and worked in Marin County since 1988. In a coaching role, he assists Marin professionals re-discover their values and talents. A recipient of a BS in Business Administration from Cornell University in 1969, Block offers his clients over 30 years' coaching and staffing experience.

After military service, he received career coaching in 1972 from Eli Djedda of San Francisco's Bernard Haldane and Associates, obtaining his first high-tech industry position through that collaboration. In 1973, he joined Robert Siegel and Company of San Francisco, establishing the firm's first retained search function. Block later co-founded a search firm in San Francisco, which performed retained search and recruitment training.

In 1986, he unveiled his own company, Block & Associates, which offered recruitment consulting and staffing workshops and retained search for high technology companies. By 1998, seeking a change, he hired a career coach himself, which led to his becoming a career transaction coach. The CPAD Network certified him as an International Career Transition and Management Coach. In 2002, he completed a 16-week course from Career Coach Academy, becoming a Certified Career Management Coach.

Sponsored by 6figures.com, Randy conducts monthly public seminars on networking and interviewing in today's economy. Combining years of content with effective tools that can translate into pragmatic career solutions, Randy is today fully engaged in his coaching and search practices. His experience as presenter and speaker include International Convention for CMI, Kiwanis Clubs and several private groups. He and his son Jeremy live in Larkspur.

SETON SMOKE

CAPITAL MANAGEMENT

Complex financial markets pose major challenges for private investors. Seton Smoke meets these challenges with knowledge, experience, and resources long valued by affluent individuals, family businesses, pension and profit sharing plans, trustees, executors, corporations and non-profit organizations. Our financial advisory and portfolio management services are time tested and designed to emphasize highly customized investment strategies, disciplined institutional level management, and sophisticated wealth planning.

Our clients come to us for the long term, to protect and grow their assets for retirement, children, grandchildren, and philanthropy. We enjoy these lasting relationships because we recognize and meet the unique individual needs of each client's portfolio, and our time tested investment processes allow each client to achieve their goals.

The key to serving our clients is our experienced team of wealth planning and management professionals. We are an independent investment management firm with no affiliation and no conflict of interest. We have no products to sell other than sound investment management and sophisticated wealth planning advice. Our clients' interests always come first.

As a committed member of the community, Seton Smoke sponsors events and programs for nonprofits and local businesses. Its principals and employees participate in research and fund raising efforts, serve on boards, and support many charitable, medical, and other organizations.

Tamalpais Bank, established in 1991, is the Marin County financial institution that helps families, businesses and the community at large realize their lifetime financial goals in a caring private banking environment, providing the best solutions to meet each customer's financial needs.

The Bank has created a new paradigm: helping customers grow and manage their wealth through consultation, planning, and a full range of banking and investment products delivered in a non-intimidating, personalized way. Key to this vision are the lifetime relationships that the Bank's experienced, responsive and friendly bankers earn and develop with their customers.

A founding principle of Tamalpais Bank is giving back to the community to help create an even better place to live, guided by the belief that its strength is tied to the strength of the communities where it does business. Branches are conveniently located throughout the county. As the Bank continues to grow, it remains dedicated to what its customers care about – personalized services, the highest ethical standards, and community commitment and participation. For ongoing accounts, Tamalpais Bank makes an annual donation to the Marin County non-profit of the customer's choice. The Bank also sponsors the annual Heart of Marin Awards, having allocated hundreds of thousands of dollars to this program since 1992.

Tamalpais Bank is a socially responsible company. Its Board and senior management are gender balanced and its policy is to promote from within and support the individual growth and achievement of each employee.

Value Magazine
QUALITY LIVING FOR LESS

Value Magazine is a community news and advertising publication that is mailed to 75,000 households in Marin County. Our logo says "Quality Living For Less" and that is our goal—to bring our neighbors in Marin the best offers, from some of the best local businesses, so that you have the best quality of life possible for you and your family.

During 2003, our first year of publication, we featured more than 100 local businesses. As we enter our second year of publication, we expect to bring even more information about—and great offers from—local companies who realize that value means providing high quality products and services at a reasonable price.

Quality of life extends beyond the physical environment we create in our home. It extends into the community of friends, neighbors and others who have chosen to live in this beautiful place. That's why every issue also included community news based on stories broadcast on Comcast Cable's popular program, The Marin Report and other fun features.

Value Magazine is published by Graphic Arts Management. Graphic Arts Management was founded by Dora Knell and has been serving the North Bay community for over 25 years. Now operated by a new generation of the Knell family, we look forward to continuing to serve our community for at least another 25 years.